THE FUTURE OF HIDING

EXPERTISE

CULTURES AND
TECHNOLOGIES
OF KNOWLEDGE

EDITED BY DOMINIC BOYER

A list of titles in this series is available at cornellpress.cornell.edu

THE FUTURE OF HIDING

Secrecy, Infrastructure, and Ecological
Memory in Estonia's Siberia

Francisco Martínez

CORNELL UNIVERSITY PRESS   ITHACA AND LONDON

Thanks to generous funding from the ERC project WasteMatters, the ebook editions of this book are available as open access volumes through the Cornell Open initiative.

First published 2025 by Cornell University Press

Librarians: A CIP catalog record for this book is available from the Library of Congress.

ISBN 9781501784255 (hardcover)
ISBN 9781501784262 (paperback)
ISBN 9781501784286 (pdf)
ISBN 9781501784279 (epub)

GPSR EU contact: Sam Thornton, Mare Nostrum Group B.V., Mauritskade 21D, 1091 GC, Amsterdam, NL, gpsr@mare-nostrum.co.uk.

Contents

Preface: Calypso in the Shadows

This book was written amid personal shifts and radically changing geopolitical contexts. Transitional phases are vigorous and experimental: they stimulate the desire for knowledge, which is not a placid state of the soul; rather it's an attitude of alert that might bring more clashes than harmony. That alone is not enough of a reason to read it. Perhaps you should read this book because it signals new recolonial arrangements amid a convoluted redevelopment of energy infrastructure. Still, I believe that you might also be transported to eastern Estonia by slipping into these pages, on a journey into alterity, the ordinary workings of secrecy, and the material culture of a liminal region shaped by mining. This ethnography traces how the repercussions of extractivist activities are dispersed across time and space, affecting not just the ecology but also the sociality of the region.

In this book, historical references serve to contextualize the legacies of mining, the topological dimensions of hiding, and the echoing practices that they both generate when aligned. The research, however, is more an archaeology of the present, an act of digging into contemporary relations while walking or drinking tea with local residents and encountering thorny landscapes of contamination. To that end, the text combines analytical and descriptive passages with more evocative and visual ones. In the attempt to show forms of non-relationality as an important part of the social order, it draws inspiration from the work of Georg Simmel and his typologies of opposition. Proximity and distance, game and conflict, bond and separation, the foreigner and the local, exposure and concealment are interactive opposites that establish a rich intermediate space.[1] Furthermore, the endeavor to observe the play between the "front" and the "backstage" behavior of informants follows Erving Goffman's analysis of the presentation of self in everyday life.[2] Indeed, my research is not limited to illuminating the shadow side of Estonian society. This book also shows how different forms, or topographies, of secrecy connect the private and the social by furnishing a space for retreat and opacity. It therefore foregrounds the potential for refusal and concealment to entail a political critique beyond traditional discussions of resistance.

We can locate shadow spaces such as basements, bunkers, garages, and dachas as part of the "right to opacity" described by postcolonial scholar Édouard Glissant. He argued that difference is the basis for relations between all things. Glissant then posed the right to opacity as a "guarantee of participation and confluence."[3] By letting things remain in their otherness, we resist the normalizing forces attempting to rule out difference. Thus, opacity refers to our ability to protect personal autonomy while expressing anxiety about how others represent us and our territory.

In a hideout, fixed and final categories become ambivalent, shaping our sense of belonging and identity in a performative way. We can designate any of these topographies of concealment as part of the anti-structure, taking issue with social ordering, potentially destabilizing cultural absolutes and institutional arrangements in turn. According to anthropologist Victor Turner, the threshold place, on the edges of structured social life, situates us in a different position toward patterns of normality, therefore facilitating negotiation of "the positions assigned and arrayed by law, custom, convention, and ceremony."[4] Shadow spaces such as basements, bunkers, dachas, and garages make room for the betwixt and between; they are essential refuges where other forms of relationality and refusal are built.

In a hideout, the current social order and hegemonic representations are disabled to create new possible belongings and to enable alternative futures. Hence, this book claims the necessity for some spaces to remain out of sight and for us to have the chance (or ability) to stand otherwise in the world and refuse the homogeneous conformity promoted by algorithms, global corporations, and state institutions. Shadow spaces are mobilized to make us appear illegible and inconclusive; that is why they are pivotal to the social reintegration of the divergent.

This book partly turns out to be about the politics of visibility and the visibility of politics. Analyzing the spatiality of secrecy is a way for researchers to inquire into social organization, belonging, and the inventiveness of relations within communities. Nonetheless, the geography of shadows remains to be mapped and tamed. The borders and echoes of hideouts shift cross-culturally; shadow spaces are rich in their imagery, indeed coral islands keep on appearing with new Calypsos moving back and forth between areas of light and shade.

In ancient Greek, there are two etymologies for the name Calypso: "the one who conceals knowledge" and "a beautiful sight." In Homer's *Odyssey*, the nymph Calypso tries to hide the Greek hero Odysseus on her island while they enjoy sensual pleasures together. Therefore Homer describes her as "deceitful." The gods, however, find Odysseus and compel him to meet his fate; the show must go on. So Calypso provides him with an axe and wood to build a boat, in addition to wine, bread, and clothing to continue his journey. Odysseus says goodbye to her, not without some suspicion that it might be a trap, and then sets sail. According to Homer, Calypso was left behind with two children and met a solitary, unhappy end.

There are better and worse ways of hiding, as well as reasonable and odd motivations to do so. The decision to wear a mask or to vanish from plain view might be a response to personal changes, political ruptures, rites of passage, or an overwhelming anxiety. Robin Hood may have wanted to retreat to Sherwood Forest because of agoraphobia. The comic character Waldo may be tired of always wearing a red-and-white-striped shirt and hiding from readers within a crowd of people, so it is understandable if he decides to quit the game for good and close down his social networks. In various novels, we have also seen how the main characters inhabit a kind of hideout. In *The Invisible Man* by H. G. Wells, the reader meets Griffin, a scientist who achieves invisibility through a successful experiment with optics.[5] There is another *Invisible Man*, written by Ralph Ellison, which is the story of a nameless Black person, invisible because people choose not to see him, who becomes a phantom in other people's minds. The invisibility of this young Afro-American is due to the "poor vision" of those with whom he comes in contact: "I am invisible, understand, simply because people refuse to see me."[6]

The idea of invisibility being the result of the terms imposed by some people upon others was also suggested by Goffman in his work on stigma, namely that social identities are constructed through the perspectives produced in interactional settings, thus emanating not from the body of the stigmatized but from the relation with the "normals."[7] Ellison's sociopolitical allegory ends with the man hiding out underground, occupying the basement as a way of surviving. The novel has, nonetheless, an existential tone that reminds me of Fyodor Dostoyevsky's *Notes from Underground*.[8] The Russian classic is told through the monologue of an unnamed, bitter narrator, a man full of shame, who tries to answer the question "Who am I?" by retreating into a hole.

In some cases, we might also need to invent inner refuges, constructed under the skin. Different topographies of concealment allow people to cope with never-ending forms of intrusion, policing, and abrasion while keeping other representations and practices unnoticed in the shadows. Nonetheless, the term "shadow" is polysemic. It may refer to a dark image cast onto a surface, a pervasive influence, a shelter from danger, a source of gloom or unhappiness, an interruption of light, and, finally, the reflected image of the one who furtively follows you. For instance, cast shadows speak about the shape, volume, location, radiation, and source of light. They also manifest the fact that nothing is always fully visible and shadows are necessary to create different kinds of shelter and distance. Indeed, poets need the dark side of the moon, and love is particularly alive in penumbral corners.

In this vein, philosopher Santiago Alba Rico distinguishes among three kinds of shadows: trees provide shade; everyone carries a shadow side; and the world is a shadow.[9] In the psychoanalytic tradition, the harder we embrace our shadow side, the darker the face we may encounter. Hence, tracing a shadow is a way to gain insight into the dark side of human behavior and troublesome parts of a person. Some people might need to do so in order to overcome their complexes, as suggested by Carl Jung—who argued that failing to integrate the shadows into one's consciousness results in their negative projection into the social world.[10]

We can find different moral fables telling us to learn to value our shadow. Arguably, the most famous one is the story of Peter Pan, whose agile shadow has been crudely amputated.[11] For his part, Adelbert von Chamisso told the story of a man who sells his shadow to the devil in exchange for a perpetual refill of gold coins. Not a bad bargain, apparently. The man nonetheless realizes he has made a mistake, since his life becomes disoriented and substanceless.[12] Hans Christian Andersen also wrote a fairy tale titled in which that naughty thing behind him not only enslaves the main character but also gets him killed.[13] So one has to take shadows seriously. They are so important that a university in Barcelona has opened a department of umbrology, as foreseen by short story writer Tim Horvath.[14] Indeed, Plato might be the father of that discipline in ancient Greece. He showed us that there is nothing innocent in making the invisible visible. Plato recounts the allegory of the cave, in which a group of people spend their entire lives chained inside an underground cave in front of a blank wall. These prisoners do not remain in total darkness but are condemned to see only those things that are in plain sight.[15] Perhaps nowadays that wall would be called a smartphone.[16] But as much as screens cannot—or should not—always be on, we should not remain in front of one all the time, because, among other reasons, there are things that we can only practice away from a screen, such as care, rest, or intimacy.

Yet vanishing today is harder than ever before, as we leave digital traces that are hard to clear out. Thus, it takes rather sophisticated strategy and logistics. Indeed, it is not enough to close down your social media, drop your phone in a river, avoid sharing data with Meta, Google, and Microsoft, and start using cash instead of credit cards. One has to work it out, and important preparations are needed to do so. For example, there are a few things that we have to keep in mind while looking for a hideout, namely, issues of size, undetectability, waterproof qualities, exposure to weather conditions, and where to run if it suddenly becomes necessary. Because the system might strike back at some point.

Exposure and algorithmic legibility appear equally central to the governance of human conduct in the present. In our societies, rendered ultra-clear, we are constantly being monitored, tested, assessed, and judged, and there is a feeling that we are becoming mere data extracted for power, surveillance, and profit.[17] Our digital screens have become our windows onto the present, promoting a new kind of seeing and novel ways of presenting ourselves; they allow us to see and be seen not just outside our homes but in faraway places. These novel forms of technological exposure and capitalization on people's data raise new political issues and challenge our disciplinary capacity to redraw the lines of sight in the field. This book shows how the invention and defense of devices for making us de-noticed or illegible allows us to remain inscrutable and unreachable in some instances. It does so by examining the spatial dimension of this specific kind of sociality and how the recursive practice of opacity can create political possibilities.

In addition, this book also reflects on the way in which practices of opacity are not the opposite of transparency but instead a recursive enactment of refusal and ambivalence. As we experience novel forms of surveillance, capitalization, and monitoring, new ways of being de-noticed, illegible, and de-algorithmed are invented in a responsive way. These are acts of cultural creation and not necessarily of confrontation, sites where we can use strategic ambiguity and render certain things unseeable.[18] Contemporary societies, however, are less and less tolerant of attempts to hide things from the system, yet they are simultaneously fascinated with those individuals who achieve an orchestrated invisibility.[19] Indeed, we expend much effort in keeping areas of our inner landscape away from both the public gaze and the capitalist gears in order to prevent graspability.[20]

Perhaps it is because being human means wearing a mask, after all. Definitely, a lot of human problems come from our inability to keep things in the dark. Hence, sites of secrecy have to be defended and updated in order to expand the margins of opacity and refuse the kind of relationality that gobbles up every critical countermove.[21] Eventually, if we adapt too well to institutions, markets, and technological devices, our sense of adventure, the possibility for dissent, and the capacity for anthropological analysis will become obsolete.[22] An ethnographic study of topographies of refusal, of spaces for saying "rather not," illuminates both limits and possibilities for self-authorization while questioning the social expectation that one must always be subject to evaluation, categorization, and capitalization.[23] In this way, the use of hideouts and shadow spaces is not a circumvention of politics but an extension of the political.

INTRODUCTION
Hiding in the Future

In the summer of 1996, a metal cylinder was retrieved from the *Glory to Labor* monument in Kohtla-Järve, the mining capital of Estonia. The capsule included a letter to the future residents of the town.[1] The message was intended to be read publicly on June 26, 2046, at the centenary of the city's re-founding. Rumors about the contents of the capsule have been in circulation since 1971, when the cylinder was placed inside the monument. The capsule is now stored at the Museum of Oil Shale, kept on an ordinary shelf alongside other objects such as mining pickaxes and helmets. "I am afraid to put the capsule on display because it might be stolen," explains Ainar Varinurm, who has been the director of the museum since 2006. "Many people know about it, and we don't have enough safety measures out there."

According to local archives, the content of the message was carefully planned by the communist authorities for over two years. The title of the monument was supposed to be *Shoulder to Shoulder*, honoring the strong sense of comradeship forged among miners. The local committee, however, suggested a more ideologically enthusiastic message: *Glory to Labor*. Nevertheless, residents renamed the sculpture—in which two miners are represented holding their pickaxes above their heads—in their own way, *The Two Sober Ones*, in a joking reference to the free-time activities of miners on their payday.

After holding heated discussions about where to relocate this "alien body disrupting the traffic," municipal officials decided simply to make the base of the sculpture on Happiness Street (Õnne tänav) smaller. During renovation work on the monument, the cylinder was stolen by a gang of kids, who are said to have

FIGURE 0.1.   The *Glory to Labor* monument in 1976. Photo: J. Lasman. Estonian National Archive.

opened it and read the message. The capsule was apparently returned a couple of days later. Both on the Internet and in newspapers at the time, one can find different versions of the message, with the shorter one reading: "Dear comrades, we turn to you as you celebrate the 100th anniversary of Kohtla-Järve, our city. In 75 years, it will not be as it is today. But we are sure that it is there, that it will be there; nothing will destroy it. It will be much more beautiful than today. Also you, the residents, will be stronger, more beautiful, and wiser. You will be happier and happier, individually and together."[2]

There was no other future inside—just one. The message reproduces the modern idea that the future will always be a socially and materially improved version of today. *But have you read the message inside?* I ask Varinurm. "Yes, no . . . Actually yes, but you cannot read it," he replies suspiciously. The cylinder is made of metal. Once it is in my hands, I start to wonder what might be inside it. Perhaps there is no letter but instead radioactive ore, or simply a fragment of oil shale. I wait until Varinurm becomes distracted and quickly try to open the cylinder. But it is not so easy; the disclosure of a public secret such as this one might require a trick, a click, or perhaps a ritual, a twisting strength I might not possess. Varinurm returns, looks at me jocosely, and comments, "Four people like you are needed to open it, or in turn, a mechanical tool with as much power." He rolls the cylinder on the table and then pretends to do gymnastics with it: up-down and front-to-back, in a playful scene that reminds me of the one in Charlie Chaplin's film *The Great Dictator* (1940) in which Adenoid Hynkel dances with a globe.

"You could say that this public secret is part of the identity of the town," concedes Varinurm. At this point I ask if we can weigh and measure the public secret: 3.002 kilograms, with a diameter of 6.7 centimeters and a length of 33 centimeters. In the meantime, the curator of the collection, Astrid Niinepuu, who has been revising files, approaches carrying several official documents related to the capsule. One of them, dated November 5, 1996, includes the weight and measurements of the cylinder, which are, to our surprise, smaller than those of the one I hold in my hands: 6.3 centimeters and 32.5 centimeters. The weight noted is also lower: 2.97 kilograms. Another municipal document contradicts the previous instructions and says that the message should be read on June 15 instead of June 26. The date is handwritten in pen. "Now you know too much; I have to kill you," says Varinurm, enjoying my awkward curiosity.

The Museum of Oil Shale is concerned with the reproduction and transmission of mining tradition in the region rather than with present-day environmental issues and social hardships. There one can find artistic representations of industrial activities as well as objects rescued from mining sites and local basements. One of the items, a painting titled *Oil Shale Chemical Plant at Kohtla-Järve* (1964), had been kept in the dark for some years. In 2003 Varinurm went to St. Petersburg and visited the artist Abram Rabkin in his studio. Rabkin lamented that he had lost track of one of his paintings and showed Varinurm a photo of the artwork. Varinurm replied that he had seen it somewhere, that it looked very familiar, but he could not remember where or in what context. Two months later, the director of a school in Jõhvi called Varinurm on the phone, saying that there was a painting representing mining activities in the basement of the school. "Perhaps it has some value? It is in very bad shape, though," he added. Varinurm went to see it and recognized it as Rabkin's missing painting. Additionally, he remembered that the painting used to hang in his chemistry classroom at the school when he was a boy.

But the painting urgently needed restoration. Apart from being damaged by environmental conditions, it was also pocked by bullet holes, as if someone had been practicing marksmanship in the basement of the school. Artist Aleksandr Igonin was put in charge of restoring the painting. The artwork was in such bad shape that once his work was complete, Igonin decided to add his signature to it, inscribing his name in a corner of the canvas. In addition, he left one of the bullet holes unrepaired as testimony to the material condition of the painting when it was found. I mention to Varinurm that the hole turns the painting into a forensic document, but he rejects my interpretation with disdain. In his view, the hole is an invitation to play. "For the same price, visitors at the museum can insert their finger into the canvas," he says, and does so while looking at me with a smile.

Then we turn the painting around and contemplate the complex architecture of patches applied by the restorer. The painting endures because of them, and previously it survived thanks to being forgotten and left dormant underground, just as with the oil shale lying beneath the region; yet in the case of this mineral, we are talking about millions of years instead of decades. The composite that gives its name to the museum is a sedimentary rock compressed through the poetic combination of meteors, centuries, soil, and fire. In reality, oil shale comes from the remains of a variety of organisms, such as algae, spores, plants, and pollen in wetlands—and thus is petrified life force. Nevertheless, the term "oil shale" is itself a misnomer, as it does not contain oil nor is it shale. It looks like a rock but is instead an organic material full of kerogen; thus, it has to be heated to a high temperature to release its energy.[3] When heated, the composite (a poisonous gift) releases hydrocarbons. Yet, in addition to energy production, the processing of oil shale also serves to produce elements for manufacturing tires, LCD monitors, and cosmetics, among other products.

Mining is understood here not as a one-way ecological incident but as an infrastructural process that fundamentally transforms places and societies simultaneously. Thus, one of the lessons of this ethnography is that oil shale is not a thing but a culture—a practical and symbolic repertoire with which a community imagines, rehearses, and organizes the world in its own way.[4] Furthermore, mining infrastructure became a locus of political belonging in the region, deeply connected to its ecological memory (notwithstanding how polluted and aggressive it might be). Extractive activities, and the related infrastructure developed for them, changed the environment, institutional structures, dwelling forms, and, overall, the sociality of the entire region. I am talking of mining as a culture that gives shape to new military, legal, religious, and aesthetic relations, not just economic ones. Tweaking Marcel Mauss's original concept about gift exchange, we can refer to mining as a totally antisocial act which brings new relations into existence with regard to infrastructural harm.[5]

In the Museum of Oil Shale, we can also find a print created in 1980 by Hugo Mitt, which depicts the mining industry in eastern Estonia in detail. The title, "Terra Cucersita" (Land of Oil Shale), sits at the top of the print. The name is Latin, and the energy infrastructure is represented with a sense of iconicity, designed to elicit awe and admiration. Energy infrastructure was indeed at the forefront of the concerns of Soviet policy-makers and Kohtla-Järve is marked with a red dot (in the decades since then, however, this city has lost part of its purpose and two-thirds of its population). The map integrates landscape and architectural details into what might otherwise seem a straightforward representation of the exploitation of nature. As a result, the things that are represented come into view as resources for humans; they have a tamed utility but not an autonomous force.

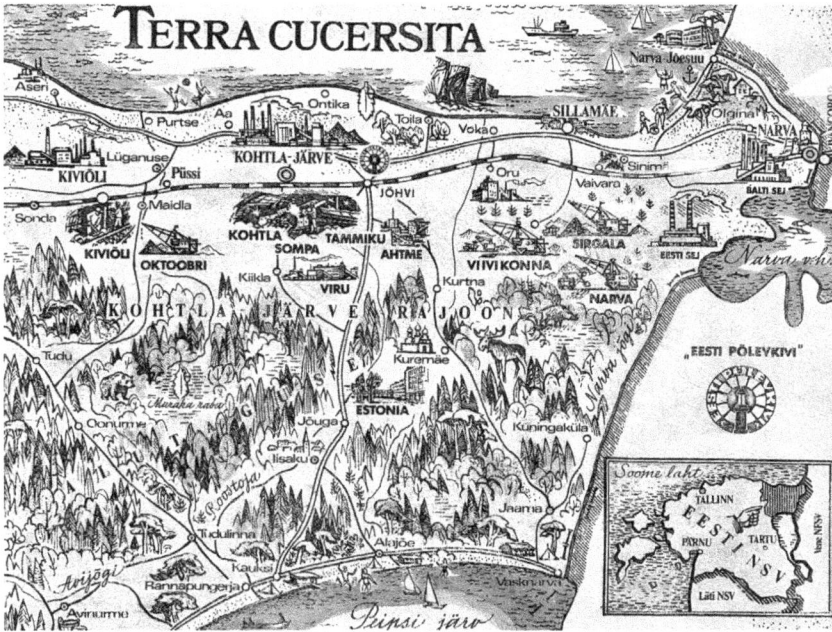

FIGURE 0.2.   "Terra Cucersita," print by Hugo Mitt.

What is identified as useful, how natural resources are utilized, and the effects of the correlated infrastructure are largely dictated by different sociocultural processes. Indeed, oil shale is correlated with the technology and expert knowledge that turn this substance into a natural resource. All these elements configure the socio-material arrangements needed for that process, which are far from neutral and transparent. For instance, the documents that circulate enable and disable what can be imagined and said about oil shale, which is a crucial step both in the making of resources and in colonizing practices.[6] In other words, modernization projects produced narratives that, in turn, framed perceptions around the oil shale and generated particular forms of infrastructural subjectivity. As a result, these mineral *gifts* appear suited for practical usage, and the territory is conveniently engineered and administered for it.

These sociopolitical forms of domination, however, are troubled by human and non-human relations of refusal and opacity. Then years later, once the geopolitical wheel spins full circle and natural resources become mere substances again, regions such as eastern Estonia are presented as remote, characterized by loss, pollution, and stigmatization. In the meantime, the evil repercussions of extractivist processes continue in the dark, persisting through leaks, escapes, aggressive reverberations, secrecy, outmigration, dispossession, and incomplete belonging. Indeed, with over 1 billion tons of industrial refuse, Ida-Virumaa, in Estonia's northeastern corner, is one of the most waste-heavy areas in the world. Alas, mining does not belong to the past, nor is it limited to Soviet modernization. Nowadays, Estonia is the only country in the world that uses oil shale as its primary energy source. But children living in the oil shale areas have higher incidences of respiratory disease and are projected to have a life expectancy reduced by about four years compared to other regions.[7]

In this sense, extraction does not end with the closing of a mine or an industrial plant, nor with the abandonment of railways, housing, roads, and power lines. Instead, it produces fundamental changes in sociality and gives shape to a specific ecological memory and asymmetric integration.

This is the dark side of the Soviet path of modernization, representative as well of the peripheral condition of this region—remote with regard to the Estonian state and identity and on the margins of global capitalism. In this context, secrecy plays a crucial role, serving as a means of everyday coping with environmental degradation and feelings of marginalization, loss, and incomplete belonging. The creation of masked geographies for enacting refusal is thus intrinsic to being part of a modern society, not residual to it, nor in opposition. Throughout its pages, this ethnography presents empirical evidence on how shadow spaces operate and novel interpretations about the role of secrecy, opacity, and refusal in the construction of the sense of self in eastern Estonia. These hidden social sites are created against the demand to be always available, knowable, and measurable by the hegemonic power.

Brown Burning Gold

There are different legends as to how the energy potential of the oil shale composite was discovered. According to one of them, a shepherd, wanting to build a campfire, gathered some branches and surrounded them with the yellowish stones he found nearby. When the fire caught, he could not believe the spectacle before his eyes: stones burning along with the firewood. The term "cucersita" comes from "Kukruse," the name of the town where oil shale was first documented. In the eighteenth century, August W. Hupel wrote that a "burning stone" was used to light fires in the distillery of a local manor. A century later, the pharmacist Juhanson brought "kukersite" to his backyard in Jõhvi and started to experiment with the material. Oil shale then piqued the interest of scientists from St. Petersburg, and in 1916 over 650 tons of the burning stone was sent to Petrograd for testing to see if it was really suitable as fuel for combustion. In 1917, imperial Russia allocated 1.2 million rubles to purchase land and start mining activities; the foundations for the first open-pit mine were aborted, however, with the sudden accession of the Bolsheviks to power.

Finally, oil production began at the Kohtla mine with an experimental factory in August 1921.[8] The Estonian state (Riigi Põlevkivitööstus) became the leading player at the time, but not the only one, as German, British, and Swedish capital arrived, enabling more factories and mines to open.[9] By 1937, there were eight mines in operation in the region, both publicly and privately owned. The Estonian government signed two contracts with the Nazis to export 44,500 tons of shale oil annually.[10] Because of the expansion of oil shale industrial activity, the region began to be called "Estonia's Siberia," an ironic nickname in sad hindsight, since thousands of residents would be deported to the real Siberia in the 1940s.[11] After the war, less than 60 percent of the native population remained in the region. Former residents were cut off from their territory, with the Soviet authorities taking over their houses and land and robbing them of the possibility of a self-determined future. New roads and apartment houses were built, as well as cooperative farms, mines, industries, hospitals, schools, even cinemas, as part of a larger process of social engineering and Soviet modernization. Hence, there were three critical moments in the development of the mining industry in Estonia: the discovery that kukersite can be used as fuel, an agreement with Germany that brought investments and expertise, and Stalin's directives to make use of the competence of local engineers to provide energy to Leningrad.

Historian David Vseviov sees a plan of Russification behind the resettlement strategies that formed novel infrastructural subjectivities.[12] By contrast, another historian, Olaf Mertelsmann, claims that the development of industrial and mining activity simply demanded a larger workforce.[13] He observes that in the early years, over 80 percent of the labor in the oil shale industry consisted of prisoners of war, and when the German POWs were released, there were not enough workers; in addition, management was poorly qualified, and wages were low and not always paid on time. Miners were still sleeping in barracks, but now surrounded by barbed wire. Indeed, the region was not simply colonized but militarized and integrated within the infamous gulag (labor camp) prison system, while living standards dropped for decades.

During the years under the communist regime, the extraction and processing of mineral resources increased about fifteenfold and the generation of electric power about one hundredfold. According to official data, by 1955, industrial production had more than doubled compared to the prewar level and risen tenfold since the end of the war, although Mertelsmann argues that the official growth figures were mainly a game of numbers, and that industrial production barely outpaced prewar levels.[14] Conveniently, military installations covered nearly 2 percent of the territory of the republic. Most of these sites were heavily contaminated

by oil products, hazardous chemicals, rubber, paint and varnish, ordinary rubbish, abandoned infrastructure, and unexploded ordnance (see chapter 3).[15] All
in all, Sovietization did not always mean modernization in eastern Estonia, and
where there was modernization, it was of a particular kind: adjusting local communities to the sociopolitical circumstances prevailing in the USSR.[16]

Before World War II, the Ida-Virumaa region was particularly multilin-
gual; one could hear Russian, German, and Polish spoken as much as Estonian,
because half of the population was foreign. According to historian Jaak Valge,
one explanation for the presence of so many foreigners in the region was "the
agrarian worldview" of the Estonian government at the time, which worked
against the migration of ethnic Estonians from the countryside to urbanized
areas, as well as, of course, the economic opportunities offered by mining.[17] In
the 1930s, journalist Osvald Tooming toured the rapidly industrializing areas,
writing a series of articles that described the competition between two towns
to become the mining capital—Kohtla-Järve, dominated by Estonian investments, and Kiviõli, where German investment was prevalent. In Kiviõli, Tooming observed dirt, poverty, and drunkenness, while Kohtla-Järve was apparently
characterized by responsibility and moderation.[18] Archival recollections also
say that at the time, every boy in the region carried around firearms.[19] Indeed,
if a show like *Peaky Blinders* were to be shot in Estonia, it would take place in
Ida-Virumaa.[20]

In December 2022, following Russia's full-scale invasion of Ukraine, the Estonian government began the implementation of a new law transitioning toward
a monolingual (Estonian-based) education system. The number of Russian-
speaking schools was reduced significantly as a result, and classes are taught in
Estonian. Since there was a shortage of qualified Estonian-speaking teachers in
the region, the government had to offer a bonus to entice teachers to move to Ida-
Virumaa from other parts of the country. Pille, who taught Estonian literature,
jokingly said that it felt like moving to Siberia.

Nationality and language have been sensitive issues here for over a century, if
not longer. Ultimately, we could date the colonization of Ida-Virumaa back to the
Baltic Germans, who established manorial estates in order to extract and process
natural resources while repressing and enslaving the local population. Estonia's history of landownership is marked by several periods of occupation by foreign pow-
ers—namely, Danes, Germans, Swedes, and Russians. In the first Estonian republic
(1918–1940), 1,065 manors were expropriated. These farms were then given primarily to those who had fought for the independence of Estonia.[21] In the Soviet
period, the very same farms were collectivized; any local resistance led to deportation to Siberia, and mass inward migration from the Soviet Union was organized.

The term "extractivism" is used to signify the extraction of natural resources with the goal of trading them abroad and without any responsibility for the future condition of the local environment. Thus, this phenomenon is often linked to colonialism and the conquest of foreign lands. In the case of Estonia, however, mining activities and energy infrastructure have been particularly concentrated in the northeast of the country, in some periods of history taking the form of an internal colonization.[22] While the Soviets did not allow the former owners to return to Ida-Virumaa after the war and decided to reorganize the uses of the territory around industrial and military occupation instead, once Estonia regained its independence, many of the recently arrived residents saw themselves as marginalized within the new ethnocentric republic. In the meantime, the energy production and distribution activity only increased, with the profits largely going elsewhere.

A Region in Need of Theorization

Within a century, Estonia experienced rapid industrialization, wartime economic conditions, the birth of an independent state, a liberal explorative period, the patronage of a nationalistic pseudo-fascist regime that chose not to fight the Soviet invasion, the devastation of war and multiple occupations, Stalinist repression and deportations, infrastructural modernization within the Soviet grid, economic and technological stagnation, the articulation of a transition economy with limited financial capacity and know-how, integration within transnational institutions such as the EU, NATO, and global markets, and the gradual introduction of green policies. Breathe, dear reader. And as if this weren't enough for one century, all of that happened with special intensity in the northeast of the country.

After a hundred years of extensive extraction and processing of natural resources, the region has been going through new recolonizations. Ida-Virumaa stands as the shadow of the larger Estonian society and as a laboratory where the future of the country is at stake, answering key issues such as the sustainability of fossil resources, disconnection from the Russian energy hub, social integration, the rural-urban cleavage, and the complex entanglement of global information highways within local contexts (see chapter 8). The infrastructural leftovers are being intensively removed or retrofitted as I write this book. Nonetheless, some infrastructures allow for repair or discarding better than others.

But what is the depth of the difference between eastern Estonia and the rest of the country? In cultural terms, the region is still not fully integrated within Estonia, yet is nonetheless part of the country and of the imaginary through which the national identity constructs its otherness or shadow. Then, in economic terms, this region is likewise not external to global capitalism but ingrained in it asymmetrically. Accordingly, in Ida-Virumaa, we can learn about complex performances of belonging, competing perceptions of the past, and the constituting of an opaque sociality through the reproduction and destruction of infrastructure. Eastern Estonia is located at the edge of Europe and mostly populated by Russian speakers. This corner of Estonia concentrates social, economic, religious, and ecological processes that differ from those occurring in the rest of the country.[23] Additionally, local residents display a particular cultural intimacy, which mediates relations to the state and might entail illegibility and the possibility of refusal.

This can be seen, for instance, in the story of Aleksandr Popolitov, who was born in Leningrad and came to Ida-Virumaa in 1947, when he was only one year old. The first time I met Aleksandr was in 2017, while searching for old postcards of the region. Those who have worked with him know that Aleksandr was very protective of the collection that he managed to put together at the Sillamäe Museum.[24] So, after interrogating me about the purpose of my research, he asked me directly, "And why would someone from Spain come to talk about Sillamäe?" Puzzled by the question, I was able only to mumble something about Soviet modernity. But was I doing research *about* this region or *in* this region? In any case, I do not think Aleksandr was searching for hidden meaning; he was just trying to understand what I was doing here. Nonetheless, the gesture of placing me as an outsider was part of the production of local cultural intimacy.[25] I recall this episode not only because I failed to give him a good answer but also because Aleksandr's question gave evidence that I was considered to be an awkward but observant outsider. As Simmel put it, the presence of an outsider, a foreigner whose disapproval matters, is often identified with transformational possibilities, as well as being threatening.[26] Nonetheless, my position as a stranger abroad, away from national hierarchies and networks of favors, was in fact epistemologically generative for research in this region, where many residents consider themselves peripheral and distrust institutions.

Fieldwork is like therapy: we can divide people into those who have done it and those who have not. Still, a dozen more times I was asked the same question. So at some point I decided to turn the query around, counter "Why does it surprise you that someone shows interest in your region?" and make my informants speak for me. Vladimir Gruzdev, owner of the SillArt Cultural Hub, replied by saying, "Because this is a strange corner, part of Europe but inhabited by Russians." Jelena Antusheva, director of the Sillamäe Museum, explained that "local people have a periphery complex and too often consider themselves inferior, even in circumstances when they should not." There was also Julia, who had moved from Karelia to Sillamäe a few years earlier, who thought, "It is because this region has been changing owners for centuries. Also, because of its current material condition; don't you see it? There is very little attention and investment coming from the Estonian state."

In anthropology we try to understand other ways of being in the world by using the self as an instrument of knowledge. We learn about others during our fieldwork and we learn again as we write books and articles. To present our knowledge, we describe relationships, tell stories, and create contexts as a way of understanding the human condition. Since the anthropologist's knowledge is based on circumstantial evidence, we spend a long time in the field building connections and documenting an array of relations and firsthand experiences in order to produce a cultural understanding of the other. Indeed, the anthropologist is the kind of expert who secretly observes while being there, relies on the generosity of others, and combines living experience with analytical distancing. Conducting ethnographic research thus entails entering into complex hosting relations that generate feelings of exposure and vulnerability. Oftentimes, a host-guest relation rests on a sense of alterity and an imbalance of power and knowledge. Still, decentering ourselves toward the world of others is part of the anthropologist's method: We see the familiar with the eyes of the stranger while at the same time retaining familiarity with what was supposed to be foreign. Perhaps because this region is largely populated by other outsiders, strangers, or non-natives, I often felt at home in Ida-Virumaa. Eventually, being considered a stranger in a strange land helped me come to terms with my own foreignness. But it also made me particularly accountable to how I represented the residents of this region. They had been depicted as an other within Estonia, a minority characterized by an incomplete belonging to the country and inhabiting a liminal world between absolute cultures.

"I am intrigued by the idea that nothing good comes from hybrids," Darja Popolitova told me at our first meeting. She is the daughter of Aleksandr and one of the artists with whom I collaborated during my research for this book. Back then, Darja was preparing her artwork *Eestimaa kodumaa* (Homeland Estonia) for the exhibition "Life in Decline" that I curated at the Estonian Mining Museum. This installation touched upon the topic of linguistic queerness in Estonia, reflecting with humor on the so-called *veneesti* (Russestonian) idiom and, ultimately, on the conditions of possibility of human inter-comprehension. To that end, Darja developed the character of Seraphita, a sort of magical trickster. A series of objects, such as an oil shale rock, an embroidered dress, orchids, and a piece of jewelry placed next to obsolete machinery, created the playful environment where the witch Seraphita tries to cure people of their cultural hybridity. This idea refers to an actual condition of mixture that presumes a narrative of

pure origin that "migrants" and those belonging to the "minority" do not completely meet. As Darja put it, "My personal trajectory followed a similarly winding
road: growing up in a Russian-speaking environment and then moving into an
Estonian-speaking one; from eastern Estonia emigrating to Tallinn; from holding a gray alien passport to gaining an Estonian European [Union] passport."[27]

In the same exhibition, visitors could see the multimedia project that the artist
Eléonore de Montesquiou made about the life of Katja Grafova, a schoolteacher
born in Narva in 1992. The installation consisted of a film and a series of postcards based on interviews with local women. In the film, Katja claims to have lost
her childhood and notes that her generation went through a social experiment,
growing up as the Soviet state was falling apart and the new Estonian one was
making Russian speakers feel unwelcome. The film conveys the anxieties of this
transitional generation and relates how Katja carved out a betwixt-and-between
identity, showing how it felt to fall between two worlds, to be rooted in neither
Estonia nor Russia, feeling like the nearby river—dividing and divided. She uses
the term "experiment" to hinge different fragments in her life and explain how
it was to grow up in "a world with no past and no future." As a result, "I finally
understand when a new experiment begins," concludes Katja retrospectively. In
that context, and as we will see in chapter 1, the basement of her apartment plays
an important role for her in testing multiple sides of the self while facing the
messiness of the actual.[28]

In another instance, in May 2024, I was arranging to screen Eléonore's film,
Kannuka Kool, at the SillArt cultural center with designer Semjon Krasulin,
painter Eduard Zentsik, and IT developer Aleksei Dorosh. At the Kannuka
School of Sillamäe, Eléonore met with a few pupils during their English lessons.
In the film, the students comment on their origins, their feelings about national
belonging, and what they know about the history of their city. While we were
setting up the film, Semjon had to go find another computer somewhere in the
building. When he came back with one, Aleksei glanced at it, then asked me:
"Do you know Estonian? I mean, do you read Estonian?" That was the operating
language of the new laptop, and none of us knew it, so we had to google how to
change the language in order to start showing a film that dealt precisely with the
issue of the different languages spoken in Estonia and their mutual incompre-
hensibility. "This is planet Sillamäe," Eduard would say later on. "Here things are
different."

Since 1991, many residents of Ida-Virumaa have left the region, and those
who stayed felt an incomplete belonging to the new collective. A sense of distance
from the rest of the country (now framed as an ethnic nation) had been spreading among many locals, a feeling that has more to do with the present accommodation within Estonian society than with roots and origins. These shifts in

identification have been correlated with new forms of inequality, dispossession, and loss. Residents grew up in a sacrificed zone, in a region that has been written off for environmental destruction in the name of the national interest. This condition evokes a sense of recolonization and a differentiated second-class citizenship within the Estonian state. Indeed, the fact that Estonians had to struggle with colonialism and endure brutal foreign domination over centuries does not prevent them from reproducing forms of colonialism within their territory and toward their own people. Quite the opposite, it partly explains it, alongside the wicked dependencies and entanglements generated by the energy infrastructure. As we will see, residents in eastern Estonia have developed forms of secrecy and opacity in response, but without establishing conflictual relations with the state.

Colonizers Recolonized?

States often foreground homogeneity and order at the expense of the actually existing heterogeneity.[29] The stigmatization of certain groups is effective in advancing that agenda, placing the other as out of time and space, emphasizing differences through stereotypes. As a result, not only is the well-being of the stigmatized population restricted, but also they are blamed for their own decline, remoteness, and pollution. Most often, *normals* don't get to know the pain of the stigma or its unfairness. After all, the other is deserving of visible discredit because of potentially spoiling a prevailing sense of identity, purity, or social order, even if the reason behind such discrimination might be publicly unknown. This was noted by Goffman in an influential study of stigma. He also observed that secrecy and concealment are part of the management strategies and outcomes of discrimination, because the stigmatized will forever remain an alien who can hope, at best, for a phantom acceptance and a phantom normalcy.[30]

Representations of national identity are articulated through the way in which certain parts of the population are visible, yet they are also arranged in what we choose to remove from public sight. An example of this is the number of people of undetermined citizenship living in the country—nearly 5 percent of the Estonian population, over 69,000 individuals who came to work in the industries of Ida-Virumaa decades ago.[31] For instance, nearly half the population of Sillamäe and Narva hold a gray alien passport, reducing them to people who have been made invisible and expelled from the hegemonic representations of national history and identity. The difficult accommodation applies not simply to citizen status—being present legally or illegally—but to a wide range of conditions in between that eventually reveal the exclusionary character of national citizenship.[32]

An example of this sense of homelessness and incomplete belonging is found in the phrase "another place on earth," which is how those holding a gray passport are defined in Estonia. Officially, the government uses the category of "undetermined citizenship" to refer to those who were living here in 1991 but failed to pass the required Estonian language exam. Nonetheless, during my research I came across multiple ways of labeling these people: "noncitizens," "stateless," "aliens," "placeless," and "*negri*" (from the Russian *negrazhdanin*).[33] All of these terms imply that citizenship is not absent but has yet to be determined or completed.

Nonetheless, the gray passports indicate not just a problem of limiting rights and not giving citizenship to a part of the population but one of a passive-aggressive sociality as well. Indeed, the sense that the belonging of the Russian speakers to the national community remains partial is also experienced by people who have Estonian citizenship, who were born here, and have even served in the army. Indeed, in the media and in different official documents, we can read a distinction between "Estonians and ethnic Russians," constantly emphasizing the latter's failure to fit into the ethnocentric understanding of identity.[34] In this way ethnicity is actively used to cultivate a sense of distancing and guilt for something that the "ethnic Russians" currently living in Estonia have not done and are not responsible for (from the Soviet occupation of Estonia to the aggressive imperialist politics of present-day Russia).

Still, thousands of the former "colonizers," now subalterns of this nation-state, cannot speak Estonian.[35] Nevertheless, they manage to sustain their social and cultural universe by carving out spaces of ambiguity, not accepting (for a variety of reasons) the national representations that underwrite their actual incomplete belonging. Indeed, after the beginning of the Russian invasion of Ukraine in 2014, a series of measures were promoted by the Estonian state to advance the integration of the Russian-speaking population. One of these measures was to launch a Russian-language TV channel "to create more cohesion in the society and give Russian speakers in Estonia the feeling that they matter," as proclaimed by Darja Saar, director of the channel.[36] *To give someone the feeling that they matter* is indeed a strange formulation. For decades, the Estonian state had been pretending to care about "the Russian minority"; in the meantime, the residents of Ida-Virumaa performed the roles attributed to them while making do apart from institutions. It was all make-believe, a theater of shadows, interrupted by the red lights of the full-scale Russian invasion of Ukraine.

This ethnography therefore questions whether decolonization implies solely the political establishment of nation-states as a historical-political ideal, challenging a victimhood-as-innocence logic as well as the assumption that efforts to counter Russian imperialism and colonial relations have to lead to exclusive, ethnocentric forms of nationhood.[37] Literary scholar Epp Annus explained that the Soviet presence in the Baltic region commenced as a foreign occupation and evolved into a late-colonial form of rule. According to Annus, in the context of totalitarian control, people defended their "emotional truths" and national continuity through the concealment of their own values and thoughts; these truths were hidden and camouflaged but not erased, since they could still be found in kitchens or basements.[38] A similar argument has been recently developed by social scientist Helena Jerman yet in a different context: Russians living in Finland, showing how they have resorted to various methods of hiding their ethnic identity (from turning their names into Finnish versions to whispering) in order to cope with the increasing Russophobia.[39]

Nowadays Estonia is a democratic state organized around a liberal market economy and with a high standard of living overall; alas, different mechanisms of secrecy persist with a special intensity in the northeast of the country. Ida-Virumaa is a prime case for tracing how the state is embedded in everyday practices, and understanding why the management of ambivalence still remains such a prized skill in the digital present. Nonetheless, decolonial, postcolonial, postsocialist, or postindustrial approaches and the like are not enough to explain the actual sociality of the region and the ongoing recolonial processes; hence my emphasis on the need to produce analytical insights that, while relevant beyond our specific context, remain based on empirical detail and attention to the limitations of the comparative or translating gesture.

The region is abundant in sacrificed zones, areas not intended for dwelling but needed for the provision and processing of natural resources—dark locations about which we don't want to know, removed from view and easily ignored, despite our responsibility for their degradation. Sadly, these zones of sacrifice seem to multiply and expand in the present moment around the planet. As the intensive industrial activity and extraction of natural resources acquired global scale, we can argue that a key problem for eastern Estonia is not its detachment from the rest of the country and from the world but precisely how it is asymmetrically connected—as residual, as a source of raw materials, and as a host for chemical processing, but where the profits hardly remain. In Estonia, the increasing need for construction materials sustains the mining activities in a region where, paradoxically, little building is ongoing. The materials quarried and processed in Narva, Sillamäe, or Kohtla-Järve, for instance, are needed for building an office tower in Tallinn and a new museum in Tartu, or for the electric cars driven in Kalamaja. Likewise, the capital from a chemical plant in Kiviõli is invested in a real estate development in the Paljassaare peninsula; yet the brutal landscape transformation, hazardous waste in rivers and soil, and continuous atmospheric emissions are left behind.

This also brings into question how eastern Estonia is represented by the media and in official institutions, making evident the need for more polycentric stories within the country. Ethnic Estonians, however, have a relative monopoly on political and representational power and too often believe that they are culturally and morally superior to ethnic Russians. In the national media, we hear of dealing with the eastern region as "a cleaning task" and that investing there is "a civilizing process."[40] This attitude affects how eastern Estonia is referred to in private and public discussions, presented as "unworthy of salvaging" or as if "nothing can be done there." Indeed, everyone seems to have a strong opinion about Ida-Virumaa. S., a friend of mine in Tallinn, asks rhetorically why the state is still supporting cultural activities in this region at all, as "it is already clear that integration has failed." He also admits that he is unwilling to visit Narva because he does not understand the local people and feels "scared because Mordor might attack us at any time." J., another friend, complains that the Estonian language should already have been imposed in all the schools in the country in the 1990s, and concludes that "Russia has always been a threat. The question is when the bear will be able to attack again." Another time I met M., who had just been in Sillamäe for a month while preparing to enter the Jõhvi Coding School. He summarized his experience by saying, "It was a strange feeling, being in a place that seems to be part of Estonia but not of Europe."

Also, negative events receive much greater coverage from the Estonian-speaking media than cultural activities organized in Ida-Virumaa. The passive-aggressive gaze of the Estonian media reflects that of the state toward the region. For instance, during my research, I met state officials who argued that "the local people are too emotional" and "they do not know how to write proposals" (which often was possible only in Estonian). Likewise, Kaarel Tarand, chief editor of the journal *Sirp,* argued in a phone conversation that the importance of the region within Estonia is relative: "Of course, a way of looking at it is geopolitical, but I can also say that it has become demographically insignificant, as it has lost half of its population since 1991." Certainly the unfavorable demographic situation of Ida-Virumaa is not a secret. The population of this region has been in constant decline for decades. In short, if in 1990 over 220,000 people lived here, by 2024 there were only 132,000. Another challenge is that while the need for social services has grown significantly (on account of unemployment, health issues, and an aging population), tax revenues have only declined. Even if industrial companies pay environmental fees to the state, municipal authorities complain that these revenues are not returned to local areas. For example, the region pays the largest share of environmental fees (68 percent of revenues), but this is not reflected proportionally in the budget lines of the local governments there.[41] The overall economic growth of the country does not always reach beyond Tallinn and Tartu; quite the opposite, it only deepens socioeconomic inequality and the rural-urban cleavage.

It is in this vein that a study of hiding places in a mining borderland, largely populated by Russian speakers (85 percent), lays out the multiple and heterogeneous connections between people, territory, and institutions. This opens the door to studying how liminal experiences sit in the territory and can, eventually, be carried and passed on through daily interactions and throughout generations. To the rest of the country, Ida-Virumaa is still a mysterious, edgy, dangerous, and depressing area. And the post-socialist experience, traumatic for many residents, still influences the way residents look at institutions and the way they relate to the state. Nevertheless, and notwithstanding the different struggles that arise out of confrontation with radical sociopolitical change, it would be a mistake to simplistically identify people in this region as vulnerable subjects, or to find easy-to-blame straw men in Tallinn or Tartu. Local people also bear responsibility for their problems. Indeed, I have also met people who grew frustrated and decided to leave the region after having been proactive against corruption and apathy there.

This ethnography therefore describes an unsettled sense of homeland among the residents of the region, being at once at home and not at home. Seeking to understand the sociality among those people who are not in dominant positions, this book gives space to studies of opacity and refusal in a post-socialist context. It describes a series of covert topographies that suggest subtle practices for disengaging dominant representations instead of public, oppositional acts of resistance. By drawing on insights from postcolonial studies and discussions of daily practices of secrecy and refusal, this book attempts to ask new questions about the post-socialist experience—in relation to the cultural dynamics of exclusion deployed within nation-building processes, the endurance of Soviet infrastructure, the right not to be transparent and not always to make sense, and the manner in which shadow spaces operate representationally and materially to maintain or challenge social order.

As Simmel noted, secrecy creates a shared reality based on concealment, an affiliative second world alongside the manifest world. Also, he foregrounded how the withholding of information demarcates different types of relationships and intimacy, articulating a sense of community as a result, though a vulnerable one because of the constant danger of being discovered.[42] More recently, anthropologist Carole McGranahan has examined forms of refusal among Tibetan refugees to show how acts of negation can be affiliative, generating novel social relations and cultural expressions despite undermining the established order and institutionalized expectations. She also shows that refusal represents not necessarily repudiation of the state but rather abstention from engaging in the present form of it.[43]

Anthropologist James Scott referred to visibility as one of the central problems in statecraft. In his view, states recurrently try to make societies legible to the apparatus of governance, deploying different efforts at domestication to facilitate the creation of accountability.[44] Hideouts are therefore needed to preserve the dissonant and different in our societies. They help us to keep in the shadows things and practices that might be antagonistic but are not necessarily incompatible. Hence, secrecy operates as a form of integration within a given system by creating spaces of ambiguity and cultural inversion.

By paying attention to shadow spaces, this book rereads the postcolonial notion of opacity in the context of contemporary problems of exposition, datafication, and recolonization. As a cultural product, secrets bring to the fore existing social divisions, yet they also provide people with tools for negotiating the boundaries of the sayable and the knowable. For authorities in turn, secrecy is often seen as a dubious practice that undermines hegemonic representations, thus an epistemic problem that demands repressive action. Concealment, however, is not always done from below; in totalitarian regimes such as the Soviet Union, the culture of conspiracy was precisely what characterized the institutional attitude toward information, with Soviet leaders and officials making use of the realm of secrecy as a part of governance.

In many cases, we enter into a relationship with society by protecting ourselves from it. For instance, in colonial territories, shadow spaces have favored an ambiguous, illegible presence safe from the eyes of those who dominated. These hidden social sites are experienced as a zone not of resolution but of cultural hybridity, one of continuous negotiation and contestation, as noted by Homi Bhabha.[45] Nevertheless, practices of concealment and refusal are contextual and show particular nuances within cultures. For instance, in Russia there is a strong distinction between the persona that is performed in public and the hidden "real" self. This has traditionally influenced the workings of statecraft as well as the experience of everyday life.[46] Sociologist Oleg Kharkhordin refers to the private-public dichotomy in Russian culture as radically different from its Western counterpart, since the primacy of the external over the internal leads to complex dispositions of dissimulation.[47] Thus, the authentic self can survive only by concealment, by the process of wary distancing from the institutions that threaten to break or obliterate it.

The idea of an inner self that is blocked from visibility as a form of protection from the authorities, while the overt is theatrically staged, suggests that communities need a front-and-back-area differentiation for social organization. Yet, contrary to what Goffman noted—social reality as crafted by the entanglement of both, front and back—in the Russian notion of subjectivity, the only true one is the private.[48] Hence the need to keep the state at a distance and to keep public speech repressed for safety's sake.[49]

Nevertheless, in eastern Estonia I found a rather fluid interplay between what is in plain view, publicly performed, and the underside of things, as well as multiple ways of dwelling on the limits of transparency. Here, social order is a dynamic process in which certain elements alternate between the forefront and the background, which are not separate but rather constitute each other dynamically. This region is itself a borderland, where binary distinctions find their explanatory limit. As noted earlier, there is a Russian-speaking majority in Ida-Virumaa because of mass migration from the Soviet Union, since the newly built cities and industries provided migrants with both work and shelter. Instead of a monolithic community, however, what we find here is a superdiversity of ethnic backgrounds. As a result, local residents show multidirectional configurations of identity that are not based on national absolutes; rather, what we see are liminal configurations of belonging and complex modes of differentiation and cultural hybridity, which are partly due to an uneasy fit in a state that deploys a too narrow understanding of national identity. That is manifested in local residents' perceptions that their views are not simply ignored but decidedly unwelcome in the national public sphere. These feelings already existed, but the war in Ukraine only cemented them. Consequently, personal agency often means working in the dark, and feelings of distrust toward institutions (but also in relation to one's own circle) are widespread.

Corners Redux

Secrets play an important role in human affairs and are central to the working of social order, not because of being true or false, but as a route into understanding the relationship between the personal and the collective, as well as between power and refusal. Yet not all secrets are alike. Digging into the operative functioning of concealment, anthropologist Michael Taussig argued that public secrets are characterized by an active not-knowing. They refer to that which is generally known but cannot be spoken, establishing a complex relationship between those who know it and those who pretend they don't.[50] As a result, the people of a given community learn what not to ask and what not to know. Taussig called this performative relation between concealment and revelation the labor of the negative, a term that stresses the social order established around the various silences and shadows taking place. Hence, they are important not in a negative way, for what they are not, but instead for what they allow (the possibility of ambivalence and adaptation).

Likewise, we can approach negative topographies as a problem space from which to think differently about social order or the modern world.[51] In this regard, corners are a fertile ground for practices of cultural inversion and the betwixt and between while also challenging the hegemony of vision. They are often occupied by "threshold people," those eluding the classifications that prevail elsewhere, at the center.[52] A corner, for instance, can be a center out there, holding a heightened symbolic, industrial, military, historical, and spiritual value, like eastern Estonia, and operate as a zone of contestation and ambivalence.[53] But corners are empirically multiple. That is why the term "corner" depicts multiple nuances in different languages.[54]

Corners often make visible the contours of a problem; they are critical zones for social relations, important because of the kinds of questions they open up for geographers, anthropologists, designers, and cultural theorists.[55] A corner is a turning edge, an area that interrupts the central modern gaze and tends to host alternative activities. It is also a symbol of solitude.[56] As corners are strongly symbolic and structural, looking at them arouses a desire to focus. In turn, dead ends refer to a situation in which opportunities for advancement are lacking, a place from which there is no exit, a path that does not lead anywhere. Still, dead ends take part in locally produced orderings and repertoires of practice, precisely by refusing to leave or not disappearing properly.[57] These oblique areas situate us in a deviant position vis-à-vis cultural conventions and dominant representations. As these dark zones of divergence spur alternative political, cultural, and social activities, they are most often negatively defined.

The ordinary demarcation of visibility is indeed constitutive of relations of knowledge and domination, not just a mirror of them. According to Michel Foucault, modern societies exert "power through transparency" and "subjection by illumination."[58] Against these modern forms of domination, and in the context of network societies, shadow spaces favor practices of critique and refusal, and not simply of an abnormal standing. In this respect, the defense of nontransparent spaces is in opposition to processes of whitening and readability that characterize modern ideals.[59] The eyes of power are manifested, for instance, in the extensive use of glass in architecture as well as mirrors in interiors, especially in institutional buildings.[60] Thus, transparency is part of the magic of the modern state, yet it has a colonial history too. An example of this is the Crystal Palace in Madrid, built in 1887 to house an exhibition on the Philippines, in which natives from the then Spanish colony were exhibited as if it were a human zoo. Categorizing and exposing something is indeed a form of control; for instance, limiting the possibility of occupying the public realm on one's own terms—thus leading to the removal of dissenting opinions from view—as a form of domination.[61]

As a technology of exposure, transparency can also operate as a tool to erase differences, overshadow social claims, and conceal hidden agendas and machinations of power.[62] Furthermore, transparency correlates with a demand for uniformity and accountability, making everything readable through the lenses of enlightenment. Not unlike bureaucracy, and arguably mobilized to articulate an ideal of democratic governance and to make the operations of power more visible to citizens, transparency is part of the ideology and practice of accountability. This way of exposing activities and representing the relation between people and institutions draws on modern thinkers such as Jean-Jacques Rousseau and Jeremy Bentham, who dreamt of transparent communities and the erasure of zones of darkness within societies. In turn, Walter Benjamin equated communism with glass architecture: Both are hard to fix and operate against secrets.[63]

Nonetheless, the Romans were the first to use glass to seal windows.[64] Then, Christian churches featured ever-larger glass windows so believers could identify God with light. As an ideological infrastructure, transparency has its particular aesthetics, materials, and history. In contemporary Western societies, the use of glass in institutional buildings is supposed to magically favor scrutiny and participation. Accordingly, transparency is not just a process, nor simply an outcome of modernity, but also a veil for the operations of power, carried out by all sorts of officials through quotidian acts of knowing.[65] Not surprisingly, transparency is often presented as a quasi-religious solution to all kinds of problems, an apolitical form of administration that can always be improved by experts and the use of technology.[66] In like manner, transparency has also been wrapped up in beliefs about the superior function of markets and algorithms. Yet organizational discourses of transparency often conceal hidden machinations of power while eliding critiques directed toward the social practices and arbitrary decisions necessary to enact it.[67] Eventually, some people end up being more transparent than others, because transparency depends on a control space that is visible only to those who are watching from inside it.

Modernity has traditionally addressed itself to the sense of sight, while opacity evoked terror and mystery.[68] Yet the practice of seeing and being seen has changed dramatically in the digital age, producing new forms of visibility and accountability through the drastic expansion of datafication. It is in that context that opacity and secrecy emerge as a form of refusal, a way of coping with the overdatafication of the present, with its arrogance that assumes that every place is known and fully charted.[69] Practices of opacity and secrecy curb the light of modern epistemology and scrutiny, referring to the demand to define and display our identity all the time as oppressive. This book points in that direction, foregrounding that hideouts help us to enact another social order, even if temporary or illusory. That is why shadow spaces, where concealment takes place, are associated with creativity, dissonance, and non-judgment.

The Eye Open in the Dark

This book asserts the necessity for some areas to be dark, elaborating an argument to defend nontransparent spaces of ambiguity, those enacting different ways of coping with current forms of hypervisibility, central accountability, and hierarchical monitoring. Hideouts connect the private and the social by providing room for suspension and retreat. In doing so, they allow diversity against the central gaze, which recursively demands transparency and accountable clarity. More than ever before, the infrastructural dimensions of secrecy and their contribution to social order need to be investigated. In this way, fieldwork on topologies of secrecy provides a dearth of information about political alterity and belonging while enabling us to map out transformations of the social over time.

This ethnography accounts for precisely what seemingly does not fit in the present or refuses to be part of prevailing structures and representations. Such under-the-radar activities are most often unnoticed because they happen with the lights out, so they have been ethnographically invisible. Territories of secrecy present difficulties for observing what is in the dark partly because their use requires ordinary obfuscation and occasional lying. Still, shadows take up a place and time, and they leave traces, despite not fitting into notions of data as measurable. Anthropologists then need to deploy other ways of seeing when they step into a basement, dance a choreography of suspicion when entering a bunker, fall into a mining hole, address the unobservable in a vacant apartment, smell the effluents of an oil shale processing plant, get lost in an abandoned library, or hear someone moving behind the half-open doors of a garage.

In shadow spaces, we find social realities that are disturbingly difficult to observe, thereby proving opaque to the methodologies we have developed. This issue raises the question as to why anthropologists should operate only within the framework of participant observation instead of trying out different ways of intervening in the world.[70] Or perhaps *intra-viewing*, as shadow spaces require other modes of seeing in, of knowing the world from within.[71] Therefore, we need to engage in ethnography in some other manner or in an expanded way. Indeed, the absence of the conditions for visually coded observations and the opacity of my experience in the field demanded the continuation of ethnography by other means, even if this entailed lacking the standardization typically attributed to methods.[72]

One way of doing so was to put different skills in relation. For that purpose I organized a series of exhibitions embedded within the respective field sites in order to explore the possibility of accessing non-formal knowledge, without sacrificing ambiguity.[73] Eventually, the artworks created for this research demonstrate the power of the aesthetic realm to think, to conduct social research, and to modify the register of the sensible. By reconsidering what to hide and what to show, by selecting who can see what, and by refusing to be accountable according to the central gaze, we also become political, or perhaps infrapolitical, as these practices happen under the hegemonic radar.[74] Thus the importance of accounting for things that can be seen only in the dark while reconsidering the conditions of their ethnographic observability.

This book describes the ways in which hiding practices take place in eastern Estonia, but it also examines how a sociality of secrecy is enacted in and by those shadow spaces and practices. For instance, basements, holes, vacated apartments, garages, or bunkers are relationally defined by what has to be unseen. The ethnography reveals in this way the actual heterogeneity within Estonian society, reminding us that national identities are not necessarily coherent, despite recurrent institutional efforts to make believe they are. Based on six years of field research, it gives an account of shadow spaces and ordinary practices concerning concealment and refusal, exploring, in turn, how they play a role in the working of social order as the elastic adhesive that connects the parts and the whole. A series of opaque topologies are thus accounted for in the attempt to include non-relationality as part of social order. Indeed, a great deal of this research studied how people engage in a form of strategic ambivalence and refusal to negotiate a sense of incomplete belonging and complex group affiliations. As a result, the contribution of this research to debates about the relation between environmental damage, political marginalization, and cultural aspects of belonging is threefold:

1. To analyses of contemporary decolonial processes, understanding the reasons why the perception of Russian speakers in eastern Estonia is not always aligned with the country's value system; therefore, it shows that the critique of Russian aggressive imperialism does not prevent us from questioning the ethnocentric construction of the nation.
2. To sustainability research, since the ethnography probes how the harm of extractive modernity and the correlated ecological memory continue to narrow down how the future is brought into the present in this region.
3. To the changing set of relations between the private and the public that characterize our world at large, since the insights challenge the institutional fixation on and demand for transparency in an empirical way.

The book is divided into eight chapters and a conclusion. Chapter 1 describes my visit to thirty-seven basements and the organization of three exhibitions on the topic. Basements are technologies of the meantime, social machines through which the editing of one's own life takes place. Cellars provide a second world of suspension and retreat; they are contact zones where the past takes up space and where cultural hybridity is stored. Thus, basements have a crucial function in societies: preserving difference while contributing to the articulation of symbolic and material order. In doing so, they allow people to cope with the changing boundaries of our private space and the invention of new forms of intrusion and ways of policing them. These underground spaces are mobilized to conceal and to regulate the amount of intimacy to be displayed upstairs, allowing other things to be seen in public. Hence, their use can be linked to wider claims about epistemic disobedience and intergenerational transfer—especially important for attending to the liminal condition of eastern Estonia.

Chapter 2 reconsiders the possibility of reparative futures by paying ethnographic attention to mine shafts. Holes are responsible for generating uncertainty and disconnections, but they also remind us of a century of extractivist modernizations. The disintegration of recognizable material forms affects the ecological memory of the region, yet it also produces societal risks and questions the prevailing economic model. These material voids contain their own forces and stand as a forensic testimony to ecological exhaustion and prolonged infrastructural harm. Today, extractive activities continue in this sacrificed area, demanding careful un-design and further unmaking. The chapter ends by paying attention to how people strive to reconstitute post-broken surroundings, describing a series of practices of public kindness that question an extractivist, industrial approach to territory. The embodied encounter with holes fosters collective responsibility, upsets modern planning, and evokes internal realms of consciousness.

Chapter 3 discusses how military remnants and phantasms of past aggressions raise questions of responsibility and disposal in the present. The discussion centers on the formerly secret town of Sillamäe, which became a closed area during the Soviet era because of a nearby uranium enrichment plant. Back then, this settlement could be accessed only with a special permit, thus pertaining to the paranoid reasoning of the Cold War. That sense of closure, along with the scars of historical battles in the area, still reverberates among the local population. Some of the numerous military bases built in eastern Estonia were demolished in the 1990s; others were repurposed or simply abandoned after the Soviet collapse. The Russian invasion of Ukraine, however, awakened unforgotten fears. As a result, basements were being inspected by the state, exploring whether they could be transformed into bunkers. Both nuclear and military wastes spread feelings of anxiety because of their wrong way of disappearing, fitting badly in the present. In their distressful resurfacing, they troubled historical representations, suggesting that there was something more to say. In this way, the research in

Sillamäe impelled me to interrogate the uneasy cohabitation of memory, history, and necropolitical residues.

Chapter 4 discusses how the demolition of Soviet housing has been undertaken by different stakeholders in Kohtla-Järve, a town developed in relation to intensive mining during the Soviet period. The regeneration-by-demolition pilot is presented as a matter of public concern by the Estonian state (thus politically loaded by reordering local relations, infrastructure, and ideas according to the normative central gaze). The project was meant to act as a normative intervention that would influence how people organize their daily life while rehearsing policy models to be applied elsewhere; therefore, it turned the locality into a social laboratory. Alas, the hope for bottom-up involvement of residents was not always met, and the intervention has been rendered as apolitical by municipal officials. The reception of this pilot by different agents has, likewise, been complex: Residents feel as if they have been placed in a social laboratory, and local authorities refuse the attributed categorization of "shrinking." The chapter thus demonstrates an acute difference in the understanding of local needs and the purposes of the enacted demolition policy experiment between national policy-makers, experts, local officials, and residents.

Chapter 5 describes a visceral encounter with vacancy as a way to understand the socio-material changes that came after the collapse of the USSR. It reflects on the temporality and materiality of post-socialism as a field of study by examining the things left behind in local homes as fossils of the transition period. Therefore, the archaeological gesture is oriented toward understanding what the experience has been in areas that are not part of the success story. After visiting twenty-five vacant apartments, I reconsider the possibilities for post-socialist material culture to become an archaeological object of study and ponder the links that tie individuals to specific locations and society at large. What might be at stake, therefore, is an entire worldview, now reduced to decomposing objects in domestic contexts and liquidated buildings. Still, future generations have the right to claim access to the past; yet to do so, they need vestiges of it alongside open historical narratives.

Chapter 6 investigates the relegation of certain places to the shadows, made redundant, off the map. It investigates how the politics of infrastructure are entangled with the production of a spatial order that might imply both the constitution and dismantlement of collectivity. Fifty or so years ago, Viivikonna was central to cartographic representations of the region. Nowadays it is not on the maps, and people come here searching only for experiences of adventure and dark tourism. The decomposing materiality invites exploration while epitomizing the contingency of Soviet power. Yet the shutdown of the mining activities that led to the fall of Viivikonna happened well before the disintegration of the

Soviet Union. In addition to discussing the aftereffects of mining infrastructure, the chapter also reflects on what it means to be in decline and how to represent it. Embracing this disheartening trope seemingly leads us to focus on exceptional situations; this condition, however, can become ordinary for many. Also, decline is examined not as an issue of being detached from the present, from the global economy, or from the state, but rather as a result of specific forms of connection, prolonged over decades as part of a systematic harm.

Chapter 7 takes us to the very edges of Estonia to visit a series of garages and dacha gardens located next to a reservoir on the border between Russia and the EU. Here, rows of boathouses lining the canals form a charming community with homemade garages and allotment gardens, producing a particular kind of bonding and feelings of being at ease. Paradoxically, a zone of tinkering and escape from the ordinary like Kulgu is situated right next to a transnational frontier that is thought of as demarcating civilizational absolutes. The great logics of geopolitics and the small tactics of an amphibious habitat meet in Kulgu. The chapter also describes the activities taking place in Sputnik, another area of dachas near Sillamäe. Overall, Kulgu and Sputnik take us to the edges of how we think about social order and our relationship to places. In this sense, I refer to this exclave as an "extopia."

Chapter 8 reflects on how cryptomining reveals a novel combination of financial exchange and technological secrecy that, nonetheless, takes place at specific sites. Since the Soviet energy infrastructure in Ida-Virumaa was underutilized, both Estonian and foreign companies have concentrated cryptomining activity in the region. Thus, a new kind of mining has partly replaced the old, which might be understood as a masked recolonialism. Indeed, cryptomining consumes a lot of electricity and water, and is seen by local residents as just another episode in a long process of resource extraction, with no clear return for them. Furthermore, the profit of large storage servers hardly improves living standards in the region. On the contrary, the ever-increasing demand for electricity to support this speculative activity has led to the development of a new energy infrastructure, which reproduces the same social and ecological harms that have been affecting eastern Estonia for a century. In this way, the chapter makes evident a continuation with the earlier extractive industrial activity, the asymmetric integration of this region within global capitalism, and the widespread territorial secrecy.

KEEPING THINGS IN THE DARK

A basement is a social artifact all the way down; nothing we do therein is untouched by the norms and expectations of life upstairs. Basements operate as the backstage of a home, where the dialectic between what is hidden (reserved for our own sight only) and what is shown to others (the stage) is performed.[1] Hence, the possibility of storing things in the dark can be viewed as a surplus of living, a generative process that plays an important compensatory role in managing a whole array of relations. In this sense, we can refer to basements as a reality-generating space that influences our standing in the world. They provide us with time to think and to explore other forms of knowledge and value, away from the conventions and scrutiny upstairs. Indeed, basements can be used in many ways: as a family archive, a material manifestation of subconscious desire, a playground of the repressed, a corner for self-expression, a room for historical and material density, and also a technology through which to rework regimes of visibility and the social experience of time. Eventually a study of storage spaces shows that some parts of our being have to descend below the ground and wait in the darkness for other parts, in turn, to enjoy the light of day. The possibility of keeping things in the shadows is thus central to the construction of a sense of self in a liminal region, where identity and memory are performed not only with regard to what is actually in plain view but also around the presence of what is not.

Between Past and Future

Once a month, Katja comes downstairs to check that there is no damage and concedes that it would be good to bring some order to her basement. We met there twice. Her basement was the most packed of all the storage spaces I have visited. Katja's basement in Narva is full of things, but also of stories. Behind a heavy metal door, and another wooden one, and after passing through a dark entryway, we encounter a family archive containing things such as a broken balalaika, which triggers stories of her grandmother playing it. "They are part of my memory," Katja says. "See, for example, these shoes from my great-grandmother or these books with old songs, which I use from time to time to get inspiration for my class [as a schoolteacher]."

Pointing at an old Soviet era radio, Katja tells me that once she has children, she will use it to explain technological change to them. Katja's radio and the children's books allow her to preserve her past but also to imagine a different version of herself. As she puts it, "What remains here might be our future." These possible futures might not come about, but the possibility of having them is part of the construction of subjectivity in the present. The same happens with Arseny. He would like to become a film director. Indeed, he has already made several experimental films, uploading them to YouTube. But now Arseny would like to produce a mainstream one. For years he has been stashing different things in three basements: items like furniture, household objects, and appliances from the 1960s and the 1990s, as that is the material culture needed to create the atmosphere for the film. He has a lot of ideas for the scenario, and storing these objects favors keeping these ideas in potency, not wasted.[2] As I am showing genuine interest in these things, Arseny closes the door that gives access to the basement and starts talking about the banner hanging in his parents' car and about a cassette of songs by the Soviet era rock musician Viktor Tsoi bought by Arseny's mother. Apparently she always listened to the cassettes at the market before taking them home, because "it happened several times that the cassette inside had a different recording from the one you had bought."

Between 2021 and 2023, I visited thirty-seven storage spaces in different towns in Ida-Virumaa to investigate which things are kept and which practices take place therein. As a technology for hiding aspects of reality, basements make some things visible by concealing others, participating in the sorting and settlement of relationships. In doing so, these shadow spaces facilitate ambivalence and the possibility of letting things go or simply remaining in their illegible otherness. Basements make past worlds available anew, reminding us of others who were here before us, and of those who will come after. They operate as spatiotemporal fixers, sites where traces of various histories and generations might meet and mingle.

There are different reasons why people keep things in a basement: the belief that they will resume that activity at some point, the assumption that things might regain value, the will to keep a connection with ancestors, or because of the human need to create distance from certain ideas or people. "You never know what use they might have in the future. Personally, they bring me happiness. I like the feeling of having the chance to revisit the past anytime I want, or to share it with my son," explains Dmitri. He likes to keep old things, in some cases items that were given to him by friends who didn't know what to do with them. For instance, he has parts of mannequins: "What if I want to open a fashion shop one day?"

We can also see sentimental material there, mostly stuff from his childhood, such as school notebooks and cassettes that would require unavailable devices to be played. From cardboard boxes, we take out a VHS of the *Nu, pogodi!* Soviet cartoons and a Nirvana cassette to be exhibited in the art installation that we are preparing (*Keeping Things in the Dark*, which I discuss shortly). These two items are pirated copies bought at the market in Ivangorod, on the Russian side of the Narva River. Dmitri is reluctant to let me use them in the installation, however, even if their present value in monetary terms would be nearly zero.

In *The Arcades Project*, Walter Benjamin suggested that old technologies influence the new in such a way that "each epoch dreams the one to follow" by engaging with obsolete items and forming past-present constellations.[3] He also observed how the value of certain possessions might appear to be irrational to everyone but the possessor. We are talking of possessors such as Dmitri, who take a given thing as a prompt to the imagination and are affected (possessed?) by the possible interactions with it.

Basements often soak up memories and distill sentiments. They allow us to pause things that cannot be easily spoken of or displayed in public while activating others. Storage spaces thus make room for a passive reconquest of time. Here, things are granted less value—for a while. And most often, this kind of value is irreducible to monetary worth and rather relates to personal history. The relation to the thing does not disappear but is instead paused. In the process, these spaces eventually contribute to resolving tensions between past and future. Nonetheless, this way of placing things at rest is different from heritage conservation, whereby the continuity of things does not arise as the outcome of doing nothing with them but is rather an active achievement of socio-technical interventions. In short, if heritage conservation requires different kinds of labor, in basements, however, things are preserved by putting them aside.

"Only When My Grandma Goes Away"

In Sillamäe, a restricted town until 1989 because of its production of uranium (see chapter 3), we meet Dima, who works as a technician. Of his storage space he insists that "this is not an apartment but a *sarai*; here, disorder is allowed."[4] Nevertheless, Dima seems to be a bit ashamed to open the door of the shed for us. He keeps things like a wooden sled and old bikes and skis, all passed along by his father. Dima says he cannot throw them away as long as his father is alive, so he is postponing putting the *sarai* in order while putting off difficult decisions. Some of these objects have accrued memories of relationships, creating a feeling of obligation to them. This, and not their economic value, is what makes them difficult to dispose of.

Somewhere between a basement and a garage, a *sarai* functions as an all-purpose storage space. There we can also find stuff such as the empty cardboard box from his old TV. Originally Dima kept it in case the TV broke down while the warrantee period was still valid. The warrantee had expired years before, yet the box remained there. This is something that most of the basements we visited contained—an empty TV carton—which exemplifies the massive expansion of gadgets and consumer goods in recent decades. This fact also shows that the basements of Russian speakers and Estonian speakers are not that different after all in terms of the overflow of things. This lack of ethnic differentiation in terms of technological goods was noted, for instance, by Mari, who lives in the mining town of Kohtla-Nõmme. She also asked several of her older neighbors to open the doors of their basements to us, and the answer was "No way, my basement is a mess." For them, opening the door to the basement was like disclosing intimacy to a stranger. I received the same answer from Aleksei, who explained to me that we could see the family basement in Narva-Jõesuu "only when my grandma goes away to visit some relative."

In this region historically characterized by resource extraction, thousands of Soviet mining and textile workers moved to the growing settlements after the Second World War, repopulating the area, as most ethnic Estonians were not allowed to return there. Besides ethnicity and obsolescence, age seems to play a key role in how basements are understood. The oldest person whom we met during our research was the seventy-seven-year-old Nikolai. He complained that his *sarai* had been robbed, but the police did not do much to resolve the case. In the break-in, he lost nearly six hundred letters he exchanged with his wife while serving in the Soviet army. His case is a reminder that storage spaces can still be broken into, since their shabby doors and locks can easily be forced. Indeed, if it were only about safety, then things would be kept more secure upstairs, in wardrobes, under beds, and in boxes on shelves, rather than beneath our homes.

Still, Nikolai keeps dozens of beautifully displayed empty jars in his *sarai*. "You cannot buy these jars anymore. They even have a different closing system," he remarks. Nevertheless, Nikolai is too old to make preserved food on his own, and the main reason he cherishes these jars is that they were inherited from his parents, brother, and uncle when they died. Even if the jars are empty and industrially produced, they are affiliative and operate as memory stabilizers.[5] They are gifts in the shadows.[6] Yet the absence of the persons they refer to might be painful, so it is better to put them away, but not too far.

We place underground what we want to get rid of, but also what we love the most. A basement stores objects that in turn store memories and relations, remaining, then, socially durable as a form of material kinship. Nikolai's case exemplifies not simply how subterranean biographies and objects co-constitute each other but also how some things create a sense of presence for those who are not physically there.[7] A sense of collective biography and of ongoing relatedness is thus established, securing our survival in the future.[8] Saving family items in the basement is, therefore, an anticipatory memory, a form of ancestralizing oneself and of generating a chronology of events and mediating with the dead.

With the gesture of storage, objects become singularized, enchanted, imbued with spirit; also, keeping things in the dark highlights a sense of intergenerational transferability, as if these items were a delayed gift.[9] These things are stored for

FIGURE 1.1.   Nikolai in his *sarai* in Sillamäe. Photo: Francisco Martínez, 2022.

others, gifts in the dark that unknown persons might someday want, favoring the creation of more fractal kinds of relations. Studies of material culture traditionally focused on objects that are present and visible. What may be absent or hidden, however, still influences people's social experiences. In other words, what is unexchangeable can be more crucial to social reproduction than the items that are actually exchanged.

Basements make room for these inalienable possessions; in doing so, they become part of a wider mechanism of inclusion and exclusion, as well as of knowledge. In this sense, keeping things underground is not just a form of storage but also a way to rework our public identity. The use of basements is characterized by a continuous discontinuity, separating us from what has no place in the present. Behind the doors of a basement, different expectations are formulated and other subjectivities find space, as if it were a laboratory of the self. Since part of our selves is archived underground, it is not that strange to find therein skeletons of a different kind. Indeed, what we hide is important precisely because it exemplifies the way people *do not want* to think, though they still do.[10] Basements are devices for conserving stuff but also for concealing potential embarrassment.[11] Certainly the act of storing something in a basement might not necessarily have a transcendental intentionality, but this gesture always refers to a relationship.

A basement is the kind of space into which all possibilities for the future can be inserted, operating as a plan B territory of inattention and ambivalence. In doing so, it helps people like Valeri to cope with the traumas caused by post-socialist transformations. In his communal basement in Narva, we found only boxes of dusty books, unopened for decades. Valeri, who is seventy-six years old, laconically states that he no longer needs to read books about Che Guevara. These books are no longer desirable but not yet torn or trashed enough to be categorized as waste. "But why do you keep them?" I ask, to which Valeri only shrugs his shoulders. For him, the basement is the place to relegate certain things in order to grow indifferent to them, but without totally breaking with the past. In this sense, his basement is a technology for the meantime, which allows not-knowing by keeping some things out of sight and out of mind.

Placing things in the subterritories of a house could be thought of as masking certain relationships and ideas.[12] Yet not all that is not shown or in the dark is actually hidden; it depends on the intentionality. In Sillamäe, I follow Jelena on a guided tour within a couple of local basements. She points out that "here you won't find Orthodox icons or Soviet memorabilia, because that's holy material," and then refers to Soviet ideology as "a form of religion." She concludes, "What you can find here is mostly emotional material." In other basements, however, I did find Orthodox icons and an array of Soviet memorabilia, some of them later included in the exhibition. But the aforementioned "holy material" is placed underground in secrecy. For instance, as we leave her basement, Irina tells us to hide the icon she has lent us inside a bag so the neighbors will not notice that she is giving it away. In our art installation, we displayed the Orthodox icon given to Irina thirty years before in the canteen where she used to work. We also included a brown leather bag used by Irina's parents when on vacation at the Black Sea decades ago. Narva-Jõesuu was itself part of that map of holiday destinations that Soviet workers could enjoy.

Stored Hybridity

Identity is what remains when you have forgotten what you are—thus something that can be encountered in basements. These kinds of dark spaces are especially useful in a borderland characterized by a performative, multifaceted construction of identity. Eastern Estonia is itself a liminal territory, standing at the border of the European Union. Because of mass migration from the Soviet Union, this is a region with a majority of ethnic Russians in a country that recognizes only Estonian as the official language. As a result, Russophone Estonians are internally "othered" because of their enduring cultural ties to Russia.[13] They are taken as *semi-immigrants* in Estonia, integral to the society in certain respects yet peripheral in others.[14] Here, belonging can be both or neither, depending on the question and the perspective.

In this context, basements extend the possibility of ambivalence and make room for multiple faces of the self and group affiliations. Basements are stateless spaces, areas where citizenship and identity have been pried apart. They shelter and mask, protecting a variety of partial identities that might be seen as contradictory from the central gaze.[15] Basements are used to seek not purity but purification; they are not about liberty but about liberation. These zones of insulation from observability are situated in the lower areas of buildings, allowing us to assign a place to what is inconvenient in the upper side of life.[16] In this sense, cellars can also be understood as the shadow of our everyday life, in a Jungian sense, referring to the dark aspects of our personality, a familiar unconscious that cannot be fully civilized.[17]

As spaces of inverted normality, basements are filled with possibility but not certainty, themselves characterized as mysterious and related to personal and collective penumbras. For example, in the nineties, Dima's storage shed operated as a meeting point for friends. At that time, he was young and still living with his parents, so the *sarai* was the place where he chatted and eventually drank with his buddies. Also Alexei tells of hanging out with his friends at Disco 5, a clandestine bar opened in 1992 in an unfinished bunker. Perhaps these young people did not have "a room of one's own" and five hundred pounds (à la Woolf), but they found a corner of freedom and camaraderie in basements. Therein they could tinker with language and visuals, testing different sides of the self in a non-designed space and experiencing things of a less consequential nature, as in an artist's studio.

Even if one can see through some of the barriers that separate individual compartments, the interiority of basements resists exposure. And through this opaque resistance, their contents become affectively charged yet inattentively accessible.[18] It is in this sense that basements can play an important role in the fermentation of cultural hybridity—as a complement or surplus to what is publicly performed.[19] Basements contribute to this form of refusal as places where multiple identity positions are stored and where new kinds of relations arise. Placing things underground is thus an enactment of opacity at the intersection between different forms of value, temporality, and representation. Here, things that can be combined not in exclusivity but only in open-ended forms enact cultural creolization. We often encountered in them a thick accumulation of layers and traces of living, looking to the generations to come and allowing different forms of gleaning to be practiced. Nowadays, these basements host unexpected coalitions such as the consumerism of neoliberal transitions with the stockpiling, kitsch, and "what you save is what you have mentality" distinctive of socialist economies.[20]

Consider, for instance, Svetlana, who wrote, "I have a very strange basement," before our meeting in Narva. She does not enter it often because every time she does so, she encounters a rat—dead or alive. Also, her father threw away all of her old toys and she was very upset. Getting rid of unwanted objects is a mechanism of identity construction; hence, when someone does it for you, it can be felt to be oppressive.[21] As soon as Svetlana opens the door to her basement in Narva, the first things we see are the remnants of the various repairs to her apartment over the years, such as tiles, door locks, and insulation material used in catching up with European building standards. She prefaces my visit with the claim that "it won't interest you, what actually interests me." Then she proceeds to rescue from the far end of the basement a wooden shipping crate that her family used decades ago to send goods to her grandmother in Pskov. Svetlana starts explaining the system, signaling with her index finger where the address was written while trying to remember the kinds of things they sent each other: candies, meat, oranges. "In terms of goods, Estonia was considered a foreign land in the Soviet Union," she notes.

Her friend Valentina reprimands Svetlana for not being ashamed to show such a basement to a foreigner—poorly lit, dusty, stinky, and with spiderwebs and cracks in the partition walls. In the neighboring building, we find that Valentina possesses three storage rooms. "What a kulak you are!" notes Svetlana jokingly.[22] The construction of basements in the region relates to architectural choices made long ago under the Soviet regime. The apartment buildings, the *khrushchevkas*— low-cost concrete-panel apartments that were developed across the USSR during the 1960s—were built according to models sent from Moscow; nowadays they are being renovated according to energy efficiency regulations prescribed in Brussels.[23]

The use of basements offers individuals the opportunity to reduce role conflict, explore alternate interpretations, and manage stigma, thereby enhancing autonomy. In Glissant's view, people are culturally opaque, and it is institutions and organizations that violate that opacity. He also pointed out that opacities can coexist and converge. In this sense, the gesture of keeping things in the dark is oriented toward a defense of our condition of minoritarian subjectivity, our not settling for a relation with those who demand we always be understood, categorized, and rendered transparent in alien terms.[24]

There Is a World Beneath the Surface

Though death may signify the biological, bureaucratic, and cultural end of someone, the legacies a person leaves might go on having a distinctly active afterlife.[25] There is the case of another Nikolai, this one in Narva. He works in construction and repair, and when someone dies, he clears out the apartment. Sometimes he puts aside some of the things he finds, hoping to sell them on the Internet, though most of the stuff ends up in shoeboxes piled up in his basement. There, he stores dozens of old mobile phones, bills and coins no longer in circulation, several icons, and rarities such as a Bible printed in "Yuryev" (now Tartu) in the Estonian language. *But are you able to read Estonian?* It is a question to which Nikolai simply smiles.

Originally, he thought I was a secret police officer. Once we started to talk, Nikolai relaxed to the point where he ended up explaining details about drug consumption among young people in Narva. Nikolai also described the disputes he had had with his neighbor about the basement. Since the space was communal, they went to a notary to define clearly which square meters belong to whom and to draw an imaginary line that neither of them could cross. Interestingly, some reactions in the field were rather skeptical or even demeaning. For example, my posts in a series of Facebook forums seeking access to basements received laughing emojis as a response and comments such as these by Anele: "And what is interesting about the basements of Ida-Virumaa? Sorry, I don't really understand the purpose of this project. . . . I went to check my shed in the old town, hoping to discover how this could be attractive to the Riga art space."

There were also cases in which local residents reconsidered the value of their basements after a stranger showed interest in the things stored there. In some instances, the research also acquired a performative aspect. Once, a resident decided to clean the basement and stage a few objects before our visit. On other occasions, such as in Narva-Jõesuu, neighbors presumed that I was a thief, checking out what was in the basement in order to steal it. This was also the case with Boriss. We agreed to visit his basement in Narva, but he canceled an hour before our meeting. Months later I met Boriss by coincidence, and he explained that his mother had come to visit him that day, casually asking, "What's your plan for today, Borya?" He duly replied, "There is a guy coming to see my basement; he's an anthropologist or something, a foreigner." Boriss's mother put her foot down, leaving him with no choice but to pull the plug. She was apparently horrified by the idea of showing the basement to a stranger and was also afraid that I might be a spy or a thief intending to rob him.

One has to learn to be in the dark. Retrieving something from the shadows takes a particular choreography; we need to slow down our pace so as not to fall or break something. Likewise, we do not get out of a basement the same way we got in. While you're descending, the acoustics change, echoes and shadows grow, and you encounter visceral smells, confusing signs, and an array of things losing concreteness and semiotic meaning. Not everything here has a straightforward sense; one needs another form of attention to see the entanglements in the making and access what silently exists incognito. As a result, what goes on in a basement stands at the limits of knowing.

Many of my visits to these shadow spaces were with artists Anna Škodenko, Darja Popolitova, and Viktor Gurov, research that led to the installation *Keeping Things in the Dark,* and to three exhibitions prepared collectively.[26] Our main installation was composed of four parts, each developed by one of the members of the group. In my case, I extracted a series of items to be displayed alongside the corresponding subterranean biographies. Some of these objects had to do with family relations, while others were holy and ideological, and there were also emotional memorabilia, preserved because of their reference to childhood.

What people do in basements is deposit things with the intention of perpetuating certain thoughts and relations, not just items. Accordingly, the gesture of revealing what was hidden paradoxically reinforces the sacred structure of concealment. Overall, what had been concealed has a particular performative efficacy while being on display—allowing visitors to see beyond the social front that informants present to strangers to the ordinarily invisible. Shadow spaces such as basements can nonetheless be entered ethnographically, thus affording knowledge that is available only to insiders and those exploring the reverse side of relations.

While we were preparing our installation, one of the discussions we had was what to do with the dust, deciding to keep it as a form of basement patina. For us, material authenticity was paramount to the integrity of the installation, a gesture that resonates with the art of Ilya and Emilia Kabakov.[27] Their installations reproduced the accumulation and reinvention of trash that characterized Soviet culture, yet positioning the ordinary as a site of resistance from which to undermine the state's desire to control memory, history, and individual representations. In a similar manner, for our installation we decided to combine ordinary objects with pictures, photographs, texts, sounds, and material culture, playing with things that appear out of time. The work with materiality gave us access to the hardware of opacity and its beyond-verbal forms of relation.[28]

Such twilight aesthetics lock out both future and past, evoking a lost or hidden temporality. Oftentimes one can also encounter existentialist forms of expression in basements. Also inverted phrases, using Cyrillic letters to write words in Estonian or English. Viktor engaged with them in *Sartre Downstairs*, re-creating the aesthetic rehearsals found underground. A half-poetic, half-archival collage was then printed on a sheet of linoleum, reproducing the rather spontaneous creative expressions of local residents throughout different eras.[29] These messages ("ghosts" in graffiti parlance) make you feel as if the basements of Soviet apartment buildings were socialist Pompeiis. Viktor also created a ceiling using fumage techniques, resonating with the postindustrial landscape of the region, with its noticeable chimneys, pipes, and factories.

In a basement, the past and the future are brought into the present, but the present is introduced to them too, making perceptible the coexistence of heterogeneous temporalities. This double capacity makes it difficult to clearly determine where the past begins and ends there. In addition, objects can have their own biographies as well, undergoing different cultural and ecological stages, existing in alternative time, separately from humans. As a result, the thing that is liberated from a hiding place is never the thing that was placed there. When something from a different time becomes relevant anew, it often does so with unpredicted associations or meanings. It is in this sense that things can threaten the stability of the present, thus holding a dark potentiality. That was, indeed, one of the key ideas of Darja's video sculpture, in which a *nevalyashka,* a Russian rocking doll, was liberated, setting off an assessment of the contemporary world through the eyes of a past cosmology. In this way, Darja transformed a cold object from the basement into a warm, unstable one—simply by resurfacing it into the present.

In her part of the installation, Anna led visitors into the basement of a five-story apartment building in Kohtla-Järve to encounter the intimacies of

FIGURE 1.2. A portion of the installation in the exhibition *Decolonial Ecologies*, Riga Art Space. Photo: Kristine Madjare, 2022.

disrepair. The building itself stands on the hollowed-out grounds of an abandoned oil shale mine, slowly sinking. Despite this, Jelena Mutonen, one of the residents, keeps decorating the building with mosaics made of leftover material from construction sites (as we read in more detail in chapter 2). For the *Life in Decline* exhibition at the Estonian Mining Museum (see chapter 6), Anna created the site-specific installation *Standby Regime*, nicely embedded in Bar Barbara, a hidden corner at the top of the building where the managers of the mine had access to privileged leisure.[30] The artwork reflected on those things that are kept pending and concealed from the gaze of strangers, things somehow suspended in the expectation of change or a better future. Anna managed to make visitors feel the overwhelming sense of standby that both basements and decline share, somewhere between rise and descent. As she noted while installing her artwork, "Basements are shelters for accumulation and future appropriation, combining both emptiness and fullness, as well as value and non-value."

Bringing Things to Light

During the opening of the exhibition, we enjoyed a concert by the local band Analogue Quattro (with Semjon Krasulin and his friends). Jelena Antusheva, director of the Sillamäe Museum, praised the band and noted that they had been practicing for many years. "We all come from a basement," she concluded. Yet her comment was not just metaphoric but also literal, since Semjon ran a club called ÖÖ in a cellar in the town for four years. Jelena herself had been leading the renovation of the museum building and its surroundings, in addition to updating the displays. The portrait of Stalin, for example, had been removed, and of the two remaining busts of Lenin, one was placed backwards and the other was half-broken. The aim of the new display was to present different periods of the city through the theme of mysteries, making use of multimedia technologies to reach various audiences. One of the installations was a virtual reality story of how it is to live in a totalitarian society, presented as a glass panopticon.[31]

Research in basements, however, entails turning the dark into an object of inquiry, accounting for things that belong to the realm of the non-measurable—the strange, ambiguous, and unknown.[32] Keeping this in mind, we also organized a storytelling workshop as a complement to our exhibition, asking residents to share personal stories and objects belonging to the dark. People of diverse backgrounds participated in our shadow play, disclosing the ways in which they experience concealment. Retrospectively, the workshop appears to me as a ritual or performance of revelation.

Fifteen people took part in the event, which started with each of the artists presenting an object rescued from their own basement. For instance, Anna brought parts of a mannequin that she had used in a previous art project and that now sits in her parents' basement waiting for a new purpose. In turn, Darja presented an unfinished handiwork produced by her father, Aleksandr Popolitov, who died during the pandemic. Then she acknowledged her dilemma about how to proceed with finishing that piece. "Should I do it in the manner of my father, or instead in my own way? What would be more legitimate?" she asked rhetorically.

We had to conduct the workshop in two languages, Russian and English, because one of the participants was a foreigner. Mark is a retired software developer originally from London. Somewhat surprisingly, he spends part of the year in Sillamäe, staying in an apartment in the center of town which he bought for a low price. Whereas many of the residents tried to move abroad, Mark took the opposite trajectory. He had yet to enter his basement because, allegedly, no one had given him a key. So Mark talked about the energy infrastructure he had seen in the intestines of the building. "The heating works in a very Russian way," he said jokingly. "Every time I came [home], I had to do a trick to make the heating work, despite paying what was written in the contract. Then, my neighbor S. helped me to turn on the heating permanently by doing something that I didn't quite understand. At some point, I tried to figure out what the problem was. Then I realized that I had been paying the wrong contract for years and also that what S. was doing was illegal, since it turned on unpaid heating to my apartment somehow."

Another participant, Meelis, mentioned a guitar that he had received as a present twenty-five years earlier. The giver expected him to learn how to play the instrument, and Meelis himself wanted to learn how. It never happened, though. In the beginning, the guitar sat untouched. Then, when he was preparing to move from one apartment to another, the guitar was put in a basement. Still, Meelis could not throw the instrument away and felt a sense of obligation toward it. "It was a present, and who knows, perhaps still I can learn." There was another participant, Daniel, who wanted to talk about two items, not just one. First, "a Soviet lock," which triggered this story: Daniel had asked his parents for the keys to the family basement several times, but they refused to give him access to it. As a result, his interest in that shadow space increased exponentially. At some point, Daniel broke the lock and went in to discover that the basement was full of food. Confused, he closed the door and put the broken lock back as if nothing had happened. A few days later, his father stated during dinner that someone had broken into the family basement but, strangely, nothing had been stolen. Daniel chose another item from the basement, a basketball: "I am a nineties kid, the time when there was nothing. Most often, we were hanging in the streets with nothing to do; in the best cases, we just played basketball."

To conclude the workshop, we performed a theater play, with the shadows of objects and drawings cast on the wall and the art installation. Overall, our project was meant to reflect on how objects become loaded with significance in the dark. Nonetheless, storage practices, as a form of memory work, are based on negotiations with oneself and others that are not always rational. This turns basements into a kind of space that cannot be contested and where remembrance and invention can happen only through traces.[33] Indeed, during the opening of our exhibition in Sillamäe, several visitors told me that they were moved by the installation, yet for reasons that I didn't quite understand. For instance, a woman named Olga told me that it reminded her of the energy of an eclipse and the lunar cycle, while another Olga thanked me for "this fairytale," which brought her "home country closer." Then, in the guest book, there was a comment describing the installation as "nicely scary."

If anything, removing things from a basement is a new start, a beginning again. Yet the underworld is fine, so long as it remains the underworld. What we were not expecting was for the placement of one of the Orthodox icons to raise complaints. V.R. saw a video report about the show on the national media and noticed that an icon of Saint George the Victorious was displayed horizontally instead of vertically.[34] She sent a private message to me as well as a complaint to the museum staff. Her first message read: "The image of Saint George the

Victorious does not look right; it is not a joyful and pleasant encounter, as it should be. But the way it is located in the exhibition would outrage any believer. Please try to do something about it. I would be grateful if you would change the current position of the holy image."[35]

I informed her kindly that I would consult with the group of artists about how to proceed. Two days later she wrote again, asking what we had decided, to which I replied that we were keeping the icon as it was because the installation represented an actual basement and how things lay there. Then we received another complaint, this time from a local priest, V.L.: "Didn't you consider that the location, surroundings, and significance of the icon of the Great Martyr George offend the feelings of believers (Orthodox, Catholics)? He is highly revered in Greece and Italy."[36]

Five minutes before the beginning of our storytelling workshop, V.R. was waiting for us at the entrance of the Sillamäe Museum with a present. As we "had no brains and no heart" in displaying the icon "incorrectly," V.R. gave us a pig's heart in a plastic bag as a present. Before she left, she explained that she had come from a distant town specifically for that purpose. "Unfortunately, I could not find animal brains at the local market," she added.

In his review of our exhibition at the Sillamäe Museum, journalist Yevgeni Ashikhmin wrote that "old things speak of many things."[37] He added that basements are places for forgetting, for casting away our burdens, which also give us signals about our present. Katja is of a similar opinion. "If we don't know how to think about the future, we can turn to the past," she said. I continue pondering these words after our farewell, and more questions than answers arise. Certainly, basements carry futurity as a storage space for things and ideas that might be experienced as new again. In that sense, some future is hibernating there. But first, what if the past has not been a preparation for the present? Second, what if the things therein refuse to be part of tidy interpretations and instead remain at the edge of signification and objectification? And third, what if these delayed gifts are not actually wanted, have no value or even place in the present anymore, and teach no lesson for new generations?

This chapter has provided an intra-view of some of the things kept in local basements, not merely on account of their economic value and usefulness in a context of precarity, but mainly because of the memories of relationships that these objects contain, creating a feeling of obligation to them. In this sense, storing things underground refers not only to the displacement of items but also to the relocation of certain meanings and actions away from plain sight.

Keeping things in the dark is a gesture that reconnects the past, present, and future, and is hence an integral part in the process of positioning ourselves within a community. Nonetheless, basements are not sites of memory, since they do not contribute to the reification of the past and the creation of expectable futures. Rather they are a social technology through which things are removed from visibility and separated from public relations, entering into another uncertain temporality. In basements, what is important is not the extent to which that "past" is real or fictitious but rather the bonding effect across generations.

Basements are entangled within wider processes that are deliberately activated in order to "make space" for other things to come in. Indeed, the use of these shadow spaces follows alternative ordering principles, providing a space for suspension, retreat, and ambivalence—without confronting or revealing, without concluding or rushing. Basements are social machines and rehearsing projects of some kind, something more than the sum of its parts, certainly not just passive repositories. Accordingly, we need to understand how spaces where the state does not enter actually matter.

A WOUND THAT GIVES OFF
A DARK LIGHT

Most often, the emergence of a hole is seen as a way to end a time and an order; in eastern Estonia, however, holes keep appearing as a post-broken continuation, manifesting a sense of post-collective loss. Local residents often refer to these mining shafts as a negative externality of industrial activity, a side effect that was not part of the original plan and design. Approaching holes as an unintended result of mining suggests that it is possible to detach these harmful consequences from the original activity. Digging, though, is a constitutive part of mining rather than an unfortunate consequence to be deplored or redeemed afterward.

Since a hole entails a particular relationship between a part and the whole, a repair intervention implies facing up to the harmful consequences of past decisions sometime later. Accordingly, this chapter raises questions of responsibility and sustainability, as well as a new awareness of the effects of modernization and of the externalities of extraction. The environmental damage caused by mining and the correlated social void have become commonplace in the region, acquiring an internal dynamic of their own while undermining the authority of both infrastructure and public institutions. On the one hand, they make evident infrastructural harm and the erasure of the continuity between human communities and ecosystems. On the other hand, the presence of holes weakens state legitimacy.

These mining shafts are a legacy from a not-so-distant past but also part of the economic and social configurations of the present. In this context, the repair of holes shows that the Estonian state is assuming responsibility for them.

Nevertheless, their "recultivation" still does not preclude further destruction, as it is not correlated with questioning the modern paradigm that brought us here. In this sense, the repair intervention seems to be nothing more than a mitigating action in a post-brokenness whole.

The Problem Is Bigger Than the Hole

When they woke up, the hole was not there anymore.

Olga used to be in charge of maintenance for an apartment building in the south of Kohtla-Järve. For many years, she neglected the threatening existence of a hole next to her living premises, despite the cracks that appeared in the walls and foundations. Olga was rather concerned, but the fear of being expropriated and uncertainty about the future made her believe that it was better not to turn to institutions. Jelena Mutonen, the new person in charge of maintenance, informed the relevant officials about the hole that posed a risk to their dwellings. Once she made the problem official, responsibility then fell on the shoulders of the state. As a result, a succession of experts began to arrive to examine both the apartment building and the hole.

Here, holes are evocative of a post-broken normality in which things have not been fixed, yet life goes on nonetheless. While the consequences of underground mining activities are hypervisible in the landscape of the region, the mining tunnels are invisible (hidden through modern technologies of excavation and subterranean domination) until they collapse. Then, a series of accidents caused by sinkholes occurs, affecting both humans and non-humans. For instance, Rene, a resident of Kohtla-Nõmme, tells how a dog fell into a sinkhole that had suddenly opened up in the middle of a park. After several days of searching, the dog was found—alive but dehydrated.

The area affected by mining is over four hundred square kilometers (almost 1 percent of Estonia's territory). Approximately 220 square kilometers of this area lies underground.[1] In autumn 2022, the Environmental Investment Center (KIK) and the Estonian Ministry of Climate funded the repair of fourteen mine shafts in the northeast of the country. First, they digitalized all the tunnels.[2] Then they identified 115 instances of ground sinking and highlighted the cases most threatening to residential buildings. Finally, they organized a protocol for fixing them and opened a public competition, which was won by the engineering company Steiger. Kristel Veersalu was the person in charge of the repair project. Interestingly, she spoke of "recultivation" and "reclamation" instead of simply repair. She also noted how the Estonian state was more closely felt by local citizens after filling the holes.

Helena Gailan, the adviser to the ministry who had been behind this project, also shared this view: "Local people notice the presence of the state through our reparations." Thus, the recultivation of these holes connects people to the institutions in qualitative ways. The repair intervention is politically charged by putting things back in order and materializing different dimensions of care by the state. The paradox, however, is that mining shafts do not quite qualify as political.[3] Still, these holes need to be repaired, not only because they are abundant and potentially dangerous, but also because they can become a sign of the inability (or lack of will) of the state to act.[4] Making these shafts absent is thus a way of securing institutional representations while reaffirming the sense of social order as a stable thing.

The emergence of holes, however, is primarily framed as an infrastructural problem that can be solved through a series of technical interventions. Gailan decided that something had to be done with the shafts when she realized that local people, "young and not that young," had been descending into the holes. Some of them were seeking adventure, while others were searching for metal and wire to be sold later on—in a postindustrial form of scavenging through which infrastructures are taken apart to sell off their materials.[5] It then took three years to start repairing the externalities of a hundred years of mining activity. And this was just the beginning, because repair takes time, money, technology, labor, and bureaucratic perusal as well. Nonetheless, new holes keep appearing. For example, in January 2023, two new ground collapses occurred in Ubja. Dealing with them promised to be easier, however, because of the existing protocols for intervention.

And yet, a Sisyphean challenge has to be faced each time: Where to find the money? In other words, who is going to pay for the repairs? The filling of those fourteen holes cost the Estonian state over 66,000 euros. Miners are not the sole party responsible for what happened in the region during the twentieth century, nor can we ask—at this stage—the Soviet Union to compensate for the environmental damage affecting local dwellings. It must now be paid for by the Estonian state. Gailan noted that the next step was to repair the nearly nine hundred shafts identified, intervention that will require cooperation between the Ministry of Climate and the EU's Just Transition Mechanism, and which had yet to find sufficient financial support.

Steiger prepared four standard procedures for the different collapse scenarios that can occur in mines. This helped in calculating costs and modeling the processual sequence (filling the shafts mostly with mining and construction rubble). To prepare these repair models and create a typology of mine shafts, experts had to do fieldwork and blend into the "holed" ecology. Often, however, the first thing they encountered were vernacular filling practices, which do not follow environmental standards. Therefore, in most cases they had to begin by cleaning up the accumulated waste before starting to fill the holes anew. Extracting natural resources is a process that rarely follows a simple linear trajectory but rather produces intertwined temporalities. Repairing the externalities of mining is no less complicated. In any case, no one has yet found the treasure that different generations were searching for with all this digging.

The Maze

Kalle Pirk, the head of the Oil Shale Competence Center in Kohtla-Järve, argues: "The key question is how to reuse the leftovers of the processing, how to recycle them or transform them into resources again. By now, after a hundred years of working with oil shale, we know everything about it. There are things we can still learn about its waste, however." Pirk shows pride in expertise and sees the extractive tradition as a source of local power instead of weakness. In the competence center, they mostly study how to give new uses to the leftovers of the process, to the industrial waste. Alas, Pirk also has a strong opinion about the place of mining in the contemporary world: "We have to use the resources we've got; we don't have to leave them underground."

To make a long story short, oil shale is a composite of organic and mineral deposits, which was formed over 450 million years ago. The organic content of Estonian shale is very high (35 or 40 percent). The inorganic part of cucersite consists of carbonates and terrigenous materials, and its processing leaves ash and semi-cooked elements. Once transported from nearby mines on monumental conveyor belts, the cucersite is crushed and burned to produce electric power or, in turn, processed into products for the chemical industry and oil, which is then refined into gasoline (to be sold mostly abroad).

"If we do not extract oil shale here, then we need to bring it from elsewhere, and the environmental impact would be the same, if not greater. Mining activity will stop only when it is not profitable anymore. Taxes and regulations are pointing in that direction. But still it is profitable to the point where a second mine will be opened in Kiviõli," says Veersalu, referring to the Uus Kiviõli II oil shale mine, scheduled to open in 2025.

Phosphorite worth hundreds of billions of euros is waiting in the depths of Estonia as well. For over a decade, there have been discussions about the potential extraction of this sedimentary rock, which is suitable for the production of fertilizer but also contains strategic rare earth metals (see chapter 3). Phosphorites, however, are a sensitive topic in Estonia because of the massive protest that arose in 1987, the so-called Phosphorite War. The Soviet project to mine this rock was finally abandoned, and the protests became a landmark of the movement for independence and eco-nationalism overall.

But what is a resource? We can find the etymology of this term in the Latin language, meaning "to rise again." From the original sense of a spring and material support, it acquired in the eighteenth century a stronger connotation referring to a country's wealth and means of raising money and supplies, in correlation to colonial expeditions overseas. Nevertheless, natural resources are neither "natural" nor always "resource-ful"; they are made so through various investments, infrastructure, and representations.[6] For instance, since the start of Russia's full-fledged invasion of Ukraine in 2022, the price of oil shale has been going up. This fact—based on both laws of the market and a geopolitical need to disconnect from an aggressive neighbor—seems to justify investment policies and the development of new mining infrastructure. The current geopolitical moment, however, not only sheds light on economic dependencies and infrastructural ties within the region but also renders visible the political dilemmas inscribed within fossil energy production and distribution.[7]

As explained by Gailan, "in Ida-Virumaa, people are used to living with the energy industry, so they do not protest against the opening of a new oil shale mine or hosting heavy industries." Nevertheless, residents of the Lüganuse municipality began to protest against the VKG (Viru-Keemia Grupp) project to develop a new pulp mill in the area. "No one in the village approves of the plan, as far as I have talked to people. There will be no benefit to the village, and we cannot see anything good coming from it. There will be heavy trucks, big pipelines, and other disturbances to our summer stay here," says Helmi Sibrits, a local elder. VKG, in turn, justifies the choice of this location on the basis of its access to water and the existing infrastructure for transporting raw material. The mill's raw water will come from the former Ojamaa Mine and be flushed into the Gulf of Finland "once it has served its purpose."[8]

There are three thermal power plants in Ida-Virumaa. We find the world's two largest oil shale–fueled power stations, Eesti Power Plant and Balti Power Plant, near Narva. Another one stands near Kohtla-Järve.[9] There I meet Õnne Pilvet, the head of communication of VKG. She began working for the company in 1992. At the time, Pilvet was paid in goods instead of receiving a salary. "What else has changed?" I ask. She pauses for ten seconds and replies, "The technology and the environmental inspections."

Entering the premises of an energy plant means stepping into a gigantic maze. Within the factory, one encounters a totally man-made intestine, a world within this world assembled from pipes, kilometers of tubes running through structures built of concrete and metal, along with multiple chimneys and smoke. And in the middle of it all, we can find a stencil of the Super Mario Brothers emerging from

FIGURE 2.1.   VKG oil shale processing plant in Kohtla-Järve. Photo: Francisco Martínez.

tubes, as in the video game. In another corner of the premises, in the older hill of ashes, there is a spot where orchids bloom in a variety of colors. I am certainly not used to wearing an industrial helmet, gloves, safety goggles, and reflective vest, nor to absorbing fieldwork through my nose. Unsurprisingly, I became dizzy in the reactor room of the plant, where strong smells and ground tremors combine with high temperatures. (The reactor reaches nearly seven hundred degrees Celsius.) There is also a strong sense of vigilance here; conducting observations under the surveillance of multiple cameras is indeed a strange experience, but while my fieldwork was a highly surveilled activity, the workers of the factory did not pay much attention to my presence.

In the engineers' room, the controls are labeled in two languages. When asked about it, Pilvet explains that all documentation and top administrative meetings are in Estonian, with everyday tasks often conducted in Russian. People of more than twenty nationalities work here, she adds with a hint of pride. Pilvet is from the south of Estonia but married a miner and moved to Kohtla-Järve. Every morning she checks the weather vane, since the wind might push the strong odors to Kohtla-Järve, eventually preventing the people living nearby from going out for a walk or keeping the windows of their apartments open. "I'm not too sensitive, but I know people who cannot stand the smell. . . . In any case, the smell is not so strong as to have to close the town," Pilvet reassures us. I visited the VKG premises with Anna, Darja, and Viktor while we were preparing our exhibition. After noting our skepticism, she suggested that we "breathe deeply; this is the smell of money."

Urbanist Andra Aaloe has studied why local residents are not complaining about it, concluding that their endurance has shifted over time exposed to the stench.[10] Still, long-term exposure to sulfur dioxide reduces lung function, damages the respiratory track, and causes bronchial constriction. As a result, respiratory diseases are more common in Ida-Virumaa than in the rest of the country. Pollution is indeed part of a differentiated belonging in Estonia. Power relations are sensorially attached to locational differences, generating in turn the experience of an incomplete belonging to certain communities. One location receives warmth and profit, the other one receives stench, harm and stigma.

A year later, I visit another of the power plants, the Enefit plant in Auvere.[11] I share Pilvet's comment with engineer Lena Kolatsk. She smiles and reminds me that "money doesn't actually smell." I keep thinking about it during the excursion. Perhaps money does not smell because it is now electronic. Or perhaps because it lies somewhere else, far from where the energy is actually produced. Kolatsk adds that "there are many potentially toxic gases that we do not see or smell either." She has been working here for eighteen years, at first in the lab, and then as an engineer. I ask her how long these plants will be operating, and she is unable to give me a concrete answer. She excuses herself, explaining that it is impossible to say because the EU regulations are becoming more and more strict, making this kind of energy production less and less profitable. Thus the uncertainty, but not because the mines might dry up or the infrastructure might eventually become obsolete.

Materialization of Emptiness

Kristel Veersalu, the engineer of Steiger, notes that "nowadays, the principles of resource extraction are not that different from those in the twentieth century, but technology and environmental protection have certainly changed." The technology that has revolutionized the planet in the last two centuries is made with resources that come from the subsoil. The first commercial oil shale plant in the area was put into operation on December 24, 1924, and subordinated to the Soviet authorities in December 1940.[12] After World War II, the distribution

FIGURE 2.2. Construction of the Kohtla-Järve–Leningrad pipeline. Photo: Grigor Akmolinski. Estonian National Archive.

of the mining industry was based on the kind of infrastructure grid developed throughout the Soviet Union. In the case of eastern Estonia, mining combined a dual displacement of mineralogical matter and people to develop systemically extractive industries that are still operating.

We can perceive in the landscape the long-lasting dependency on oil shale mining and chemical processing that shaped eastern Estonia. That dependency also came to shape how the region is seen in the rest of the country, its governance, and also the kinds of relations existing among municipal politicians, the state, private companies, and local residents. Thus, the actual shafts testify to the unsustainable character of the human presence in Ida-Virumaa. Holes render visible the dark side of modernity, whose emergence requires territory and bodies as sacrificial zones and is premised on extractivist systems such as colonialism, capitalism, and communism.

Mining, as an ecological incident as well as a source of strong smells, does not end once the workers go home or the mine is closed but rather continues to generate present and future pollution even when the activity is over. Its extractive effects linger on as a form of post-brokenness, a leaking time of agony. These mining scars appear as the hangover of a century-long extractive process with all the associated environmental and sociopolitical impacts. Hence, when exploring post-extractive futures, we also have to reconsider the social costs of infrastructural residues and the need to deal with the negative consequences of Soviet modernization. Filling land is not the reverse of resource excavation but an extension of it, a gesture of repairing the problems created by previous generations. Most of the industries, however, are still active.

A drive around Kohtla-Järve or Kiviõli shows leftovers of mining that resemble lunar landscapes—deteriorated buildings and rusting machinery but also spacious urban planning. When stepping out of the car, you can smell the chemical odors related to the processing of oil shale. Social order and stigmatization are also a nasal phenomenon.[13] In eastern Estonia, the historical disregard of the environment led to a deterioration in the quality of the air, which is one of the reasons behind the current outmigration. Since 1991, some cities have lost two-thirds of their population. Subsequently, the number of people here aged sixty-five and older was expected to increase by more than 40 percent between 2020 and 2030, resulting in a greater need for social support in parallel with a decreasing capacity to address that need in terms of human, political, and financial resources.

Outmigration has also been related to the high unemployment rate, which has risen in recent years as a result of corporate restructuring connected with the European Green Deal Investment Plan. Alas, it is not only the implementation of the EU's strategy at stake here. Since the full-scale invasion of Ukraine started, the Estonian state pledged to reduce to the minimum its energy dependency on Russia as early as 2025. Ivan Sergejev, who manages the EU's Just Transition Mechanism at the Estonian Ministry of Finance, explains that the residents of Ida-Virumaa are those most affected by the change of script in energy production and consumption.[14] Eastern Estonia exists in a social laboratory mode, in need of a future while seeing parts of the region recolonialized and sacrificed even now in the present. A sentiment of collective loss that appears as the opposite of a future has been spreading since 1991. Indeed, the local residents I met refer to Kohtla-Järve as a futureless town with too much pollution and too few opportunities for young people.[15] For instance, Jelena doesn't talk of cultivation or of ground collapses. The problem, in her view, is "the emptiness from mining" (*pustota ot shakhta*). At first I thought she was talking about holes, but then I realized that what she means is bigger than that—a void that generates stress, affects the value of local apartments, and disintegrates social bonds.

"For many years, we had to pay for the repairs, cracks, and façades on our own, with no help from institutions. It was difficult, and people dealt with the consequences of mining as best they could. Loans were taken out to make repairs. Then, the KreDex program came," Jelena says. Her friend Anya adds: "This is the southern microdistrict. Underneath us, we have mines that are no longer in use, but we might fall through, since shafts continue to appear everywhere." Indicating the buildings around us, she remarks, "I don't know when these buildings might fall as well." According to Pirk, however, the head of the Oil Shale Competence Center: "The construction was experimental from the beginning. They knew where they were building, the kind of ground they had."

Holes are often thought of as putting an end to a time and to a socio-technical order, but in the case of Ida-Virumaa, they stand as a continuation of both: an unsustainable extractive approach and a vulnerable condition.[16] Here, shafts and ecological damage became ordinary and remain as a lasting state of affairs, with their own internal dynamics. They point to a condition of loss whereby multiple destructions have not yet been sorted. Anthropologist Dace Dzenovska has developed a similar argument in relation to the Latvian countryside, where locals use the term "emptiness" to name a condition characterized by loss (of schools, transportation systems, neighbors, jobs, purpose).[17] As Dzenovska notes, emptiness attests to the process of restructuring the entire economy and society after 1991, built upon neoliberal capitalism, which brought the revision of the state's economic role and the liberalization and marketization of natural resources.

For local people, the repair of mine shafts has been a way of making order out of the chaos brought about by the post-socialist change of scripts. While considering these holes, however, we also need to pay attention to the principles that brought us here. This makes the unmaking and redesigning gestures preconditions to a sustainable future.

Digging Shadows

In *The Foundation Pit*, Andrei Platonov describes the endless labor of excavating what seems to be a shelter. One of the workers, Voshchev, says that he is digging in order to find meaning in the ground. But instead of meaning or, at least, happiness, what Voshchev finds is darkness, rendering his labors existentially futile.[18] In this allegory, Platonov contraposes the Soviet infrastructure projects with the idea of building into the ground, downward, thus for the dead. While I was reading the novel, the newcomers who began to move to eastern Estonia to work in the newly constructed factories after World War II came to mind, as well as the nothingness that came after, in the 1990s, once the industrial activity was first reduced and then integrated within the global market of commodities (see chapter 5).

Rather than existing a priori, the underground—as we know it—comes to be through extraction, thus through human intervention. According to sociologist Lewis Mumford, mining was a prime causal agent in the emergence of modern industrial production and capitalist exploitation. He writes, "The methods and ideals of mining became the chief pattern for industrial effort throughout the Western World." Indeed, mines are "the first completely inorganic environment to be created by humans. . . . Day has been abolished and the rhythm of nature broken: continuous day-and-night production first came into existence here. The miner must work by artificial light even though the sun is shining outside; still further down in the seams, he must work by artificial ventilation, too: a triumph of the manufactured environment." This extractive logic, Mumford concludes, also applied to the relationships between people: "Human beings were treated with the same spirit of brutality as the landscape: labor was a resource to be exploited, to be mined, to be exhausted, and finally to be discarded."[19]

Historically, mining was a type of labor regarded as worthy only of slaves; the idea of excavation, however, gradually acquired an aura of reverence and mystery, as if it were a solemn task. In *Notes on the Underground*, science and technology studies scholar Rosalind Williams explored the significance of spaces below the surface in past narratives, especially at the beginning of the Industrial Revolution. That was a period when mining activity grew, forming modern infrastructures that were part of a wider "dialectic of progress and destruction." "Since the nineteenth century," Williams writes, "narratives about underground worlds have provided a prophetic view into our environmental future." Some of these narratives referred to digging down into the earth as a form of truth-seeking and as a journey of discovery, turning the underground and excavation projects into social metaphors.[20]

Kohtla-Järve has been considered the mining capital of Estonia for a century. It is located on deposits of oil shale, and the extraction and processing of this composite is still the main industrial activity here. Kohtla-Järve received city status in 1946, but settlements in this territory have existed for a long time. The name of the city was borrowed from the neighboring towns Kohtla and Järve, on which the city was established after World War II. A few other settlements were swallowed by the mining industry and the subsequent foundation of Kohtla-Järve. The biggest one, among those fallen into oblivion, was Käva, which had its own monument to the independence of Estonia. Paradoxically, its vestiges are now buried underground.

The early years of Kohtla-Järve have been studied by folklorist Tiiu Jaago, who focused on residents' life stories and their relationship to the place.[21] The infrastructural provision of electricity and running water and the development of railroads and pipelines were taken as the arrival of civilization itself. Yet in an interesting play of mirrors, Jaago contraposed what people confessed in their diaries with what they were writing on postcards they mailed. The public narratives (on postcards) presented a tale of progress; by contrast, private observations (written in diaries) remarked on the gloomy and unsafe experience of living there, alongside tales about how the old village community was broken. In addition, early accounts foregrounded hard living conditions and continuous fights based on ethnicity, noting that after the war Estonians were still cursed as "fascists." The process of Sovietization, which took decades, was accompanied by terror and irreversible changes in the structure of society. Nevertheless, as noted by Olaf Mertelsmann, it would be an oversimplification to refer to it only in terms of Russification, since indigenous cadres were preferred for promotion, schools operating in the local language were better equipped, and folkloric festivals were sponsored by the regime.[22]

FIGURE 2.3.   A view of Kohtla-Järve in the mid-1950s with a bus driving down the street. Photo: V. Gorbunov, 1955. Estonian National Archive.

The territory consisted of clusters of villages around particular mines, in some cases towns of thousands of inhabitants such as Kohtla-Järve, Jõhvi, Ahtme, and Kiviõli, but also smaller settlements such as Sompa, Kukruse, Viivikonna, and Sirgala. An extractivist archipelago was then formed to secure the provision of raw materials for the Soviet grid. Overall, energy infrastructure served as a tool for integrating Estonia into the Soviet political space. Likewise, the correlated migration contributed to give shape to sociality in Ida-Virumaa. At the time, the newcomers saw no reason to foreground their own ethnic identity, as they identified with the Soviet supranational one. Furthermore, schools, jobs, and various cultural and sports facilities could be accessed in Russian. Thus, there was no need to learn Estonian.

During the Soviet period, the municipality greatly expanded, rapidly establishing modern settlements for miners in former rural areas and reaching over 87,500 inhabitants (2024 population: 33,197). The first mention of the villages of Jeruius (Järve) and Kukruse in that area dates back to 1241 in the Danish land register and Sompa in 1420. Some of these settlements experienced the Livonian War in the sixteenth century and the Great Nordic War in the early eighteenth century.

The villagers had built their individual houses and farms themselves, or inherited them from their parents. After the Second World War, they had to relocate into five- or nine-story concrete-panel apartment houses provided by the state.[23] Two cultures were thus on a collision course with each other: the newcomers thinking that it was now their country, and those who had stayed, believing that this was still their homeland. Once the Soviet Union collapsed, the newcomers found themselves aging in a world that was becoming increasingly strange to them.

Estonia's political elite then opted for "an intentional and complete break with the Soviet past and everything that reminds [people] of it," as noted by sociologist Marju Lauristin.[24] At first glance, the post-socialist "transition" in eastern Europe appears to be a success story when we consider the financial and political macro-levels. And among all the former Soviet republics, there is one that is often presented as the role model: Estonia. But anthropologists need to peek behind the curtains. Indeed, the present that has resulted from the restoration of an independent republic disappointed some of the residents in the eastern part of the country (for instance, many of those who still hold a gray alien's passport).

Indeed, Ida-Virumaa has often been described by the national media as a land without roots, reduced to polluted surfaces, underground tunnels, and residual occupants from the Soviet era. In this context, anthropologist Eeva Keskküla has studied what it means to be a miner once the job has been stripped of its glorified status, being rather stigmatized and suffering from a loss of the sense of community. In the Soviet Union, industrial workers were elevated to a particularly honorable rank, one whose hard labor served to construct socialism. The regained independence of Estonia, however, along with the new market economy, meant the miners lost their political and economic—as well as sociocultural—significance. They then had to readapt to increasingly rapid technological changes and a competitive moral economy to be a part of global capitalism.[25]

Even though some of the mines had already been abandoned during the Soviet regime, a sense of cultural loss and social void has been a growing reality in eastern Estonia, due to the outcome of the neoliberal economic policies and narrow national narratives adopted as well. What used to be collective then became privatized, neglected, or demolished. Yet we are talking not only of a dispossession of properties but also of losing social status.[26] This part of the Estonian population was not *possessed* anymore by industrial corporations, farms, or youth organizations, thus being left as part of nothing. This sense of a collective loss is still latent. Indeed, during my visit to the Enefit premises in Auvere, Jekaterina Muravjova, the communications manager, emphasized several times that "the workers of the energy plant are proud to be a part of something big."

Post-Brokenness

The energy system of Estonia has been dependent on oil shale for a century.[27] Nowadays, it is the only country in the world that uses oil shale as its primary energy source. Five mines remain in operation: three are open-pit mines and two are underground mines. In 2022, according to the Statistics Estonia office, the country generated approximately 57 percent of its electrical power through combustion of the burning stone.

Rurik Holmberg, analyst of the Swedish Energy Agency, notes that the processing of oil shale has been a guarantor of electricity supply and a refuge for Estonian investigations in science and technology.[28] In his view, the survival of the oil shale industry in this country has been a result of its variety in technology, end products, and ownership structure. Additionally, he observes that elements of the interwar period and the Soviet culture have remained operative in the Estonian oil shale industry, even in today's global market economy.

In the 1990s, the industries at Kohtla-Järve and Kiviõli were merged into a single company called Kiviter. In 1999, Kiviter went bankrupt, leaving thousands of people unemployed. Activity continued, thanks to the seasonal demand in road construction, as well as the sale of scrap metal.[29] The mining and processing infrastructure was then taken over by a newly established private company called

Viru-Keemia Grupp. The power plants in Narva, however, were left under government control; Eesti Energia, the corporation that now runs them, has become the world's largest oil shale energy company.

I take a walk in Kohtla-Järve and see other people walking their dogs, putting gas in the car, watering their plants, or buying ice cream. They might also invite you in for tea, such as in the case of Jelena. The overwhelming first impression of disrepair and pollution in this town is contested when we pay attention to the ongoing interventions that establish socio-material stability.[30] In 2010, the EU allocated nearly 4 million euros to build and repair roads and sidewalks, as well as to replace the street lighting system. The central square was also renovated, becoming primarily a pedestrian zone. Hundreds of trees were planted near new benches, flowerpots, and rubbish bins. Yet processes such as ecological pollution, outmigration, and peripheralization have put the local population in a precarious situation.

One of the side effects of this socioeconomic shrinkage is that the real estate of Kohtla-Järve has radically lost its value. Apartments are often worth less than a secondhand car, as thousands of them continue to remain vacant. Following the outmigration trend in this town, hundreds of privately owned properties reverted to the municipality, which, in turn, compelled the Ministry of Finance to react and intervene. This phenomenon is referred to as contagious by different stakeholders, potentially leading to a negative spiral that could put an end to the local sense of urbanity. After decades of approaching this societal issue as merely a local problem, the Ministry of Finance initiated a pilot project in 2020 in which the demolition of half-empty apartment houses was proposed as a future-making intervention intended to bring back order to the urban fabric (see chapter 4).

Post-brokenness is a condition in which recovery has not been achieved, yet many things continue in the meantime, including suturing practices. Manifestations of post-brokenness make evident that disrepair might last in time, have different socio-material manifestations, and also be a part of multiple endings.[31] As we saw at the beginning of this chapter, Jelena lives in one of the buildings that are being considered for potential demolition and which had a mining hole nearby. While the liquidation of architectural objects is under consideration, she has been refurbishing the basement, entrance, and attic of the building with creative mosaics, made by hand from leftovers taken from nearby construction or demolition sites. She confronts the damage of mining and tries to find ways of mitigating it as a matter of public kindness:

> I started because it was terrible, terrible. At some point, I had to throw a lot of tiles into the garbage container, and I felt some pity, so I created a bird out of them. First, I tried doing so on my own in the basement, to

see what I was capable of. It was in such bad condition; it was terrible! My husband helped me to clean it a bit and said, "I hope you know what you are doing." I am not a professional, but with patience you can do it. It's always in my free time, two hours here and there. Later, I also made it beautiful upstairs, at the entrance and in the attic. With the mosaics, I can fill holes and cover horrible places with beauty. . . . I want to make the lives of people less stressful. . . . I believe these installations contribute positively to how people organize their everyday life.

Jelena has been finding value where there was none. In doing so, she deploys a critique of the finality of brokenness and practices care beyond the logic of capital. Perhaps it is because life seems easier when you fix things; perhaps because repair work can be experienced as a form of material participation,[32] an infra-political intervention that addresses social issues via politically disqualified means;[33] or perhaps because the reworking of things that are public can operate as a form of contestation, one working from within, redesigning who and what counts as well as who is entitled to what.[34] In some cases, it might be that repair is performed without our knowing clearly where the problem lies, what the damage might be, or even what we are really doing. As Jelena demonstrates, we can still rework the point of brokenness as a generative gesture, improvising, once the limits of normalized procedures have been reached.[35]

Voids on the Way

In their study of repairing infrastructure, Christopher Henke and Benjamin Sims differentiate between the vertical repair practices that uphold power structures and the horizontal interventions that transform relations around the repairer.[36] Jelena's interventions belong to the latter type, bringing up new configurations of endurance.

Repairing involves paying attention to a problem and responding to a break, failure, or error.[37] It has two interconnected dimensions: a practical attempt to fix what has been broken and the symbolic charge that honors care over abandonment. It is repair that reestablishes a sense of how things should be, acting as a normative suture between separate parts.[38] In addition, repair interventions also have a political component, as something performative to be seen and noticed as a symbol.[39] Repair studies, however, have traditionally prioritized the material dimension of the act, neglecting in turn its symbolic-political level.

Etymologically, the word "repair" comes from Latin, where it means "to prepare again." Thus, it is a transitive verb, that is, it requires an object which

receives the action. You can also fix yourself, improve your appearance, or intervene in your body or even your mind.[40] As a way of calibrating, intervening, and
reconstituting, repair plays an important role in the constitution of the everyday
environment, too. While the repair models point to a *whole*, holes materialize a
fragmentation into different parts. Nonetheless, we can distinguish between preventive and corrective maintenance. Also, there are repairs that are done according to plan, others that are unexpected, and finally upgrades that have to be done
on time but might be delayed for different reasons.

Still, repair is rarely considered sufficient for future-making strategies, despite
its capacity to create favorable conditions and mobilize socio-material care. In
accordance with this logic, planning and financial efforts have to be allocated to
amending modern infrastructure. Nevertheless, there has been criticism which
argues that what we need to do is to undo and design away the principles that
brought us to this situation, as we live in the aftermath of previous making and
policies. By contrast, repair might end up feeding into new iterations of a harmful
model, so we should begin by unlearning and undoing extractivist paradigms.[41]
Indeed, extraction reorders things and relations. It is mining plus infrastructure
plus an ideology of grabbing and taking without giving anything back regardless
of the possible consequences (or externalities, as they are called). Extractivism is,
therefore, the expression of an overwhelming and unsustainable idea of mastering and dominance.

Nevertheless, ground is not broken only to extract resources. In addition to
sinkholes erupting from past mining activity, we can also find wells, potholes,
and the foundations of vanished buildings. Wells take on a poetic manifestation in Mäetaguse, where spectacular fountains spring up through the mining
shafts, since oil shale excavation has influenced the movement of groundwater
in both horizontal and vertical directions.[42] Potholes can also result from diverse
nonstructural causes, such as diesel spillages, animal hooves, vehicle rims, rocks
falling into asphalt cuttings, as well as from structural reasons such as poor road
design, dispersive soils, weaknesses in the base material, or a lack of regular
maintenance. To paraphrase Paul Virilio, every pothole contains its own form of
an accident.[43] And to paraphrase the well-known dictum in *Anna Karenina*, all
happy roads are alike, yet each hole is broken in its own way.

Potholes direct attention to the contingency of infrastructure; through disruptions we perceive the fragility of the things we construct. Inadequate preventive
maintenance of roads might lead to the development of surface cracks. If they
are sealed, or the spalling is repaired in time, no significant damage will occur
to the pavement. But if they are left open, the access of water through the cracks
results in deeper deterioration of the road. There are, nonetheless, several ways of
treating the problem. The easiest and cheapest method is to fill the potholes with

sand or crushed stone. This formula is mainly used in cities. A more expensive alternative is to fill the holes with cold asphalt. The third option is to cover the whole potholed road with a new asphalt surface. Much depends on the financial capacity of the municipality—for example, in the Jõhvi municipality, the volume of pothole patching was 1,500 square meters in 2022 at a cost of 180,000 euros— and also how close the election date is.

Potholes are first of all a local government problem but also a symptom of the reduced funding for rural areas in Estonia. In general, April is the time of year for pothole repair. The work involves a certain degree of normalization across the country. Asphalt is typically between twenty-five and fifty millimeters thick, unlike the much thicker surfacings used in most other Northern Hemisphere countries (one hundred millimeters plus). Nevertheless, independently of latitudes and infrastructural traditions, all potholes have something in common: the bigger they get, the faster they grow. Hence, the corrective maintenance of potholes happens every spring. Preventive repair, however, is what Erik Väli, an engineer at TalTech, proposed to the Ministry of Climate: to blast the old mining tunnels that remain close to the surface in order to avoid future risk of collapse. Or perhaps it was rather a form of iconoclasm.

Looking from Below

How can holes transmit information? And what kind of light do they give off? Mining shafts are a specific form of material failure, a normal accident that is, nonetheless, intrinsically unpredictable. A hole cannot be known in full and always looks up at us from below. Obstinate and always unresolved, it demands too much attention and is hard to replicate; hence holes have to be made invisible for something to keep working. Yet as with our bodies, some orifices are needed for systems to be operational. Mining shafts, however, are *the other* of modern planning and its grammar, with the ability not only to interrupt the designs of humans but also to act with their own trajectories and entropic propensities. We are talking of *hole power*.

Despite having no specific function, neither symbolic nor practical, shafts unequivocally affect the surroundings, from social relationships to mechanical functions and the organization of the space. Hollowed-out spaces are spectral in their withdrawn condition, a negative symbol or black trope. That is why physicist John Wheeler coined the term "black hole" to describe a self-contained universe from which nothing, not even light, can escape. This astrophysical phenomenon is black because of its inability to emit light and a hole because of its gravitational pull (swallowing nearby objects).[44]

As negative spaces, holes are part of the whole and simultaneously excluded from it, thus a part that has no part.[45] Still, they are capable of stretching or interrupting social relations, of changing the directions that we take, and of keeping things in potential—because holes leave no room for negotiation. They come as an offense against the neat and tidy, reminding us of the interdependency of our worlds. Shafts also invite us to account for more than human relationalities. On the surface, a hole signifies a scar, since the ground falls because different agencies meet and interact entropically. Holes generate collateral realities and stir up existential rumination along with sentiments of social and ecological responsibility. They have entries and exits, and give access to the subterranean, yet socially they appear to us as a reminder of a century of modernization, largely based on the extraction and processing of natural resources.

These holes make visible the destructive forces of human intervention and spatial abstraction, of withdrawal, exhaustion, and the negative effect that leaks and remains behind.[46] Nevertheless, these ideas are removed from the recent musealization of this region through tourist campaigns with the anthropocentric slogan "Land of Adventure!" (*Seiklusmaa!*). Nor are the energy plants producing the majority of the energy consumed in Estonia represented in the new promotional maps of Ida-Virumaa. Perhaps a better way of advancing a new awareness of the effects of modernization and of reminding us that it costs a lot of time and money to recover contaminated land is to keep one of these mining shafts publicly accessible. Such a hole-monument would then become a sort of entropic heritage, maintained in its ruined state through careful stabilization while time and ecological damage are allowed to continue working on its shaping.[47] That form of *land art* would stand in the same way as the mine-waste hill in Kukruse. There, local residents have expressed their opposition to the Ministry of Climate's plans to remove the waste hill full of ashes. For them, the hill is a landmark of the town. Meanwhile, the experts at the ministry are worried about the potential leaking of chemical elements into the groundwater, since semicoke is a residue classified as environmentally harmful.

Still, the landforms generated by mining and oil shale processing became a part of local inhabitants' identity. The hills and the sinkholes show an interesting correspondence, indeed, one oriented upward in relation to the surface, the other downward as a depression. The highest artificial mountains in the Baltic region are situated in Kohtla-Järve and Kiviõli, semicoke formations over one hundred meters high, while in Narva we encounter two ash plateaus occupying 860 and 570 hectares, respectively.[48] Over 15 million tons of oil shale are mined annually in Estonia, and its processing leaves over 7 million tons of ash.

Paradoxically, as early as the 1970s it was suggested that the *Glory to Labor* monument be relocated to the Kukruse waste hill. Leonid Ananich, the first

FIGURE 2.4.   Monument to Lenin in Kohtla-Järve. Photo: V. Gorbunov, 1951.

secretary of the Kohtla-Järve party committee, proposed that measure; archi-tect Udo Ivask and sculptor Olav Männi (the creators of the monument) were strongly opposed, however.[49] In the end, *Glory to Labor* is still in its original location, though the monument to Lenin that used to stand at the gate to the town (on the corner of Järveküla and Vanalinna) was sacrificed on February 13, 1992. The bronze statue was fifty-two years old, a few years ahead of retirement. Nowadays, the nearby VKG factory is still operating, and vegetation has taken over the monumental void.

Mining shafts are signs of how the ecological consequences of human actions might be beyond our control. These voids are the side effect of previous infra-structural designs and modernizing policies. In the present, a study of these situ-ated forms of collapse compels us to reconsider who has, or should have, the responsibility to fix what is broken, and how repair is linked to issues of the future, care, and redesign. Thus, in projecting post-extractive futures, we have to confront the need to undo the side effects of modern projects and reconsider the social and ecological cost of extractive industrial activities. Yet the para-digms underpinning Estonia's fossil energy supply are neither exhausted nor fall-ing apart. Here, holes are referred to as belonging to the past, not the present, whereas the future is imagined as flat and digital. The paradox is that these holes cannot strictly be called "Soviet" and that the digital future still relies on extrac-tive infrastructure, at least partly (see chapter 8).

Some of the underground mines began their activities as early as the interwar period, and the holes, as a materialization of social emptiness and excessive exploitation of ecosystems, spread after the Soviet Union was thoroughly deceased. The aging of ecologically harmful infrastructure and the correlated risks are an actual problem. A mining shaft demands efforts to fix it that generate further care infrastructure, models, and labor. That effort requires time and resources but also a reconsideration of what brought us here (so we do not simply reproduce the present). The persistent emergence of shafts shows us how territorial control is constantly troubled by unruly, dynamic matters, thus reminding us of the wickedness of oil shale extraction and processing. Holes not only refer to design imperfections or material weaknesses but also upset the canons of modernity and the delusional belief in a consequence-free extraction of natural resources by means of increasingly powerful technologies.

The unsustainability of mining activities also invites us to question whether it is enough simply to replace existing infrastructure with more ecologically friendly ones. Indeed, the impact of industrial mining continues with infrastructure that narrows down future prospects aboveground, and as a void in the living conditions of local residents. Hence, in thinking about the afterlife of mining, it is not enough to physically fill the hole; the process also requires making sense of the social afterlife of the correlated infrastructure while unmaking the principles that led to this situation. Otherwise our future, not just our present, will take the form of a black hole.

NEW HIDEOUTS FOR AN OLD FEAR

In August 2023, Viktor and Mari were taking a walk near Sillamäe when they found a suspicious military-looking box with Cyrillic lettering hidden in the bushes. They called the police, who arrived along with a bomb squad. This kind of incident is relatively common in the area. In the first four months of 2024, over two thousand explosive devices were found there. Hence, in early May, the Estonian Rescue Board published a message in Russian informing locals about the cleanup:

> Our bomb squad and their assistants will be searching for wartime explosive devices between May 7 and 9 in the areas of Sinimäe and Sirgala. During this period, you will see more special equipment and hear more explosions than usual. ⚔ If you also find a suspicious object, for example, in the forest, a pond, or in your grandfather's attic, do not touch it, and immediately call 112 and act according to the rescuer's instructions! We remind you that you do not need to fear punishment for the voluntary surrender of an explosive object. Just that under no circumstances should you attempt to transport it yourself![1]

Decommissioned military ordnance is a flagrant example of what humans leave behind and the need for new generations to work with scraps, rubble, and in some cases the toxic debris of past conflicts that are not all that past, as we can see in eastern Estonia. The past is actually re-lived in the present through necrological remnants. In Sillamäe, the resurfacing of military and nuclear remnants forces us to notice the coexistence of parallel timelines and historical representations.

This chapter thus reflects on how problematic legacies are capable of generating social effects not just in their preservation but also in their disposal.[2] Indeed, industrial and military pasts have an enduring impact on the sociality of this city. For instance, the same week that the rescue board was de-mining the area, an anonymous user posted a series of photos on a local virtual network showing how the red carnations placed at the war memorial in Sillamäe had been collected and thrown into the garbage. A heated discussion followed, which led to the return of seven bags of flowers to the memorial, now ornamented with even more care and attention. "Nobody is forgotten and nothing is forgotten! Happy Victory Day," a woman named Viktoria wrote in a comment, adding, "You can't erase or throw away human memory and conscience!"[3] Some locals even called the Vaivara cemetery to complain about its employees for removing the flowers. The board of the cemetery had to hastily release a press statement explaining that they had had nothing to do with it.

The Least Estonian City in Estonia

Sillamäe is the most non-Estonian city in Estonia. For decades, local residents lived separated from their surroundings, as if the town were on a different planet. In 1502, this settlement was mentioned in reference to a tavern for pirates run by someone called Thor Brugen. Back then, the territory belonged to the Livonian Order of knights. In the eighteenth century, the area was populated by fishermen and later on became a popular holiday resort among Russian intellectuals and aristocrats. In the 1920s, Swedish investments helped construct a slate factory, a power station, and a port, with over one thousand people on the payroll. After the Second World War, Sillamäe was developed from ruins as an industrial military town, supplying nuclear materials to power plants and weapons facilities until 1989. During that period, Sillamäe was governed through opacity; the very existence of the town became a public secret. Because of the correlation of risk and secrecy, the supply of nuclear material was enclosed within security buffer zones with special restrictions.[4] Indeed, Sillamäe was surrounded by barbed wire, and visitors needed a special permit (*propusk*) to get in.

Between 1947 and 1952, over 250,000 tons of Dictyonema shale was mined in the area, from which the town was able to produce approximately twenty tons of pure uranium. Then, the Kombinat Number 7 plant and the so-called Krasil'naya fabrika (Paint Factory) began enriching the gray chemical element, and Sillamäe was adopted into the uranium brotherhood. In 1947, the area was given the code name R-6685. The plant was even forbidden to use its street address. (A mailbox bore only the number 22.) The word "uranium" was also taboo, and other terms

FIGURE 3.1. An oil shale extraction plant in Sillamäe, 1930. Estonian National Archive.

such as "product A-9," "metal," "tar," "silicon," "tin," and "aluminum" were used instead.

In 1949, uranium from Sillamäe was used in the first Soviet-made nuclear bomb, and thousands of workers relocated to the town. There really wasn't any uranium there, however. The yield was poor, and the processing left behind a significant volume of solid hazardous waste. By this time the communist leaders already realized that they would have to start *importing* uranium from Bulgaria, Czechoslovakia, Poland, and the Kola Peninsula to make good use of the newly built facilities.[5]

According to old postcards and photos, boathouses and summer cottages were the most common buildings on Cape Päite, on the Gulf of Finland. Then, from 1946 to 1959, waste from the uranium processing was kept aboveground on the cape. This means that radioactive dust was being stored out in the open on the Baltic Sea. Then a pile of waste tailings was established. Thousands of people lived with dangerous residues for decades. Nowadays the site contains over 12 million tons of different types of wastes, including oil shale ash and waste from processed uranium ore. In terms of area, volume, and radionuclide content, the Sillamäe tailings pond is one of the largest deposits of these materials in the world.[6]

Nuclear waste is not simply active but radioactive, and for a long time. Containing and keeping these residues in a stable form is thus a matter of life and death. Still, nearly six hundred tons of radioactive residues are stored in Sillamäe—and are expected to remain hazardous for thousands of years.[7] Once Estonia became a member of the European Union, funding was given to clean up some of the residues and partially dismantle the old industries. A total of 28 million euros was allocated to cover the kilometer-long, half-kilometer-wide pile of tailings near the Baltic Sea. The required containment and the importance of communicating its meaning to future generations might be conceptually linked with heritage management, alas in a necrological way.[8]

In Sillamäe, the nuclear heritage is commemorated in the most central location in town, where a statue of a man holding a model of an atom welcomes visitors to a Stalinist promenade. The monument was erected in 1987, only three years before the energy plant stopped processing uranium. At that time, Sillamäe had a population of over twenty thousand residents; by 2024, it was a mere twelve thousand. The official slogan of the town is "the city of fresh winds." After visiting Sillamäe in 2013, journalist Andrew Suttaford wrote an article presenting the waste dump as "a Leninist lake, toxic and vile."[9] Still, radioactive dust cannot simply be thought of as Bolshevik or Soviet; rather, its more-than-human timescale is a novel feature in world history.

In 1997 the plant was privatized and renamed Silmet. Most of the shares belonged to the US mining group Molycorp until 2016, when it filed for bankruptcy. Then it was acquired by Neo Performance Materials to process imported rare minerals that are later sold in the global market of electronic industries. Per annum, this plant produces 360 tons of niobium, 84 tons of tantalum, 4,800 tons of lanthanide, and 1,800 tons of ammonium fluoride. The seventeen rare earth elements have valuable electromagnetic properties, so most chipmakers today are fighting for a share in their extracting and processing market. Neo Performance Materials recently built a magnet factory in Narva to serve electric vehicles and wind turbines, thus creating a mine-to-magnet supply chain (the first of its kind in Europe). It is expected to support the manufacture of approximately 1.5 million electric cars to advance the EU Green Investment Plan (see chapter 8).

What Else Can We Do in Silki?

"From what kind of dark film have you escaped?" Reimo jokingly exclaimed. He gave us a curious look, as if we were in the middle of a ghost-hunting foray. Reimo, who is employed in the production of naphtha, saw us wandering around Sillamäe with no guiding force apart from guesswork. Once he left, we jumped over the fence of the now abandoned *kazarma* (a Soviet-era army barracks), venturing into the dark of military waste, despite the real chance of bodily harm. Not that long ago, these premises were used as a dormitory for soldiers of the Red Army. Today, the building is deserted and stands between the actual and the phantasmal. Its abandonment, alongside the decommission of the nuclear power plant and related infrastructure, might be considered, even if paradoxically, a destruction of the collective memory of this town.

In the *kazarma*, we discover surviving traces of old graffiti, including one asking, "Nu a che yeshche v Silke delat?" (What else can we do in Silki?). We also find different forms of military art there, such as nicely drawn landscapes, so a number of conscripts may have had an art school background.[10] The night before, we were hanging out with designer Semjon Krasulin (aka Simon Red) and one of his two bands, Smoke&Smile, who kindly invited us to a jam session. The place had a cave-like atmosphere, cozily dark, so we were inclined to stay for quite a while in this cool cavern. Later on, I discovered that this basic structure at Majakovsky 12, which somehow reminds me of a barracks with squat toilets, is the oldest building standing in the town—built right after the war.

Semjon talks about *Vernanda*, a film shot in Sillamäe in 1988 (directed by Roman Baskin). In his view, this film conveys well the spirit of the town: simultaneously claustrophobic and permissive, with an air of secrecy and retreat, as if the battle were over and we were left with nothing much to do. The surreal plot starts with a train passenger who is left behind in an eccentric town called Vernanda. A man (played by Sulev Luik) buys a loaf of bread in a local shop, only to discover it has a bomb inside. While the man desperately wants to get rid of the bomb, he realizes that gifts of this kind are the town's trademark, learning that in this town the unseen realm has quite visible effects.

A few months later, I met Semjon again at the jam session hideout. Before his friends (from his other band, Analogue Quattro) arrive, we start listening to music from YouTube. After a few minutes, he plays "Nuclear War" by Sun Ra (1984), "one of my favorite songs":

> They talkin' about . . . nuclear war
> . . . if they push that button,
> your ass got to go
> gonna blast you so high in the sky,
> . . . radiation, mutation, fire, hydrogen bombs, atomic bombs.

Sillamäe certainly has a sense of creeping unease. After a quick visit, Marina repeats that it is "a dead city." For her, it was interesting to walk around. "But I cannot see myself living here. Only those who have no choice stay. It is a dead city and it smells bad there." Or, as observed by Mari, "The architecture blows your mind, but there is not a good vibe here." That creepy feeling is not just because streets are rather empty of people. "I don't know how to explain it. It is the vibe," Mari insists. Eventually, that vibe refers to how Sillamäe was built as a secluded town with a bunch of bomb shelters and military secrets, but also to the chaos and nothingness experienced in the 1990s, leading to "a sense of panic," in Semjon's words: "You ask me how; this is just Sillamäe. All this secrecy has affected the locals too; people here try not to stand out and avoid gossip in every possible way. . . . This is a town where time stopped, like in the film *Zerograd*—have you seen it?" *Zero Town* (1989, directed by Karen Shakhnazarov) tells the story of Moscow engineer Alexey Varakin, who comes on a business trip to a small provincial town that he can never leave. From the beginning, everything seems to be a bit off there, and despite his repeated efforts to escape, all possibilities mysteriously disappear.

"Why did you come back, Semjon?" I ask during a break in one of the jam sessions.

"This place gives me stability, because of living by the sea. Because in Tallinn I was no one, and here I know everyone and everyone knows me. Here, I don't try to belong; I know the seashore up to Narva-Jõesuu by heart, and I can go to the sea in the winter and in the summer. . . . I have friends to play music with, which is what I actually like. I just need an instrument and a couple of like-minded people."

No-Man's-Land

The term "no-man's-land" is often used to designate the area between two enemy trenches, a strip of mud and barbed wire under artillery fire that neither side can claim as its own. At the end of World War II, the Sillamäe-Sinimäe area was a no-man's-land in a military sense. Over sixty thousand people died here in the decisive battle of the Tannenberg Line, in which the Nazi army was retreating after the blockade. Ivika Maidre, director of the Military Museum in Vaivara, gave this synopsis: "In July 1944, the Leningrad front started to move. German troops had surrounded this city for three years, but then the front reached the Narva River in just a few weeks and large forces gathered around here. Then our former prime minister Jüri Uluots gave a radio speech and said that all Estonian men had to go to the front because it was the Second War of Independence."

On display, we can find assorted memorabilia and military discards from the area. In addition to anti-tank cannons, minesweepers, handguns, helmets, and uniforms, the collection includes soldiers' personal items, newspaper pages, and propaganda prints. The sensory impact of these residues of past conflicts is profound, ranging from a sense of horror to recollection and existential musings. Perhaps the most impressive items to me are the things related to leisure and ordinary life, such as the board games brought by Nazi soldiers. Many of them were kept underground, wrapped and hidden by local residents.

One of the games, a beautiful wooden chessboard, was handmade by a prisoner of war and exchanged for food during the construction of Sillamäe. In the spring of 2023, this chessboard was exhibited at the Sillamäe Museum in the *Keeping Things in the Dark* exhibition, along with thirty other objects extracted from local basements (see chapter 1). Among them, one object was rescued from a bomb shelter located fifty meters away, under School Number 1: a clock that stopped working at precisely six o'clock. This item was exhibited with a newspaper dated September 4, 1993, which emphatically states, "Look forward to school!"

The school itself closed in 1999. Then, for seven years, the building hosted the ECOMEN Institute of Economics and Management; later it was abandoned. Fortunately the library, which comprises a strange array of books, such as *Windows 95, The Internet, How to Become an Entrepreneur,* a biography of Lenin, and *Technological Advances in Mining Engineering,* was left behind. Darja, one of the artists participating in the exhibition, used to organize art events in the bomb shelter of the school when she was a teenager. We can still find the self-portrait of one of her friends there, Anton Serdjukov, along with a series of Estonian national symbols lying on the floor and Soviet machinery designed to produce breathable air in case of a nuclear attack.

Tõnis Tolpats, the other person behind the Military Museum in Vaivara, explains the operational details of the Tannenberg Line, also known as the battle of Sinimäe, in a passionate way. In the meantime, I wonder to what extent these military objects are deemed to be representative of the regional identity. Sadly, we cannot understand the twentieth century in Estonia without paying attention to the vast destruction caused by war and the social and ecological consequences that followed.

A war happens in a social time, not a geological one; nevertheless, it is capable of changing the course of rivers, dismantling mountains, and altering the territory with kilometers of trenches, just for the sake of destroying someone identified as our enemy.[11] We could even argue that the destructive capacity of modern warfare is anti-planetary. Wars are wasteful and a vector for the spread of different forms of toxicity. They leave destructive traces, lay different sorts of waste to territory, and cause human loss and trauma. During a war, humans appear to be a failed species.

War follows a specific logic of confrontation and domination, bringing certain ideas and relations up front while placing some others at the back; refusal, however, is about making claims from the shadows and without entering into direct confrontations with institutions. Yet war preparation also permeates ordinary life and interweaves military and civilian worlds, even nowhere close to a front or base.[12] In his study of ordnance in Bosnia and Herzegovina, David Henig notes the unruly temporalities of military waste and how it mediates the way in which landscape is perceived, creating situations of emotional distress and indeterminacy even in peacetime.[13] Reminders of war lead us to reconsider the separating logic of the aftermath of military conflicts, as well as the supposed newness of the actual assemblages of vigilance and security. Additionally, this issue raises questions about how to represent hazardous military waste. For instance, the National Museum of the History of Ukraine responded to this question in 2023 by displaying artifacts retrieved from formerly occupied areas. The exhibition was composed of boots, dosimeters for measuring radiation levels, ration packs, and destroyed signage. The idea was that the display of fresh vestiges of violence might help visitors sense the horrors of war from a safe position. The curators actually ended up living in the museum for two months at the very beginning of the war when they had to pack up and transport the museum's collection to the western part of the country.

Leftover weapons might end up in museums such as the one in Vaivara, and former military installations might become attractions for dark tourism. The actual destruction and trauma caused by violent conflicts is preferably forgotten, however, since it is almost impossible to write military waste into grand narratives of success and national identity. Nevertheless, violent episodes still resonate and affect younger generations: they linger on phantasmagorically, despite leaving minimal tangible traces. Although violent events might have occurred in the past and been officially concluded, their effects reverberate in the post-broken present and their negative repercussions are dispersed across space and time.[14]

There is another military museum in the region, located in the basement of the Kohtla-Nõmme House of Culture. It is run by Rene Pedak, an amateur archaeologist and military aficionado who has assembled a collection of items from World War II based on his own findings in the forest and a few donations. Rene presents this display as a "history room" (*ajalootuba*). There, we can see items such as gas masks, radiometers, machine guns, photos, and uniforms from both the Soviet and Nazi armies. Rene could easily have made his way into Ulrich Seidl's film *Im Keller* (2014).[15] Seidl emphasizes in the film the sordid weirdness beneath the surface of bourgeois society, in contrast to the rather ordinary use of the spaces that I have encountered in eastern Estonia.

One Thousand and One Nuclear Nights

While reflecting on the impact of the war in the region, we might distinguish between those who left and those who came after. Since the Estonian residents were not allowed to move back after the war (being considered too untrust-worthy to be employed in strategic sectors), the region was repopulated by new arrivals from all corners of the red empire. Ida-Virumaa lost over 40 percent of its population as a direct consequence of the war. Most of the existing housing and infrastructure had been destroyed. Very few farms survived.

After World War II, the Soviet Union established two nuclear complexes in Estonia, forty-five missile bases, nine military airports, and four large areas for military training.[16] War-torn villages became industrial and military towns, which followed the principles of modernist planning and Soviet ideology. Historian David Vseviov has called this phenomenon "an urban anomaly," since the density of apartment buildings and the mono-functional organization of towns is more intense in this region than in the rest of Estonia.[17]

Sillamäe was built as if it had fallen from the sky, as in *One Thousand and One Nights*. The planning of the town was a task for the Lengorstroyproyekt state office in Leningrad; the Department of Architecture of the Estonian SSR, however, adapted the plan somewhat to local circumstances.[18] The first inhabitants of Sillamäe were teenage survivors of the blockade of Leningrad. From one year to the next, a battalion of young factory workers, engineers, architects, teachers, historians, artists, and nurses came to this location. The town was built in a very short time and without financial restrictions in order to exemplify Soviet modernity. But Sillamäe was determined not to exist, claims Vseviov. "There's practically no archival material: it looks like the city doesn't exist. Not only on maps, but also in history."[19]

None of those who provided the labor—neither the thousands of German, Romanian, Hungarian, or Estonian POWs nor the Soviet political prisoners—were fully aware of the kind of infrastructure they were building. They also constructed the key buildings in Sillamäe, including the boulevard and grand staircase (which followed the model of the Alley of the Heroes in Stalingrad). "Builders were needed and there were no professionals. The local leaders made a proposal to the prisoners who lived here in the center, under the current promenade. They promised to reduce the detention time for those who were willing to work. So, to some extent, we can say that they were volunteers, though only 2 percent of the workers were really free," explained Aleksandr Popolitov at the local museum.

Sillamäe was something close to a proletarian utopia, built according to a modernist plan, with high salaries and stores well stocked with products including perfumes, suits, coats, and fur articles.[20] The isolated nature of the city was not always easy to handle, however, and many residents felt as though they were living in a cage. Journalist Andrei Khvostov, born there in 1963, looks back at his childhood and recalls what it was like to have asthma, a condition that did not seem to exist as far as the Soviet doctors were concerned. He also remembers playing with other children while throwing and exploding homemade bombs from the edge of a cliff. As Khvostov concludes, it was very easy for them to forget that they lived in Estonia.[21]

In the early years, most of the town's population was under twenty-five, mostly young graduates who moved into communal housing with the prospect of getting a separate apartment after a few years and having a career. One of them was Alfidina Orlova, who worked in the city library from 1960 to 2004. She has written several books and articles about the cultural history of Sillamäe "in order for the new generations to know how it was, and for the old-timers to remember the beginnings," as she explains. Orlova divides the history of the settlement into two periods: before and after perestroika.[22] In her view, the first period, characterized by the industrial processing of uranium, can also be divided into two parts: the village of Sillamäe (from 1946 to 1956) and the city (from 1957 to 1991).

Our place attachment is frequently rooted in memory. For Orlova, local history begins in 1946. This past, however, does not fit Ivika Maidre's past and has no place in the Estonian present. "For them [the Russians], there was nothing before and history begins in the 1950s. That's why they were so surprised when we recovered our independence. Aha, so there was something like an Estonian Republic before us. And these guys are now equal, or superior to us. Also, progress stopped in the 1990s, industrial jobs were lost, and they were not that young and pretty anymore," Maidre says as she lists her complaints in a sort of stream of consciousness. "We were treated like Aboriginals in Australia. Back then, I could not buy goods in a shop if I was not speaking Russian. 'Speak a human language!' I was once told. Nowadays, most of the guys living in Sillamäe are unable to buy a bus ticket in Estonian. They have been here for fifty or sixty years and hardly speak a word in our language."

Then, Maidre refers to the evidence of several labor camps in the region under the Nazi occupation as "a fantasy, stories fabricated in the 1950s. . . . Here, there was just a transit one, which had no gas chambers and all that." Then, in the middle of these phantasmagoric temporalities and counterfactual narratives, she suddenly stops and says, "I look at you and reckon this guy must have a Russian wife, don't you?"

Nevertheless, the existence of a camp for Jewish people in the region was not just Soviet propaganda, and it was not just for transit. When the Nazi army retreated from Rostov-on-Don (thus losing access to the natural resources of the Caucasus), they made the extraction of Estonian oil shale a priority. For that purpose, Hermann Göring ordered the deportation of Jewish people from all over the Baltics to the region to work in the mines. The Vaivara concentration camp was under the jurisdiction of the German Main Office for Economic and

Administrative Affairs (SS-WVHA). It was established in August 1943 as part of the Nazi war industry, and Jews from other parts of Europe were brought here for forced labor. Over ten thousand Jews passed through the Vaivara camp system, which consisted of the main camp and about twenty sub-camps located throughout Estonia.[23]

Survivors

Ultimately, a nation always refers to a community built around a shared mistake and dislike toward a neighbor.

In August 1939 the Soviet Union signed the Molotov–Ribbentrop Pact with Nazi Germany on the partition of eastern Europe. Estonia's fate was assigned to the Soviet sphere of influence, and in September 1939 the government of Konstantin Päts decided not to resist, allowing over 25,000 Soviet troops to settle in Estonia. During the first Soviet occupation, over two thousand people were killed and over ten thousand deported in less than two years. In the course of Operation Barbarossa, Nazi Germany invaded Estonia between 1941 and 1944, after which the country was again occupied by the Soviets. With memories of the first wave of brutality still fresh, approximately seventy thousand Estonians left during the autumn of 1944, escaping first to Sweden and Germany, then to Australia, Canada, the United Kingdom, and the United States.

Before fleeing, some of them hid family possessions—pots and pans, cutlery, linens, books, photo albums, and so on wrapped in rags—by burying these items in the ground, anticipating a return that did not happen until fifty years later. Archaeologist Mats Burström has talked with thirty descendants of those families, who explained that Estonians were so used to war that they made use of hiding as a cultural praxis to cope with violence. They also explained that hiding things in attics, inside walls, or under the floorboards was not safe, since houses were often burned down, so the safest hideout was underground.[24]

Hideouts have the ability to make things (and us) disappear when faced by a threat, using tree hollows, wardrobes, sewers, caves, holes, empty graves. Often, however, a successful hideout refers not only to the agency of a single heroic individual but to a support network as well: think, for instance, of the Forest Brothers. In 1944, after the Soviet occupation of the Baltic republics, over sixty thousand partisans took refuge in underground bunkers and tunnels dug inside the dense forests of the region. They survived on food donated by local farmers. In the early 1950s, they began to receive supplies from the British and American governments as well. Most of them, however, were killed or sent to Siberia. The last Forest

Brother, August Sabbe, drowned in the Võhandu River (Võru) in 1978 while try-ing to evade the KGB. He had remained in hiding for more than thirty years.

Hans Pekk, one of the characters in Sofi Oksanen's novel *Purge*, also seeks refuge in the forest during World War II and has to hide in his own house for years.[25] Yet not only is this story about war and men, but also it focuses on themes of betrayal, pettiness, and women abandoned to terrible violations. "I write about survivors and most of my characters are survivors. . . . I was interested in the fact that victims of human trafficking had similar traumatic reactions to women raped during the war. . . . The relationship between men and women is one of my favorite topics. I am also interested in power relations, traumatic reactions, and what is considered a mental disorder—overall, everything related to ways to heal the past," Oksanen tells me in Tallinn.

A similar case of guerrilla warfare was that of the Maquis in France and Spain.[26] Following the Republican defeat, and after fighting for the Allies in World War II, hundreds of Spaniards tried to reach the groups that had remained in the mountains since 1939. They were unable to choose between exile or surrender, and continued fighting guerrilla style first to overthrow the regime and then later for their own survival. The repression of Franco's regime in Spain forced many people to invent hideouts where there were none; indeed, there were dozens of Topos (the Moles) who spent decades in closet-like spaces.[27]

Moments of hiddenness are symbolic passages that can generate different forms of personhood. The material properties of confinement also infiltrate the lives of those in hiding, becoming part of their subjectivity. There are things that cannot be said, and also hiding places that must not be found.

Bunkerology

In Ida-Virumaa, we can still find dozens of bunkers from the Cold War, a period that demanded an unprecedented level of militarism in everyday life. Traditionally, the erection of underground bunkers is meant to convey safety while materializing imaginaries of threatening futures. For that purpose, officials and engineers use diverse means of camouflage when planning these military structures, blending bunkers into the landscape.[28] Overall, bunkers have faced different fates since the Soviet collapse: from demolition to simple abandonment or refurbishment for another use, such as data storage.[29] Still, it is not the same for a bunker to suffer the indignity of destruction during a time of war as in a time of peace, once the military conflict is over (or never actually began, as occurred during the Cold War).

Many of the basements of Soviet buildings were designed to be converted back into refuges in case of an emergency. Nowadays, some of these fortifications are regaining a new life in Estonia because of feelings of fear. For decades there was no need to prepare for total war; after Russia's attack on Ukraine, however, the scenario changed into one of a "hybrid peace."[30] As a result, and apart from the militarization of contemporary public discourse and the extension of military expertise to all manner of social, moral, and cultural problems in Estonia, as of 2024 the government planned to build six hundred bunkers along its border with Russia, creating a Baltic defense line with Latvia and Lithuania.[31] Authorities also started to inspect cities from below. As a side effect of the Russian invasion of Ukraine, Andrei Mitkovets received multiple visits to his underground gym from various state and municipal officials. The spacious gym (called Albatros) was located a few meters from the Russian border, next to the former Kreenholm Factory in Narva. This space has been a gym for over forty years, and it was filled with old and new exercise machines, some of them from the Soviet era. Following the repeated inspections of the gym, the municipality finally reclaimed it, and he decided to move to another town, while the workout machines were taken for scrap metal.

Geographer Bradley Garrett has visited bunkers in North America and Australia, meeting the people actually constructing them as well as the advisers working for bunker-building companies. In his view, bunkers are not just defensive structures but a metaphor for contemporary feelings of existential threat across the globe. At first glance, one might think that rich people decide to hide themselves in a bunker after giving up on the idea of fixing the world. But they might have some hope, after all, as they are preparing a secure hideaway in expectation of another kind of future to come. I keep thinking about what it is that these extremely well-off people actually fear, to discover that for them, bunkers are not just shelters but also spaces of rebirth.[32]

Bunkers mirror collective anxieties and become the source of them simultaneously. In Estonia, the renewed demand for bunkers causes traumatic phantasms and past sensations of endangerment to resurface.[33] Most of the Cold War bunkers were subterranean and utilized the shielding and camouflaging properties of the ground. Unlike castles, however, bunkers cannot become ruins and be incorporated into nature afterwards.[34] Bunkers are incapable of cultural recuperation and spatial assimilation because of their intrinsic political culpability, being stuck in a kind of ambivalent attraction/repulsion.[35] The case of bunkers might be one of those prescribed for heritage erasure. According to archaeologist Cornelius Holtorf, destruction might not always be a threat to the fabric of memory. In his view, a selective loss of heritage is fruitful and necessary, since the meaning of legacies changes along with the social and political context.[36]

Interestingly, we hardly recall bunkers as part of the collective memory of a nation, but when we stumble upon military fortifications, they possess the power to draw us to them.[37] Anthropologist Mads Daugbjerg describes bunkers as "invasive materialities," in many ways foreign, and most often considered out of place.[38] In some cases, such as during postwar reconstruction in the UK, the demolition of bomb sites turned military ruins into an unintended playground for children, fostering a habitat for "feral youth."[39] As the Atlantikwall that Hitler commanded to be built demonstrates, bunkers a rather useless legacy after a war. Their passive-aggressive architecture barricades us, separating us from the surroundings. Certainly we can sleep, eat, and use the toilet therein, but a bunker necessarily reminds us of military aggression.

The word originates from the Old Swedish *bunke*, which refers to an assemblage of boards used to protect the cargo of a ship. As modernity brought more refined forms of artillery, defensive military fortifications were designed to protect people and things from falling bombs, including nuclear ones. Alas, the technologies of modern warfare require increasingly sophisticated defensive installations to be hidden, even in cyberspace.

FIGURE 3.2. Destroyed World War II bunker near Narva, November 17, 1944. Photo: F. Olop. Estonian National Archive.

The complex reverberation of past conflicts in eastern Estonia invites us to reconsider what the cultural role of military remnants might be in postwar contexts, along with acknowledging the eventual failure of dark heritage to heal open wounds.[40] Yet it is also interesting to pay attention to how different communities chose to live with dark legacies that should not, or cannot, be considered heritage. Nevertheless, the endeavor to combine heritage-making with the cleaning up of radioactive and military waste is not easy, if not impossible. In any case, it reminds us that heritage is not always something positive and functional to community bonding; it can also contribute to raising new tensions, particularly in cases when historical narratives and the dominant understanding of identity are too narrow.

Even if we designate a bunker as heritage, it can only be a difficult, dissonant, and undesirable one, and thus a negatively labeled heritage.[41] A bunker is a particular kind of remnant that offers up a narrative that many of those in the present wish to distance themselves from, despite having strong historical significance and didactic potential.[42] Perhaps no bunker from the past is actually safe or valid anymore. Just in case, I go downstairs to review my own bunker. I live in a building dating from the 1930s, constructed in the center of Tallinn right before the Second World War. The bunker has not been in use for many years, and it now looks more like a series of catacombs than a military structure. It is actually a failed bunker. I can't even keep my bike there, because the rise of the Baltic Sea water table produces a seasonal inundation of the cellar through two holes in the foundation. Despite the failed utility of the bunker for military purposes, what does work well there is the assemblage of infrastructural arteries that make my life convenient and warm. This is because the underground of my building is part of wider global networks and the circulation of substances and ideas through wires and pipelines.[43]

Anthropologist Tamta Khalvashi describes how a similar situation occurred in Georgia when Russia launched the full-scale invasion of Ukraine.[44] "Where is a bunker?" asked many Georgians, anxious about a possible spillover of the conflict into their country; they then discovered that the underground spaces of Soviet-era buildings were not available anymore, as these subterranean areas had been privatized and transformed into shops, bakeries, beauty salons, and even homes for those who have not been able to afford rising real estate prices in residential buildings (such as refugees, the homeless, and students).

Ethnographic Darkness

Aleksandr Openko is a popular guide, much sought after in Narva, who knows the secrets of the city. In his everyday life, he works as a history teacher at School

Number 6, but his main hobby is to lead tours and tell stories. He speaks of underground passages, horror stories, and conspiracy theories.[45] One of these stories is about a family who relocated to Narva in the late 1940s. At the time, there were many people living in the ruins of buildings, especially in the basements. This particular family saw a young girl in a white dress emerge from under their bed, dance in the center of the room, and return to her place under the bed again. They didn't say anything, but the next night, another family living in the basement saw the same ghost. Some colleagues appear rather skeptical of the veracity of Openko's stories: "He just tells people what they want to hear." Others revere him as "a local hero."

There is also the memory of the destroyed Narva, which has been reconstructed in a 1:100 scale maquette. For over thirty years, Fjodor Šantsõn has been creating a model of Narva before the Second World War. "It is sad to work with something that is lost," acknowledged Šantsõn on one of our encounters at city hall. Nowadays, the maquette is located at the Narva Museum and the hidden remains of this city lie beneath the postwar architecture. Likewise, there is another underground city—the medieval bastion—designed to be camouflaged within its surroundings. In the Swedish-Baltic provinces, Narva was the second-most-powerful fortress (after the one in Riga).[46] It is not a surprise that the bastion was built here. Within the not-too-distant history of the area, key battles of the Livonian War, the Great Northern War, and two world wars took place in Narva.

The belief that there is more to the political reality than meets the eye has been widespread in the post-socialist world, prolonging the atmosphere of suspicion that characterized the Soviet regime through the circulation of rumors, conspiracy theories, tales of magical creatures, and fears of unseen enemies.[47] Since the restoration of its independence in 1991, Estonia, however, has become an advanced digital society, and discourses regarding e-governance and e-residency have been an important part of Estonian statecraft and policy (see chapter 8). This has happened in parallel with extensive institutional efforts to establish a homogenous society based on a restricted understanding of the Estonian nation (in some cases contradicting EU values regarding preservation of difference and multiculturalism in our societies), and an ideology of restoration was institutionally arranged to recover the legality and traditions that were interrupted during the long Soviet occupation.[48] This process was not free from tensions and anger, even injustices. They all reignited after the Russian invasion of Ukraine.

Conspiracy theories often revealed themselves through the research, and I saw myself refusing my informants' refusal to the state. For instance, in some of our visits to prepare the installation *Keeping Things in the Dark*, my colleagues and I entered into unpleasant discussions about the war with those who had agreed to show us their basements. This was the case with Vladimir. One of the artists, Anna, observed a dozen large bottles of drinking water and asked if they were for an eventual recurrence of military conflict in the future, a question that led Vladimir to tell us about "the truth" in Ukraine, arguing that we, the "young people of Tallinn," were being manipulated by Western media. "The difference," Anna rightly stated, "is that here you can express these opinions, but on the other side of the border, you end up in prison for doing so."

I also had a disagreement with Graf, a taxi driver in Narva. The paradox in this case is that Graf is a French citizen, born in Lille yet relocated to Ida-Virumaa after marrying a Narvitian. "Who started the war? It is obvious: the country that is benefiting the most from it—America," he concluded. During my fieldwork in the region, I also met several people who irrationally referred to Vladimir Putin as their president, despite living in Estonia. Some of them were Cold War nostalgists with whom I strongly disagreed, or whom I even disliked, but whom I met and tried to listen to nonetheless. After all, conspiracy theories and misleading statements from informants are also data, influence how we conduct fieldwork, and give shape to the actual structure of feelings. And you don't have to defend something in order to understand it.

As soon as you become an anthropologist, you join the shadows, the underground, the dirty track of life where the counterpoint lies. People like Vladimir and Graf were talking openly about the war, reproducing the twisted view of things propagated by the Kremlin. There were also cases of local residents who openly questioned the sovereignty of the Estonian state or shared the view that this country, because of its small size, was too dependent on global actors such as NATO, the EU, or the United States. But political shadows in the ethnographic encounter were also reflected through hesitance and silence. Oftentimes people were careful in their speech around those who came from elsewhere. Indeed, I met local residents who did not dare to express basic dissonant opinions and feelings on sensitive matters to the powerful. They narrowed their eyes, looked down at the floor, made a sour face, or asked to be kept anonymous afterwards. Perhaps they did so because, in the Estonian media, those who remain politically Russian and do not speak Estonian (the only national language officially recognized by the state) are presented as belonging to a "bad" minority. Thus, they engage in conduct that radically contradicts what is said in the public sphere of the country and does not fit the current hierarchy of ethnicity in Estonia.[49]

These kinds of shadow encounters resonate with the work of two anthropologists. Susan Harding criticized the resistance of anthropologists to considering those who display a wrong way of unfitting. In some cases, researchers might find their views so "repugnant" as to make these people appear illegitimate as an object of study. All the same, she argued, these radical cultural others should be studied with the same care as those maintaining other positions, humanizing their behavior as a form of political action and as a way of destabilizing prevailing "us" and "them" categories.[50] In a like manner, Sherry Ortner coined the term "dark anthropology" to describe research dealing with the disturbing realities of social life.[51] Ortner also criticized as ethnographic refusal the situation in which researchers choose not to share certain insights because they are worried about the political implications of their findings.[52] In this case, ethnographic darkness refers not to something that is hidden but rather to something that is untamed—a blindspot that we fail to include in our texts.

Idiotic Memory

In Andrei Platonov's novel *The Foundation Pit,* the worker Voschev is called an "idiot" for not having fought in a real war.[53] Sadly, the reactions that Vovan Kashtan received after his actions in Narva regarding the war in Ukraine have been even more offensive.[54] On April 14, 2023, Vovan left graffiti reading "We will defeat everyone, kill everyone, rob everyone we need. Everything will be as we like" in the spot where a Soviet memorial tank used to stand. That threat came from the "Z" propagandist rhetoric of Vladlen Tatarsky, a blogger who had recently been killed in St. Petersburg. The T-34 tank had been relocated to a forgotten military museum a few months before. This warlike monument marked the location where troops under the command of General Ivan Fedjuninski crossed the Narva River in July of 1944.[55]

The prime minister at the time, Kaja Kallas, justified the removal of the tank as a way to counter "the increasing tensions and confusion." Minister of Culture Piret Hartman claimed, "It is also important to understand that the current state of the world is inextricably linked to security."[56] Also local artist Maria Kapajeva created an artwork responding to these events, titled *Enforced Memory.* In a two-channel video, we can see footage of the tank's removal and Kapajeva herself screaming, on-site and at home, using a therapeutic technique for ridding the body of anger. In turn, Vovan's "intervention," as he prefers to call it, was more ambivalent.

I tell Vovan that many people in Estonia do not understand that kind of public art, precisely because of its ambiguity. Many in Tallinn believed that he was reproducing the Russian theology of war, many in Russia believed that he was supporting them, and many in Narva thought of it as a needless provocation, considering that "he's not one of us." I sit with Vovan at the entrance of the Sillamäe Museum and listen to his description of events. "I went at around four a.m.," he says, "and started to write the graffiti with a Church Slavonic typeface, but I realized I wouldn't have enough paint. So in the end I made it simpler and more readable, while keeping a sense of Russian holiness." Vovan adds: "I was not hoping for understanding. I wanted to provoke an internal protest in people and express my own condemnation of all kinds of violence by representing the cult of war in a grotesque way. . . . For me, the tank was a disgusting symbol to honor war victims."

A month later, on May 8, Vovan made another intervention in the public space, this time writing the word "Children" in front of the former House of Culture (a Stalinist building) in ruins that resembled the infamous theater of Mariupol. In a tragic, disgraceful episode of the war, the Russian air force bombed the theater full of children and women despite the word *DETI* (children) written in capital letters on the pavement outside. In this instance there were also those who misinterpreted Vovan's intervention and read it instead as an invitation for Russians to bomb Estonia or to "rescue" us. In the meantime, the Russian state brought a similar tank to Ivangorod, right on the Russian side of the Narva River, and organized a pro-war concert on May 9.[57]

Vovan's interventions bring past fears and present violence to the forefront, pinpointing the complex continuities of military aggression. As a result, he was detained three times in one month by police and faced a court case in which he stood accused of supporting the Russian war against Ukraine (for the graffiti on the absent tank) and of vandalism against private property (for writing "Children" in the Victory Park of Narva). Interestingly, in other locations in Tallinn and Narva, public messages against the war and Putin were allowed, or even institutionally promoted.

"I accept my punishment like Dostoyevsky, with a clean heart," Vovan concedes, adding that one of the books that he read while detained was *The Idiot*. As he shows, different forms of recognition are at play while refusing the prevailing historical representations and military legacies. One of them is the idiot, a character who is revealed to us in a pathological misunderstanding of social order. The idiot puts hegemonic notions of the useful on standby, ignoring the consensus way of doing things while making the seriousness of the dominant position appear rather ridiculous.

This chapter has shown how military and nuclear remnants stand not as a negation of war but as an extension of it instead. They are the symbol of a violent colonial legacy, the material sedimentation of multiple destructions. Nonetheless, necropolitical residues do not necessarily exemplify the failure of communism as an ideology. Both military and radioactive waste represent a new kind of residue, indeed, one that resists its own containment and demands different conceptions of temporality and entanglement. This particular type of waste has serious socioecological costs as lethal material that endures, but it also produces a reverberating negativity that is almost impossible to contain. Hence, it cannot simply be considered pollution, matter out of place, but is rather matter with no place.

Thus, the problem with necropolitical residues is not merely their potential danger but also the fact that they can remain only in the wrong way—implicating elements of non-relationality in relationality while having the capacity to kill. This form of alienation is spectral and physical all at once, felt as a shadow world, speaking through traces that had been nearly erased from view but keep on reverberating.[58] The presence of this kind of waste also threatens symbolic contamination, becoming subversive by undermining actually existing categories of order and representation. Uncanny structures of feeling (seemingly forgotten) then resurface, making visible what we were good at not seeing. As a result, ideas and emotions that were left behind intrude on the present anew, turning historical interpretations of how the war was, is, and will be into a battleground.

The problem of these ghostly remnants then lies in their wrong way of disappearing, generating a phantasmagoric quality. They set in motion visceral dynamics that might rest beneath reality while silently nudging our thoughts and understanding. In doing so, military and radioactive waste animates another understanding about history and its relationship to the present, exemplifying the coexistence of parallel timelines, showing how violent pasts and present fears are intertwined. Yet what used to be history has become a possible future; certainly war is felt as more than history in this region. So this chapter has also described how both necropolitical residues and social tensions are inscribed on the territory as a form of ecological memory. They remain as a refusal against forgetting as much as an invitation to remember wrongly.

4

THE SOCIAL LABORATORY

This chapter discusses the state-led regeneration-by-demolition plans for housing in Kohtla-Järve, a half-empty mining district of eastern Estonia. Based on observant participation, it examines a pilot project that set out to make room for the future through the liquidation of apartment buildings. Nevertheless, this normative intervention was meant not only to secure socio-material stability in line with emptying problem but also to produce political legibility by reordering local relations, infrastructure, and ideas. The state authorities hoped that this new pilot project would also bring national institutions closer to communities that had been neglected and set a good example of governance for other municipal authorities. The production of this pilot, however, followed an experimental process in relation to its practical *hows*, as well as a speculative idea of the future to come. The demolition-based regeneration entailed a move away from something half-known but simultaneously toward something else that remains unclear—since market forces are supposed to finish the work initiated by institutions in the testing project.

Likewise, the project has been received differently by the multiple actors involved. For instance, the municipal authorities took the outsized housing as an obstacle to increasing the competitiveness of Kohtla-Järve; yet they were afraid that discourses of shrinkage might lead to a diminished version of the present. Thus, the municipality continues to maintain the paradigm of growth and allocates funding to construct new infrastructure such as sports venues. For their part, local stakeholders felt that the application of the pilot plan was turning their town into a social laboratory. As a result, the project is viewed by many of the residents as having a merely mitigating purpose, as if it were being applied as a Band-Aid for wider sociopolitical problems, many of which have little connection to the physical fabric being demolished, and have more to do with pollution and a suspicious relationship between citizens, the municipality, and the state.

A Testing Ground

"I don't want to be part of this social laboratory," yelled a resident of Kohtla-Järve. This middle-aged man was not referring to the consequences of the pandemic and the subsequent vaccination plans, nor to how social networks make us hypervisible while storing our data. The resident, who refused to share his name, felt this way because of a pilot project initiated by the Estonian state to scale down the real estate of Kohtla-Järve. The pilot involved different agents with the idea of crafting a socio-technical model to be applied in other locations affected by half-emptiness. These concerns about the emptying problem were institutionalized through the requirement to create a single, translocatable model and to protocolize interventions in a predictable manner. Indeed, the success or failure of this experiment would affect other municipalities, thus transforming the locality into a testing ground for prototyping urban governance in a real-life setting, while asserting that the state is everywhere.

A laboratory has traditionally been a paradigmatic site for experimentation, thereby producing the possibility of inconsequential actions while differentiating a controlled inside from an uncontrolled outside.[1] Alas, experiments in social laboratories are not without consequences, nor can the elements involved in the test be controlled from beginning to end.

The state's plan for a subsidy program (financing demolition and relocation) was based on the belief that the physical liquidation of parts of the urban fabric might be enough to facilitate the local recovery. Accordingly, the Ministry of Finance assumed that the sacrifice of vacant apartment buildings might positively transform a district characterized by outmigration, economic decline, pollution, and aging while making institutional governance visible and increasing the value of what was left standing. Administrative attempts were therefore linked to a series of performance indicators as well as to normative codes, presenting the pilot project as a moral imperative.

In this town, however, partial demolition of a series of buildings may have started well before their institutionally prescribed liquidation, thanks to insufficient maintenance by unmotivated residents. Still, many of these apartment buildings remain in disrepair because of longtime disinvestment and minimal value in the real estate market. In some cases, local tenants might be the first to

consider their properties redundant. Given the low market value of local apartments, along with the fact that local people have neither easy if any access to loans
nor motivation to take out a loan, investment in real estate maintenance and
renovation is most often insufficient. Indeed, as soon as they can, those living
in half-empty Khrushchev-era flats move into a better apartment building or a
private house, leaving only a few people to inhabit these cold, unrepaired apartment houses. This is the case for older residents, who do not have the means to
improve the condition of their dwellings. As explained by Valeri, a resident who
had already moved out of one of the buildings slated for demolition, "Only Soviet
people stay behind, marginals who don't have money, and also elderly ones."

The lack of financial means is also reflected on the exterior of some of the
inhabited apartment housing, which might be painted only on one side or on
the ground floor of the building, where the entrance to a shop is. The owners of
local businesses may feel responsible for only their part of the façade; thus the
phenomenon of half-painted buildings. Ninety percent of Kohtla-Järve's housing
stock was built after 1946, and the proportion of uninhabited apartments doubled
between 2008 and 2018.[2] This town is a distinctive socio-spatial formation in
Soviet planning and ideology, a fact that was referred to by experts as hinder-
ing the effectiveness of their development strategies and modes of governance.
Accordingly, the pilot project proposed the elimination of a number of buildings
as a way of dealing with the negative social imagination and low market value
affecting the town. What we are dealing with, however, is not an apocalyptic scene
of ruination and failure but rather a process of infrastructural endurance against
the grain, in a context in which normal functioning has fallen away, while the
required socio-material adjustments have not yet been made—at least, not fully.

A lot has been written about shrinkage in eastern Europe but not so much
about decline.[3] The difference between the two is that shrinkage, as a concept,
is mainly focused on economic and demographic data (thus useful to planners,
and more calculative and programmatic, leaving aside the affective and cognitive
aspects of that process, which are included in decline). Decline is by contrast a
prolonged condition of discontinuity, but not a closing chapter. Unlike crisis,
which entails a return to normality at some point, in decline, the brokenness and
de-structuration persist over time. And while the concept of crisis impels us to
look into the past and critically assess how the rupture has occurred, the repercussions of decline affect our critical capacity because of the enduring nature of
the experience.

In recent work, Dace Dzenovska has defined the concept of emptiness as space
between orders, a transitional formation between a bygone past and a future that
has not yet arrived. She has unpacked emptiness as an ethnographically derived
analytical category consisting of (1) an observable reality whereby places lose

their constitutive elements—people, schools, shops, infrastructure; (2) a series of concrete practices and relations that emerge in a condition of negative capability; and (3) an interpretive framework through which people make sense of a precarious reality once political stability, industrial purpose, basic services, and fixed past, present, and future horizons have vanished. Dzenovska sees emptiness as an incremental and relational process emerging from the experience of loss, dispossession and outmigration. As a result, she concludes, the future within the space of emptiness is radically uncertain rather than passively awaited.[4]

While, for Dzenovska, emptiness connotes a formless space-time between orders in the Latvian countryside, the demolition of vacant apartment buildings in Kohtla-Järve is an experimental, top-down act of ordering, thus a spatio-temporal repair, yet one that does not put an end to the partial absences of the state, of neighbors, of jobs and services, and of collective belonging. Hence, emptiness is merely mitigated, reinforcing, in turn, the local sense of incompleteness and uncertainty. Prefixes such as "half," "quasi," and "semi" thus capture the circumstances in which things are less than fully, almost but not quite. Half-emptiness is not simply a matter of sparsely populated buildings; it also frames the scene in a way that affects local orientations toward the future and generates further relationships of mistrust and skepticism toward institutional interventions. This phenomenon has wider cognitive and affective consequences, for instance, in influencing how the town is perceived both by locals and within the rest of the country. Half-emptiness therefore does not simply call out a present absence; it materializes how a locality is burdened by its prior occupations. Burdened but not erased; degraded but not abandoned; enduring somewhat apart from the rest of the country, whose future filling seems certain. Hence, the concept of half-emptiness indexes how decline is experienced in aversively degraded locations that beckon intervention, yet where people continue living.

Indeed, what I encountered in 2020 were formations in which apartment buildings (privately owned) were quasi-vacant but not quite; basic services (doctors, schools, public transport) had been reduced but were partially operating; the constituting purpose of the town (mining) was still active though with uncertain prospects and not providing a collective labor identity as it did in Soviet times; the population had decreased by two-thirds since the collapse of the Soviet Union, but over 33.000 people still lived there (most of them Russian speakers, thus displaying an incomplete belonging to the present Estonian state); and, finally, the regeneration-by-demolition solution was tackling the local economic, affective, and environmental problems only halfway.

The idea of being neither empty nor full is important because it frames social relations and narrows the horizon of opportunities. Currently, vacated apartments are scattered throughout the different neighborhoods of the town, not concentrated in one area. Indeed, half-emptiness is always site-specific and projects its own affective vision, even though it is noticeable only through the absence of maintenance, lighting, and social contact. In this way, half-vacancy erodes the conditions for many types of agency and results in increased vulnerability. Therefore, even if half-emptiness is less visible than rusting machinery, ash hills, and lunar landscapes, it is still equally part of the same extractive externalities—simply invisible from the outside.

Demolition as Repair

In cooperation with three municipal governments, the Ministry of Finance has been prototyping new urban governance in real-life settings. The main aim of the pilot project is to test solutions to the problem of half-empty real estate. Once the ministry got involved, a series of demolition strategies were discussed for reordering the local urban fabric. In none of the scenarios, however, was the Soviet-era housing referred to as requiring technical retrofitting; instead, the state officials presented the demolition of this inherited infrastructure as part of a future-making gesture. Thus, the pilot comes with a sacrifice being translated into a top-down intervention, assuming that processes of regeneration just need to be activated and then accomplished by the market—raising the value of real estate by reducing the supply and increasing the demand. Or so state officials believed.

The pilot therefore approached Soviet-era apartment buildings as a burden. The key turning point in the elaboration of the strategy of demolition and relocation came in 2017, when the Kohtla-Järve municipality decided not to accept any more donations of apartments to them, asking locals to give the properties to the state instead. In doing so, the municipality transferred the real estate problem to the ministry, compelling state institutions to take action on a matter that had not been deemed to be within their competence until then.[5]

From the point of view of Western societies, this divergent local sense of ownership might seem peculiar. In the case of the apartments built during the Soviet period, which constitute a majority in the region, most of the real estate was granted as property in the early 1990s, not bought and sold as in a consolidated market economy. The apartments in Kohtla-Järve had previously been allocated to mining workers on the basis of Soviet notions of social rank. The new inhabitants have had a relatively short period of ownership, which may have been insufficient to generate a binding relationship to the property as such; they have had to learn how to be owners.[6] Another explanation for the ambiguous relation to ownership could be the sense of an incomplete belonging to the new Estonian

Republic based on the ethnicity of the residents. Indeed, while Estonian speakers in the region tend to live in houses in the rural areas (often inherited from their ancestors), Russian speakers mostly live in urban apartment buildings in which they settled in the second half of the twentieth century. These noticeable differences were referred to by several Estonian speakers as indicating in their case a deeper attachment to the land.[7]

For years, the municipal authorities had been maintaining that the scale of the problem was greater than their means, and thus they tried to engage the Estonian state in resolving it. As one local official pointed out, they saw the accumulation of half-empty buildings as a state issue; therefore, the ownership of newly vacant apartments (and with it the responsibility for solving the problem) had to be transferred to the state: "So far, we have been waiting for the state to deal with this problem." Nonetheless, officials of this municipality often downplayed the political charge of the project, referring to the demolition as an acupunctural intervention. Additionally, they were reluctant to use the term "shrinking." In meetings they would insist, "We are not shrinking; we just need to take down a couple of buildings to improve the quality of the urban fabric."

Perhaps they were reluctant to call their town shrinking because this terminology makes it possible to justify the alien imposition of a remedy. Instead, in the expert group meetings, "future" was among the most frequently repeated terms, along with "potential," "scenarios," and "visions"; alas, "growth" was hardly mentioned alongside the sacrifice of the existing infrastructure. During the meetings with both municipal and state experts, a list of worrying numbers and forecasts was often put on the table. The repetition of these negative estimates acquired a performative character during the meetings, making it difficult to question the demolition strategy as a whole. As a result, the liquidation of buildings also assumed a normative aspect which entered the vocabulary of local officials, turning the pilot project into a process of both learning and intense negotiation of procedures for goal-setting, monitoring, and evaluation.

Actors agreed on what was not known and took this into account for future planning, designating this acknowledged ignorance for further action. This testing method for dealing with complex issues was not unknown to municipal authorities, who have had to work with very limited financing, and not always with reliable information regarding the actual ownership of the housing stock, while also having to adapt to new forms of (neoliberal) governmentality and distribution of resources. Indeed, the municipality of Kohtla-Järve lacked a definitive list of the unoccupied housing stock; nor was there always consensus on whether apartment buildings were empty or just in seasonal use.

Thus, the pilot not only provided subsidies for the demolition of buildings but also demanded collaboration between local councils, the state, and experts in setting up development plans. The actors involved operated with a sense that they were testing the very process of working, rehearsing different ways of approaching the emptying problem. Even if most of our conversations were held in Estonian, municipal, regional, and state experts seemed to be trying to figure out what each of them meant by such terms as "future" and "scaling down." This was not simply due to the different agendas at stake in the meetings but also because of the need to learn how to cooperate, establish a common ground for mutual understanding, and overcome the feelings of suspicion that tended to haunt these discussions.

The process of experimentation unfolded through site-specific forms of negotiation, following iterative development. In general terms, the pilot project was structured in three phases: (1) preliminary research to understand the nature of the problem, including policy analysis and extensive work revising and mapping the experience of local authorities; (2) field interventions based on policy recommendations, along with prototyping practical guides and trying to accommodate the expectations of both municipal authorities and local residents; and (3) summary and assessment of the experience based on the existing reports, and suggesting protocols and legal recommendations to support future measures.[8]

Given the probationary aim of the pilot, different counterparts were immersed in prototyping relations and questions. This was also the case for the ethnographer, as I too was learning in situ what to ask and identifying issues that were not initially considered to be relevant.[9] On the one hand, the testing character of the project allowed mistakes to happen, and formalities were somewhat relaxed. Conversely, some of the actors also commented negatively on the horizontal nature of the relations experienced in the pilot because of the confusion created over the corresponding roles and responsibilities. For instance, a municipal stakeholder objected, "I do not want to have many bosses, just one." Accordingly, the prototyping character of the project and the cooperation with both experts and inhabitants also influenced the data collection as well as access to knowledge, since I enjoyed a certain sense of openness and unconstrained opportunities for asking questions and observing. Nonetheless, the invisibility of half-emptiness became an analytic problem to me, as much as to the state in its capacity to understand and classify the issue, and eventually to put things to rights again.

Your Order, My Demolition

This chapter looks at the state as a set of spatial practices and procedures that make its presence material through demolition. The research is based on observant participation in the design and development of the pilot aiming to make room for the future through the liquidation of apartment buildings in Kohtla-Järve. I joined Keiti Kljavin's team at the Estonian Urban Lab as an ethnographer, yet in some instances I also had to advise on the participatory dimension of the project in the way social designers do.[10] This approach draws on the assumption that in some cases, or in some instances of the research, it is not enough to be in direct observation of how people act; we also need to be part of that action, intervening in the unfolding of the events and discussions in order to understand how they experience those acts.[11] The research thus combines field descriptions with materials from policy and project coordination and internal letters, as well as meetings with both state and municipal officials and interviews with local residents. For instance, as part of the consultation work, the Estonian Urban Lab conducted a series of twenty-two interviews with residents living in the apartment buildings chosen for demolition. The interviews reflected little faith in the real impact of the pilot project; nonetheless, residents readily identified several factors that compromised the region's future, such as pollution, unemployment, and limited integration within the country.

Eventually, reparative strategies can manifest two different kinds of urban planning: top-down policy based on demolishing the existing infrastructure (preparing for a distant future), and bottom-up intervention by residents wishing to hold on to their way of life (as a matter of maintaining life). Demolition itself is a multifaceted intervention, with a variety of sociopolitical, economic, and cultural meanings and not free of indeterminacy and conflict. The political polysemy of demolition was indeed exemplified in how the pilot was received differently by the actors affected by its impact. In the case of Kohtla-Järve, the liquidation of Soviet housing was meant to favor socioeconomic regeneration and political legibility (by reordering relations, infrastructure, and ideas according to the central gaze) after decades of state retreat.

Emptiness in rural areas is often perceived by local residents as the outcome of state retreat, whereas the same phenomenon is seen by policymakers as a manifestation of market development. In other contexts, such as the Latvian or eastern German countryside, it was residents who maintained the buildings to avoid the expected infrastructural endings and instead practiced a bottom-up modality of endurance.[12] In Kohtla-Järve, however, it is the sacrificing of buildings itself—rather than their maintenance—that entails a general promise of a future.

After several delays owing to the COVID-19 pandemic, on October 12, 2020, different stakeholders organized a public event to meet the tenants of two apartment buildings slated for demolition in the pilot. The aim was to inform the affected residents about the various options that the liquidation and relocation strategy was offering. A white tent was set up in the courtyard of two of these buildings, and pastries and tea were provided. Around twenty residents showed up (six men and fourteen women). I observed a certain choreography of suspicion, in which residents would walk around outside the tent observing what was going on and who was inside, stand at the entrance for a few minutes, and finally either step inside or go away.

The representative of the municipality played the leading role in the meeting and, speaking in Russian, patiently and professionally explained the details of the pilot project and the possible options for relocation. "We are going to liquidate buildings that have already been amortized," the representative announced before referring to the "independent experts in Tallinn" as leverage for the strategy. This comment made me feel that I was not simply an ethnographer anymore but an "expert" invited to "confirm" the participatory character of the pilot, an ornament in a ceremony of public consultation that operated as a technology of transparency.

Since the choices for relocation always depended on the availability of publicly owned apartments in other buildings, a few residents expressed disagreement over the compensation. During this meeting, the official stated, "We are not offering newly built apartments because, as you know, there is no construction going on here." A local resident asked in response, "But do you pay for capital or sanitary repairs?" The municipal official then replied, "Hear me out until the end." The representative from the Ministry of Finance tried to help, adding, "Later, we can discuss individual cases." But the upset resident continued: "Thanks for not helping. You just want to cheat me!" The municipal official remained calm and explained, "Our intention is to offer a better living environment." Then a resident from Kiviõli, a city in the municipality of Lüganuse, stepped up and talked about her case. She had agreed to swap her property for a municipally owned apartment. It measured fewer square meters than her previous one, but she had made use of the repair fund to improve the sanitation of the apartment she received. A female resident then asked what she had done with her furniture and if she was happy with the decision. The resident from Kiviõli responded that she had been able to take all of the furnishings (including the front door) from her old apartment to the new one and was happy because the heating and surroundings were better.

The discussion then moved outside the tent, where complaints and opinions that would have been imprudent if addressed to the officials were shared. Different notions regarding the value of a building were also expressed among some of the neighbors. Then someone said, "If you don't want Kohtla-Järve to end up like Viivikonna, then we have to do something." (For more on that ghost town, see chapter 6.) "Instead of demolishing our building, give us the money, and we will buy whatever we want, or go away with it," another resident added. Suddenly, one resident asked the representative of the ministry, "Are you Jewish?" Not knowing what to reply, the representative of the ministry appeared to be puzzled by the question. "Your plan sounds like the 1930s policies of Stalin," yelled another. The representative of the ministry then replied, "The plan is well intentioned and in the interest of the state—" Before the representative could complete the sentence, a resident demanded, "And why not in our interest?"

After the meeting, and in light of the opposition of the residents, the municipality and the state representative decided to reconsider which buildings would be demolished. Finally, only two apartment buildings were designated for liquidation in Kohtla-Järve, and the funding was mobilized to proceed with the operation in 2022. Among the forty-four apartments originally identified for demolition, only six residents agreed to an exchange of properties in the mining capital. Most owners preferred either to receive financial compensation and leave town or to find an apartment on the market instead of moving into a municipally owned unit.

Also, there were local residents who perceived the scaling down of the city as a de-modernization after its being part of the construction of communist progress during the dawn of the mining industry. Although, in the case of municipal officials, I could observe a certain gratification about the newly gained attention of the state, it was unclear how and where to direct this attention. Indeed, one of the aims of the pilot project was to help local residents—traditionally invisible citizens as most of them hold a gray alien's passport—make their situation visible by becoming "legible" to the state in giving feedback. There were, however, various signs indicating a lack of trust among local residents toward both the municipality and state institutions. They see themselves as on the margins of power and with little capacity to challenge the state's means and discourses. As one of the residents interviewed by the Estonian Urban Lab argued, "If something has already been decided, it will happen, notwithstanding what we say." And as Julia, a resident of Kohtla-Järve, confessed: "Changes? People are just busy finding solutions to everyday problems and have no time to imagine things otherwise."

Paradoxically, one of the aims of the Ministry of Finance was to develop a culture of transparency among the local population. Still, as many of the local people saw it, institutions had suddenly decided to knock on their door and offer an advantageous deal that couldn't be refused: distributing apartments and funding for repairs in a kind of gift-giving potlatch.[13] For residents of Kohtla-Järve, institutions are located (mentally) in faraway places like Tallinn, and power operates in unpredictable and capricious ways. This sense of insecurity was another source of reproach ("But Jelena was given money for her apartment!"). In turn, mutual suspicion spread, as conflicting information circulated about the pilot ("They will take you out of your apartment and force you to move to a dormitory").

There was also a rumor in Kohtla-Järve about receiving some families from India and Ukraine, as well as hopes of foreign investment, creative economies, and the arrival of skilled workers. All these hopes were unsubstantiated, though, revealing themselves to be an exercise in wishful thinking that actually signaled a climate of distrust.

In the context of prolonged decline, the sacrifice of half-empty apartment buildings was presented by the Estonian Ministry of Finance as a way of putting things in order anew. The gesture of creating order through demolition combines both making and unmaking in an indeterminate scenario; it is thus an institutionalized social laboratory that suggests a process of testing in a context in which normal functioning has ceased, basic services operate only partway, and the constitutive purpose of the locality (mining) is uncertain. While the mining purpose and function have partially collapsed in Kohtla-Järve, a new orientation toward the future is being experimented with by reordering the urban fabric, though in a way (regeneration by demolition) that does not follow the linear logic of development projects.[14]

Interestingly, the liquidation project reproduces the logic of sacrifice that has characterized the region for over a century, namely, that this territory was written off for destruction in the name of a future goal or higher purpose. The success or failure of this urban experiment will widely affect regional development. Thus, the Estonian state is approaching Kohtla-Järve as a testing ground in which reparative actions are rehearsed and from which new policy models (and knowledge) will emanate. Nonetheless, for an experiment to work, it has to be deliberately arranged to generate surprises; alas, in real-life settings, uncontrolled tests are unwelcome.

Once the demolition was accomplished, the issue would be transferred from public institutions to the market, which was supposed to do the remaining work. The unfinished, open-ended quality of the process raised further questions, such as who is allowed to take part in the decisions, how the main goals of the pilot should be interpreted, and how success would be measured. For some, demolition might materialize aspirations for a better future, while for others, it elicited negative responses. Indeed, the research presented here demonstrates an acute difference in the understanding of local needs and the purposes of the enacted demolition policy experiment between national policymakers, experts, local officials, and residents. For instance, the municipal authorities refused the political charge of the project. Instead, they defined the outsized housing as a burden on efforts to increase the competitiveness of Kohtla-Järve and were expecting to return to the path of growth once the selected buildings were liquidated. In turn, local residents did not fully foresee the positive outcome of the project and dismissed the pilot as merely mitigating wider social and environmental issues. Perhaps, in the end, the point missed by them all is that the pilot project was not anymore about making things whole again, desiring to return to or restore a lost fullness, but about making things possible while imagining different forms of politics. In that sense, demolition was an act of repair.

INTERIOR EXTERIORITIES

In some locations, political, economic, and environmental changes made dwelling spaces superfluous and eventually wasted. Kohtla-Järve is one such area, dismantling identities, materialities, and social relationships all at once. In this chapter I describe my impressions after visiting over twenty-five of the Soviet-era apartments in the mining capital that had become empty. The observation of lived things that do not belong to the present is juxtaposed with reflections on how the so-called transition was experienced through multiple devaluations—of skills, technology, social bonds, collective memory, and people's sense of belonging. The confluence of revulsion and materiality manifests a haunting disorder that questions both Soviet ideals of linear progress and post-socialist success stories. Remains of the recent past, however, are rapidly disappearing in Estonia, turning the study of the transition into an exercise in accelerated archaeology. Paradoxically, the observation of domestic materiality that had been *socially frozen* in recent decades (time capsule–like) is an opportunity to reflect about what came after socialism but also against it.[1]

In these time capsules, I encounter traces of past life that nonetheless resist a clear interpretive framework and give few signs about the future. I run into a pile of wreckage that vacancy has hurled at my feet: lived things that have no place in the present yet remain valueless, unusable, or even disturbing by confronting aspects of mortality and belonging. Their heuristic relevance, though, is also close to zero—to the point where their past use and meaning are constitutive of nothing; they hold no lesson or value in the present. Instead, they decompose in an unruly, malodorous way while impelling me to think of everything I own in my apartment, of my own interior exteriority.

Years of Vacancy

Buildings fall into disrepair not only because of engineering problems but also because of being either behind or ahead of their times. Nonetheless, socialist housing has demonstrated a surprising obduracy, despite the oversized, rigid planning and the negative symbolic meanings attached to it.[2] For instance, literary scholar Thomas Lahusen refers to Soviet apartment buildings as "zero-value rubbish" on account of their ubiquity and suboptimal construction methods and materials, concluding that they hardly have a place in a market economy.[3] Accordingly, the destruction of socialist legacies has been presented as imperative in order to move back to the future through an active dis-inheritage, following the logic of sacrifice. Indeed, the deterioration of the housing stock has been due not only to the perishability or life span of the Khrushchev-era flats but also to how they are devalued and made expendable.

During the transition period, many apartments and houses were abandoned in Kohtla-Järve; then time stepped in and did its work, reminding us that a home is always a ruin to come. I can only say "many apartments and houses" because there are no definitive statistical data regarding the abandonment. In some cases, one can see that no one turns on the lights in a particular home, day after day. Indeed, local authorities try to figure out if anyone lives in these places by checking invoices for electricity and gas consumption, hoping to catch a hint regarding the (seasonal or permanent) vacancy.

One way of noting the convoluted unmaking of the Soviet world is to pay attention to the different *remonts* (renovations) performed and undone during the 1990s.[4] Domestic spaces (invisible through the uniform façades of the apartment blocks) went through substantial renovations, to the point where the *euroremont* (Eurorenovation) became similar to the wearing of blue jeans—a defining cultural trend and part of the construction of a post-Soviet identity.[5] This vernacular term appeared in the 1990s in relation to the practice of mimicking what seemed to be Western homemaking standards, tastes, and materials. The *euroremont* therefore emerged not as a way of attending to shortcomings but as an endeavor to achieve a social status—often done in postmodern taste and contributing to (per)form the national identity.[6]

In some of the apartments that I visited, I still found traces that had been covered by new layers of *euroremont*. This phenomenon expressed idealistic imaginaries of Europe and national identity, yet conditioned by local traditions and material affordances. Indeed, as few could travel to the "real Europe," people created their own image of Western comfort based on movies and glossy magazines, making reforms to reproduce it in their dwellings accordingly. These repairs did not simply copy Western interior design solutions; they also staged new kinds of social relations. Even though aesthetic standards have changed since, and retro design trends suggest an increasing appreciation of past materiality, Soviet remains in Estonia are still considered something just to rip up and throw away. Nevertheless, things seem to be gradually changing, perhaps because of generational replacement. In cities such as Kohtla-Järve, Narva, or Sillamäe, I noticed that more and more apartments are being refurbished again and that an increasing number of residents are paying attention to stairways and front areas. They might still use the plastic windows typical of *euroremont* and get rid of Soviet stuff; repairs, however, are no longer being done to bring Europe to the East, but instead as a form of putting *things* in order anew, enacting a novel standing toward the world, including self-respect.

In a context of pollution and half-emptiness such as in Kohtla-Järve, domestic care and maintenance routines underpin a moral navigation.[7] And yet the twenty-five vacant apartments that I visited in this town did not reflect any sort of enduring sense of belonging or attachment to the locality. Instead, they appeared to me a space of dis-inheritance produced by abjection and pathological misalignment. As part of the domestic materiality therein, one can see such things as the portrait of an unknown young lady, unwashed dishes, dirty diapers, unfinished medicines, empty bottles of hard spirits, worn-down mattresses, tired wallpaper, bulky furniture, Soviet and Orthodox religious symbols, CDs, plastic flowers, foreign flags, broken glass, newspapers from October 2009, and so on.

The things that are visible at vacated apartments are no longer informative and are in the process of becoming waste. They are indeed turning back into matter while losing their concreteness as objects. These things left behind appear before us as a civilizational residue, even a sort of anti-politics. They are not mere litter (matter lying out of place in a transitional state), but they evoke loss, estrangement, and disgust, opening the gate to the dark side of post-socialist change.[8] Everything in there is already beyond repair, reflecting a post-broken present. In some cases, material disaggregation entails a rather positive symbolic power, comparable to a patina. But that is not the case with the lived things encountered in these apartments. They anchor no identity. Rather, they display a dark potentiality, threatening the stability of the present.

Indeed, can we find any heuristic potential in this trash? Or does the wasting of traces mean that something loses all power to signify completely? What we encounter is part of a mass of stuff rather than discrete objects. Stepping into these apartments turns into a visceral experience of solitude. Then you perceive that smell—effluviant of long vacancy—and feel like vomiting. Years of vacancy are, first and foremost, a sensory experience, yet one that generates further uncertainty and refers to failed social relations. These remains do not trigger memory, identity, or meaning but decompose them instead, thereby impeding the possibility of being passed on to coming generations, or of ending up in a history museum or being made into heritage.[9] They materialize a discontinuity, a gap, a lack of meaning, a disconnection, a loss of objectness; they are socially dead. It is a deserted cartography, the dead ends of emotional veins and arteries.

We understand the experiences of decline and not-belonging once they have come indoors, into our houses, and sleep with us. I am talking not merely about a limited sense of belonging to the present or to the nation, but also about individual self-worth. Still, the first impression is one of stepping into a time capsule. For quite a while, nothing has been coming in or out of these apartments. Because of the death of the owners, there have been neither additions nor withdrawals. The officials, however, do not divulge the identity of the previous tenants. Only in talking to neighbors am I told that here was an elderly couple, there a person who committed suicide, and over there a drug addict. Only inside an apartment can there actually be this kind of solitude. These dwelling spaces display intimacy in reverse. The lights do not work, the dishes are dirty, the windows broken; in some the paint on the walls is cracked, and in others the wallpaper is falling off. It is a radical, unsettling confrontation with what has no place in the present, indexing an inhospitableness. Clocks have stopped working, and the calendars hanging on the wall or lying on the floor refer to 2007, 2008, 2003. These technologies for ordering time (for marking seasons and events) are now useless.[10]

Traditionally, studies of domestic material culture have paid attention to the way the things visible in a home are informative.[11] Oftentimes, households are referred to as being key in the production and reproduction of social life; yet there have been fewer investigations about those situations in which one's domestic materiality is far from reinforcing identity or generating predictability. Architect Tomás Errázuriz reflected on this issue while dismantling his apartment in Santiago de Chile. Homes are characterized by a predictability factor, which is experienced both sensorially and intellectually, he argues.[12] Going back home means returning to oneself, to the frames of reference that safeguard our identity, and to feelings of circularity and a series of familiar senses such as smell, hearing, seeing, and touch that are associated with habitability. It does not matter whether our home is a trailer, a cave, or a hotel. The problem arises when we cannot return to something we can recognize, an experience that troubles our inner landscape.

In the case of the vacant apartments I visited in Kohtla-Järve, however, they do not provide an interiority in the present but instead refer to a prior social knowledge that has now been rendered obsolete and wasteful. The discrepancy between the longevity of homes and the relative transience of their occupants can indeed be problematic.[13] The publicly owned apartments in Kohtla-Järve are now supposed to host a home again, yet those directly affected by the demolition program are not always interested in relocating to the apartments offered by the authorities. Indeed, most of the residents prefer to take the money and find themselves an apartment on the market or move to another town. It is difficult to imagine these apartments as livable.

As with a hideout, providing shelter is just one of the mandates of a home. At this latitude, homes need to provide an interiority, but they must also be warm, and the roof should not leak. Unfortunately, there are many apartment buildings in Ida-Virumaa where even these basic needs are not met. For instance, in Sirgala and Viivikonna (see chapter 6), we can find buildings containing dozens of apartments in which only two or three people live. The heating, electricity, and water may be turned off, probably because of unpaid utility bills. Thus, it is not that rare to see traces of bonfires inside. In some cases, these vacant apartments have been broken into, and anything of value—from radiators to faucets to light fixtures—was stolen long ago. In such a context, the apartment becomes a trap. Owners cannot sell it because the value is nearly zero, and, lacking money, they can hardly relocate elsewhere.

Two important elements in the creation of domesticity are windows and doors, which create a sense of control and form a link between the interior and the exterior of a house.[14] Through windows and doors, social lives are made into homes. Then practices of accommodation such as sorting and storing become part of a domestic system of exchange.[15] A home is also a floor plan. The differentiation between front stage and back stage is arranged in the distribution of bedrooms, kitchen, and doorways, turning homes into a site of performance of the self. Households self-consciously present their public selves on the façade and the entryway, signifying perceptions of appropriate, ordinary behavior, as they want others to see them. In the bedrooms, however, people can let down their hair, be freer, and hang an Orthodox icon or a poster of t.A.T.u.

Overall, a home is the material manifestation of a series of aspirations and modalities of dwelling. Accordingly, domestic untidiness and clutter have been recognized as both a symptom and a cause of mental disorder.[16] The issue is not simply that when things become clutter, they change from comforting to disruptive, but that a *wrong* ecology of things is an indication of a disturbed psyche in those who inhabit it.[17] In a similar vein, after investigating thirty households in London, anthropologist Daniel Miller finds that the physical condition of a dwelling expresses social relationships, since people who develop a careful rapport with things are the same people who develop multiple social relationships. One of the examples that Miller provides is the flat belonging to a man named George: disorienting because of its emptiness, a chilling absence that is experienced by the visitor as violent, tense, inhospitable. The material void of his apartment comes to represent all that has happened to George: his forced retirement at the age of fifty-five, his previous work as a clerk in a large company, his difficulties in making individual decisions and taking responsibility, his loneliness, and perhaps also his depression. There were no decorations because there was just no point, Miller concludes.[18]

The poet Joseph Brodsky also found no point in the Soviet partitioning of apartments. In his memoirs, he refers to his family's home in Leningrad as "a room and a half." The space was allotted by Soviet officials, who calculated the area in a nonfunctional, abstract way, as if it were not a living room with family memories but just *space*: not functional for living, but perhaps effective for social engineering, refurbishing Soviet fantasies of an interior completely revealed in order to gain complete control over it.[19]

Secrecy was deeply embedded in socialist architecture, turning buildings into the clothing of the body politic. As a result, communal living spaces shaped both the Soviet subject and the domestic perception of the state. Conceived of as part of the public sphere, homes were open to the intrusion of the authorities. In addition to the publicity of privacy under the Soviet power, the spatial limitations imposed in *kommunalkas* (communal apartments) also contributed to reformulating the domestic sphere. As the collective became interiorized in people's domestic lives, their private lives often moved out into public settings. Nonetheless, Soviet citizens managed to find inventive ways of crafting multipurpose living spaces within communal housing. For instance, a sense of privacy was frequently experienced in the kitchen, where a close circle of friends recursively gathered for *obshchenie* (free communication). These practices of domesticity were socially significant, as they allowed for the construction of a position apart from the official regime.[20]

The term "domesticity" thus has distinct connotations in Russian culture. It is located between what pertains to the individual and what is collective: partly a gift bestowed by the state, partly an illicit haul. Nonetheless, the *kommunalka* was not an exclusively Soviet product but a practice rooted in the Russian collective psyche. Living in common, sharing facilities and resources, was simply part of being Russian, the worldly manifestation of a spiritual union (*sobornost*). Historically, the number of peasant communes was significant, sharing land and livestock and redistributing crops between families (*obshchina, mir*). It was not uncommon even for marriages between young men and women to be publicly consummated; likewise, in some localities, it was accepted practice for fathers-in-law to have sexual relations with their daughters-in-law in the absence of the son (*snokhachestvo*).[21]

On the basis of fieldwork carried out in the late 1990s in St. Petersburg (which had the highest percentage of communal housing among Soviet cities), sociologist Ekaterina Gerasimova notes how complex tactics of indifference turned neighbors into mere elements of the setting. In her view, domesticity was intensively played out in the interstices between what is hidden and what is revealed.

Gerasimova's informants recount how their lives had to be lived in the sight of others, lacking the possibility for retreat, while they struggled to maintain privacy for issues such as the maintenance of bodily hygiene. Even using the toilet was done in recognition of an audience (of people who were not members of the family) waiting just outside the door. Thus, she points out, "It might seem that the inhabitants of communal apartments were unaware that they lacked privacy, but the concept of privacy has never been a feature of Russian and Soviet culture, and, in fact, the term itself is hard to translate into Russian."[22] Waiting for the bathroom, residents lined up in the corridor, itself cluttered with laundry, newspapers, drunks, and whatnot. As Gerasimova concludes, domesticity did not fully belong to the public sphere, but neither can it be defined as private space. It was rather a struggle between what is given by the state and what is defended from collective seeing. Still, private life was not entirely abolished by the Soviet power, as proclaimed by the character Strelnikov in *Doctor Zhivago*, and as foreseen by Walter Benjamin when he visited Moscow in 1927.[23]

No Future for the Archaeologists of Post-socialism

Upon her return to "Piter" (St. Petersburg, the most foreign city in Russia) in 1989, Svetlana Boym found her old house in a state of disrepair. For her, both the façade and the interior felt "numb."[24] That sad visit led her to look into migration and the idea of home with an unexpectedly ambivalent result. Something was lost and something was gained in a rather forced way. Both experiences, migration and colonialism, are unhomely.[25] But can we say that post-socialist materiality has been ambivalent?[26] And which traces would be heuristically meaningful, allowing us to learn from and about the daily domesticity of the post-socialist *byt*? In my study of Soviet remains in Tallinn, I claimed that the pastness attributed to Soviet things, people, and ideas came not as their intrinsic quality but as a contested practice.[27] In eastern Estonia, however, I found myself gathering remains of the so-called transition in the form of fossils, skeletons, and leaking traces. Here everyday life involves managing contradictions between different times embedded in objects, infrastructures, and spaces.

The Soviet Union ended politically but persisted materially, continuing to shape everyday life in different locations of Estonia. The tension around what to preserve, destroy, or ignore reflects ongoing ideological struggles over belonging and historical representations in this country. What is preserved, forgotten, or destroyed becomes then a political act, revealing how materiality mediates memory, identity, and future possibilities. But the impermanence of the object of study, likely to disappear, complicates research on post-socialist issues and demands that the field be understood not solely as a spatial concept but also as a temporal one.[28] Perhaps the exercise of accounting for post-socialist remains that endure in the present is not just accelerated but also hopeless, once we assume that it might take several decades for something contemporary to become an archaeological object.[29]

The vanished world of Soviet socialism represented a civilizational enterprise now discarded but not entirely forgotten. The extinction of a political regime causes not only ideologies to disappear but also visions of the future in addition to skills, habits, and political kinship. Interestingly, their wrong way of disappearance, or incomplete vanishing, tells us about the world we have created for ourselves. In Estonia, an accelerated reconfiguration of social relations and change of institutional scripts correlated with the speed of material destruction, producing a complex mix of interruption and persistence, of abandonment and reprogramming.[30] A practical consequence of this disorderly state of existence is the difficulty of thinking alternatively, along with a sense of disappointment and hostility toward new state institutions.[31] That feeling of loss is explained not only by the radical changes people went through per se but also by the consequences of the ways of coping with them.[32] Dace Dzenovska has noted that those left behind in the rural countryside of Latvia also experienced dysconnectivity and the sense that the future was being made elsewhere.[33] Hence, the sentiment of loss and the experience of emptiness appear as the opposite not of fullness but of a future.

Another complication is that what has remained from the Soviet past often goes through a social and institutional disinvestment. An example of this is Kino Rodina (Cinema Motherland), one of the two buildings listed as heritage sites in Sillamäe. Kino Rodina fell into private hands during perestroika, functioning as a cinema until 1995, after which it was used as a nightclub for several years.[34] The club was named Korrida, and neon pink and green colors were added to the neoclassical ornaments and walls to create a more festive atmosphere. Rumor has it that the club was closed when drugs began to circulate among the clientele. In 2023, I visited Kino Rodina with Aleksandr Starodubtsev, one of the three owners of the building. He reiterates that he is old and lacks the motivation to do anything with the building, complaining that the electricity bill is too expensive.[35] The impressive façade is decorated with figured molding and has a sign that reads "Kino Rodina" in a beautiful old script. The building has a rich ornamental décor. The front room of the cinema is a spacious lobby, and the second floor once hosted a restaurant with a dance hall. Nowadays, the chairs are lying on the floor, a short glass for vodka is hidden in the waiter's pantry, and a package of chocolate covered with mold sits forgotten in a corner of the kitchen.

The architectural project was designed by the architectural firm Giprokino, the Soviet State Institute for the Design of Cinema Theatres, which operated across the empire. Indeed, a similar movie theater was built in Ashgabat, Turkmenistan. The building was part of the progress and prosperity symbolized by industrial activity, which often went hand in hand with locations such as cinemas, theaters, sports venues, military bases, hospitals, schools, and media offices. In Sillamäe, some of them stand as ruins, such as the Soviet-era *kazarma* (see chapter 3), or the building at Rumjantsevi 3, once the headquarters of the *Sillamäe Herald* newspaper. I also entered this building. The heating system there had been stolen, as well as the lights. While strolling around, you can detect traces of previous trespassers, such as graffiti on the walls and excrement on the floor. Someone certainly seems to have used this dark corner of the world to serve his scatological needs. A feather on the stairs might also be testimony to how the building has been transformed into a pigeon loft. I keep walking and see a series of toy guns lying on the floor, indicating that the building has become a playground for some. In addition to the playful graffiti on the walls, there are also matchboxes, broken glass, peeled-off wallpaper, headphones, books, banners from the Social Democrat Party, and random sheets of newspaper from various years strewn on the floor, which itself is full of assorted obstacles. Then I found some discarded shoes. And rotting animals. They both unsettle me. How shall I interpret this rubbish? And can we extract any learning from it?

Some of these traces of previous habitation might create unease; after all, we are confronting the social postmortem existence of places, ideas, and relationships. Certainly, things tend to generate anxiety when they do not disappear properly. Yet the wrong ending of things has not got the attention it deserves, especially in relation to how this act works representationally and materially in the present. Likewise, the vanishing of socialist materiality makes it difficult to understand the recent past. This impels us to reconsider how to trace the unknowables related to the post-socialist experience of unmaking and devaluation. Furthermore, the collapse of the Soviet Union also meant the weakening of actually existing ties and circulations across the empire, eventually reducing the possibility of studying how much variation, as well as connection, there was among cities of the socialist world.[36]

The ruination of Kino Rodina has occurred within this sort of context; hence, the building is not simply a symbol of the abnormality of socialist architecture in terms of size and a denial of the effects of time but also a signifier of official indifference, negligence, and disinvestment.[37] In Estonia, the wasting of Soviet legacies was part of a wider political process of disqualification enmeshed in new relations of power. In their devalued traces, wasted legacies appear as a forensic manifestation of an uneasy integration of the Soviet past into the present, as not belonging to us. The very wasting of a legacy is dissociating; it makes sensorially perceptible the discourses attributing to socialist ideas an intrinsic failure and reinforces a sense of residuality to the recent past. As a result, the Soviet experience is approached as a historical and political error instead of as a social and cultural reality like any other.

Self-Made Heritage

Post-socialism also resonates with global change and the neoliberal restructuring of societies, too, thus referring to both: a transitional devaluation experienced locally and processes that have been happening in connection with other processes elsewhere.[38] The disintegration of the USSR led to an exercise of undoing through the unmaking of both infrastructure and the cultural collective memory of the past regime. In Estonia, an accelerated reconfiguration of social relations correlated with the speed of material destruction. The experience itself was underlined by a strange combination of euphoria and loss, escaping into the future while looking backwards—with a reverse gaze. The way we sensorially experience and make sense of our surroundings is directly dependent on the prior knowledge of things; but in this case, the frames of reference from the past had become obsolete. As a result, many of the residents of Ida-Virumaa faced not only unpredictability about the future but also a sense of displacement in the present and uncertainty regarding the interpretation of the past.

In the middle of that state of displacement and uncertainty, people have been negotiating their belonging and sense of place in circumstances that were not of their own choosing. An example of this is Chudamäe, meaning "Wonderland," located about three kilometers from Sillamäe, in the forest and not far from the coast. In 2014, a group of retired people decided to build their own eventual resting place. Every time I visit, it looks differently refurbished, with garlands hanging on the trees, over a hundred toys carefully staged, benches, tables, banners, carved figures, a canopy, a booth.

It is not rare to find two of the founders there, Jelena Tulženko and Tatjana Mikhailova, as I did one day in August 2023. "We came from swimming and wanted to hang out a bit in Chudamäe, have a picnic and see if there was something to do," says Tatjana energetically. Then, Jelena explains the impetus behind the installation. "We had no place to hang out and started to get a little bored. And our grandchildren grew up and the toys remained behind. People walk along this path, especially elderly people. At first, someone made benches in this clearing so that we could rest our feet. Later, a table for picnics was built, then old toys began to appear here, and local carpenters agreed to carve various wooden figures," like the smiling sun and the gate with the inscription "Dobro Pozhalovat!"

Chudamäe is not merely affected by seasonal changes; it displays a sense of unfinishedness, or ongoingness. Perhaps that is because of the emotional materials with which it was constructed, revealing nostalgic affectivities. Little by little, the women have been developing the look and the comforting ambiance of the place. Five members of the group had died since Chudamäe was built, and two others had grown tired of working on the project, leaving only Jelena and Tatjana to take care of the glade. "This is a place for making new friends. Many people have helped us to construct stuff like the booth and arcades. We could not do all of that on our own. But still, we don't have enough men," says Tatjana.

Unexpectedly, Jelena and Tatjana take sandwiches and a thermos of tea from a bag, and then the picnic begins. They have also brought fruit from their dachas. "This is from our garden, not from the shop. Natural, with no chemical products," insists Tatjana. Unconvinced when I decline their offer of food, she is upset because I am not eating anything. "But I am not hungry. I just ate, Tatjana." Finally, I have to eat a piece of candy and take an apple. In the meantime, two men

FIGURE 5.1. Tatjana Mikhailova and Jelena Tulženko at Chudamäe. Photo: Francisco Martínez, 2023.

have arrived at the site, surprised by what they're seeing, and exclaim, "Where have we ended up?"

This fairytale corner of the world, this hideout for a whimsical Robin Hood, is not on any map or in any tourist guidebook. Nevertheless, for some visitors, especially those from out of town, the glade has become part of the excursion route. It is indeed experienced as a very real spot, the opposite of a non-place. Still, not everyone seems to love the glade; several times it has been vandalized by someone mutilating toys, breaking a table, tearing down the well, scattering bird feeders. Igor Malyshev, the head of the Sillamäe Open Youth Center, comments that the elderly people who maintain it should receive some help from the local municipality. A few years ago, for instance, his center installed benches along the sidewalk, but they were gone after a few months, apparently looted for the local summer cottages.

"Those who only sit on the benches criticize us. I tell them not to come if they dislike it that much, that we do it with love and soul, and that the world needs more actions with goodwill," says Tatjana with a beatific smile. As the years have passed, the glade has gained some distinct recognition. In 2021, the president of Estonia, Kersti Kaljulaid, dropped by Chudamäe to meet the creators. For journalist Irina Kiviselg, Chudamäe is like a public dacha, available for all to rest.[39] Tatjana and Jelena have created this place with vernacular tools and amateur skills (in the same fashion as Jelena Mutonen's mosaics in chapters 1 and 2). Their labor is devoted to putting things together rather than breaking things up. They work with abandoned objects and ways of doing things not traditionally identified as political or belonging to discourses of resistance, yet becoming so because of their practical and symbolic impact. The recovery of used materials also means recovering oneself, establishing a sense of socio-material continuity and a stronger connection between people and the territory.

This chapter has discussed the heuristic importance of haunting traces, not only for understanding what communism has done to us (as the usual accounts claim), but also for seeing what we have done to the Soviet legacies and, eventually, what such leftovers and the remains of the transition period continue to do to us in the present. In eastern Estonia, an investigation of traces from the transition period enables us to better understand the experience of negative capability and hyper-precarity that also occurred during the process. This *sui generis* object of study shows how post-Soviet changes happened through a general experience of unmaking instead of a cumulative linear evolution, at least in some locations. The observation of the residual and the unbecoming shows that the spread of vacancy is intertwined with empty future horizons and the externalities of extractive activities. Yet the lived things found in vacant apartments do not simply evidence loss and disinvestment; they remain as objects of misfortune and dis-inheritage.

In the vacated apartments, the pressure of post-socialist iconoclasm and the work of *euroremont* were paused until further notice, giving access to untimely domestic domains that are socially dead. These leftovers also reveal that in some places, post-Soviet changes occurred not as a continuum but rather as a simultaneous experience of loss, disinvestment, and remaking.[40] The temporalities at work here are thus neither developmental nor progressive ones. Apart from the multiplicity of devaluations that occurred during the post-socialist experience, ethnographers now face the problem of investigating things while they are actually vanishing. Consequently, we can question whether what is actually vanishing is the possibility of learning from history, since past things allow future generations to gain insight into the societies that produced them.

This chapter has also reconsidered the reparability of things as a form of public kindness and as a constantly updated relationship with the past. The DIY practices of Jelena and Tatjana exemplify how life is maintained in exhausting conditions, showing that we can still rework the point of brokenness as a form of redesigning the social. In this context, improvisation becomes a key survival skill under conditions of uncertainty and with lingering remains. The forms of redoing that may sprout up despite the condition of precarity invite social researchers to pay attention to new configurations of endurance that might alleviate an overwhelming problem despite not reaching a state of full repair, bringing to light the ambiguity and multiple meanings of repairing.

6

LEFT-BEHIND PLACES

This chapter describes the possible forms that endings might take and the creation of remoteness once infrastructure cease to be. Only a few dozen people live in Viivikonna nowadays, but we are still confronted with the enduring effects of extractive activities. Grass has grown back on the trodden dirt tracks of the mine whose activity stopped long ago. Once, this was a "central" mining town in Estonia, hosting over two thousand workers who were building communism. Today, it is a remote village, off the map, out of the history books but still in time.[1] I can still hear the metallic sound of a train just beyond a hill—so close and simultaneously so far, as it no longer stops here. The train connects an always new point of extraction with an existing infrastructure for processing natural resources and distributing energy and goods, leaving behind a sacrificed, barely habitable landscape and a sense of extermination.

There were places that vanished under Soviet infrastructure after World War II, which themselves created other kinds of places, now deserted in turn. Eventually, the rise and fall of Viivikonna was not just a glitch in the Soviet system but part of a colonial project to turn Estonia into the economic and infrastructural hinterland of Leningrad. As this chapter shows, the effects of relocating people to work at these sites and the development of an extractive infrastructure might last for decades, suspending the conditions for reproduction of life. A series of industrial rubbish dumps, territorial scars, and monumental buildings are left behind, spectacularly reclaimed by nature—the very same nature that we were supposed to dominate and necessarily sacrifice.[2]

Not to Be Found

In the twenty-first century, Soviet modernization is our antiquity. Yet abandoned infrastructure, polluted soil, and ruins are still available for study. Alas, to find the fossils of this particular form of the Anthropocene, we have to go to sites where human interest was evacuated, remote locations waiting to be found anew. People filled sites like Viivikonna with meaning by modifying and emptying them, turning such places into areas of industrial activity. When a site becomes a mining area, it is then emptied, capitalized, and surveilled. And when an industrial area becomes ecologically exhausted, human presence vanishes along with the capital. These places then lose meaning, connections, and purpose, and they host new smells and activities instead. In the narratives of modernization and extractive imperialism, natural resources are presented as separate from society; they become united again, however, when mines stop being profitable. Thus, as we will see in this chapter, acts of dwelling in such contexts of sacrifice and decomposition appear transgressive.

Processes of intensive industrialization, migration, and development of infrastructure were arranged according to where natural resources were found. Mining activities are always decided in a political center; likewise, the correlated infrastructure is also designed in the engineering center, and it is then built in the periphery *as a gift*. Remoteness therefore stands as a condition of imposed receptivity, as locations like Viivikonna could not refuse what the center chose to give despite the dispossessing consequences.[3] The unsolicited gift came along with schools, hospitals, cheaper commodities, and a new political era. The gift of modernization, however, is hardly based on mutual agreement; on the contrary, in practical terms it means a loss of sovereignty.[4]

In Viivikonna, the first settlements were established as early as 1935, next to a new oil shale mine. The extraction started in the interwar Estonian Republic (1920–1939), but under the Soviet authorities, the settlement became a town with nearly 2,200 inhabitants. Its rapid growth was linked to the production of 200,000 tons of oil shale annually for use all across the Soviet Union. The town was populated by young people, and planning it was the task of the Lengiproshakht office in Leningrad. They used ordinary, straightforward grids and orthogonal geometry, following the government order of the USSR's Ministry of Coal Industry for the Western Regions, passed on August 28, 1946. The construction had to be accelerated and completed within months in order to fulfill the five-year plan of the state. Architecture historian Siim Sultson notes, nonetheless, that the Estonian Soviet Socialist Republic's Gosplan (planning agency) proposed another, drier location for the town, since the peat land was unsanitary.[5] Construction work, however, was already underway and progressing rapidly. In a secret document

FIGURE 6.1. Australian-Estonian joint mining venture in Viivikonna around 1938. Estonian National Archive.

FIGURE 6.2. A freight train in Viivikonna, 1956. Photo: Semjon Školnikov. Estonian National Archive.

FIGURE 6.3. Freight cars being loaded with oil shale at a Viivikonna quarry in 1958. Photo: G. Paas. Estonian National Archive.

FIGURE 6.4. Workers in the oil shale quarry of Viivikonna around 1955. Photo: Gunnar Loss. Estonian National Archive.

issued in 1951, the Department of Architecture of the Estonian SSR proposed increasing the number of stories of the projected buildings in order to reserve the surrounding territory for oil shale mining. All in all, only half of the master plan was implemented in Viivikonna. Similarly, in Ahtme, only one-third was realized, and in Sompa and Kiviõli, merely one-fourth of the master plan, while the construction of a new Kohtla was canceled altogether.

Still, the infrastructure of the town (streets, water supply, sewage, electricity) was periodically maintained and renovated until the mid-1970s, when the downfall of Viivikonna began. Then, the mine dried up and people started to move away. At the same time, oil shale became less relevant in the Soviet Union, since energy from nuclear plants, oil, and gas was becoming more affordable and efficient. Thus, as mining activity was the sole rationale for this (expendable) town to exist, the settlement vanished from the map for the very same reason once the oil shale dried up and its importance to the Soviet economy decreased. After all, the dark specter of exhaustion always hovers over a mine.

Certain substances—such as oil shale—become productive through complex arrangements of extractive infrastructures, calculative devices, political discourses, archives, and labor.[6] In simple terms, oil shale is the result of the transformation of organic matter from living beings, both animals and plants, into a productive "resource."[7] Both resources and infrastructure are socially produced themselves: they refer not to a single, concrete thing but rather to a particular kind of relationship between different material and non-material elements.[8] Yet building an infrastructure can also be considered a modality of conquest and dispossession, one that often hides a political project.[9] Infrastructures are correlated with particular configurations of power and transform territory into an object for administration; in doing so, they become fundamental to rendering people governable in rather colonial ways.[10] Thus, infrastructures are important sites of culture and power. Indeed, how we see and represent infrastructure conditions our understanding of territory, the natural world, and the people living thereabouts.[11]

Originally, the term "infrastructure" was used in military parlance to designate fixed facilities. Now, however, it refers to complex processes of system building, network extension, energy transportation, and socio-technical standardization. Overall, the planning and building of an infrastructure involve not only money and knowledge but also a normative rationality, deploying assumptions of command and control while exemplifying the power of numbers to produce social order and enact modern statecraft. The normative significance of infrastructure, however, is always due to its capacity to link political, material, and economic processes, including institutions on various levels.[12] For instance, the construction of roads, mines, pipelines, and power stations was part of the effort of building communism; yet, years later, some of these infrastructures were no longer needed, and the Soviet political regime fell apart, thereby signifying failure. The idea of the state's timelessness was thus contradicted by the ruination of its infrastructure, and the dark side of modernity then became perceptible through rot and rubble.[13]

In accordance with modern ideals of the domination of nature, Soviet engineers approached infrastructures as collective undertakings capable of circumventing geological conditions.[14] Now, however, many of the spaces of Soviet modernity are meaningless or forgotten, in decline, facing multiple endings and very few new beginnings, if any. Back then, mining sites appeared "out of nothing," and then collapsed back into nothingness once the industry was gone. Nevertheless, anthropologist Anna Varfolomeeva notes that two kinds of nothingness were portrayed by her informants—one by negation, or a blank page, and the other by extinction, or a void.[15] This distinction was also reflected within social perceptions of time: while the past was viewed by her informants as the period when young people were developing the industry together from scratch in a line of progress, the final deindustrialization of the area was in turn taken as a sign of stagnation, aging, and failure. If nothingness in potential preceded Soviet industrialization, a void is what remained after deindustrialization—a nothing defined by what it was not and a shadow of what used to give meaning to their lives, to the settlement, and to the entire Soviet Union at large.

Heritage in Reverse

The optimism of modernity and of socialist visions of progress has long vanished in Viivikonna, leaving behind in-between materialities, belonging neither to the realm of the urban nor to that of the rural. Those are also consequences of the extractivist approach to our planet, a form of colonialism that pretends to have no responsibility for the future condition of sacrificed areas. Here, the passage of time makes itself visible in the magnificent Stalinist architecture standing in ruins and the bushes growing in former roads and façades.[16] The buildings were designed as solid representations of power and domination; seventy years later, they remain as a mélange of strange fossils and non-human actors—an ironic aftermath. Solid, monumental housing of the Stalinist style was, after all, built for an intrinsically temporary and unsustainable use of the land. Another irony is that the etymology behind the name of the village also indicates impermanence: in Estonian, *viiv* means "for a short while," and *konna* is a term for a settlement. Nevertheless, *something* is lasting here, yet beyond human interference and intention, *something* inviting us to a deeper reckoning with socio-material instability and historical discontinuity.

Eventually, what is not taken care of tends to vanish, but something else then reappears in its place in a different form. Sites such as Viivikonna are marked by a long absence of human activity, leaving them abandoned, dormant, and expected to disappear.[17] In the brief instant during which the mining place was being developed, human action colonized both territory and resources; yet that was only a momentary mirage. Nowadays non-human agents make visible the actual disordering of a previously regulated space. Thus, dichotomies such as finished or unfinished, grand beginning and modest finale, do not fully apply here. In Viivikonna, its ending is an entropic one, ongoing and multifarious, thus not simply the aftermath of modern order.

When people started to leave and the elements left behind began to deteriorate, the site was reclaimed by vegetation and animal life—in the form of an ecology of agencies and mutations to be found in feral trails, plant seeds, mouse droppings, fungi, rusting pipes, leaks and drips, weeds growing from a concrete pillar, and newfound shelters for different species. In some cases, we can also observe animal architectures such as those of bees, wasps, ants, spiders, moles, and termites, excavating and engineering their own infrastructure.[18] Those ongoing agencies are removed from unity; paradoxically, the myriad of life-worlds that are present in polluted landscapes and seemingly vacated settings in decline are made possible by the absence of humans, manifesting the fragility of what seemed indestructible.[19]

After having moved forward during the Soviet era, these processes are perceived by some residents as de-modernization. Nevertheless, infrastructural integration in one period may imply a future disintegration in another future, due to the exhaustion of resources and environmental pollution. Indeed, as the quarry and mining industry moved farther away to find new territories for exploitation, the town of Sirgala was created four kilometers from Viivikonna, yet this time with *khrushchevkas*—the cheap concrete-panel apartment buildings that were common across the USSR in the 1960s—instead of monumental Stalinist architecture.

Originally, the decay of Viivikonna had more to do with the exhaustion of resources than with the collapse of the Soviet Union. Then, the abrupt change of political regime exacerbated the decline, for there was no place in a market economy for towns that had lost their extractivist purpose. In Estonia, these postindustrial sites are taken as remnants of a now discredited political order, and therefore somewhat different from capitalist deindustrialization processes. In this vein, we can distinguish between two kinds of infrastructural harm: (1) the super-destruction of life and matter entailed by modern extractive industries; and (2) the posterior abandonment of leaking remains once the mining ceased to be profitable. They are both associated with the delusional belief in a consequence-free abuse of "natural resources," and they both have repercussions that go beyond the infrastructural and the economic.

Over the past few decades, the population of Viivikonna decreased from 2,200 to barely twenty-five inhabitants. As a number, twenty-five does not say much. As a community of residents, each of them is deemed very important to keeping the settlement inhabited. Various hints indicate that a termination of continuance between the past and the present has been taking place, but other things continue to happen here in the meantime.[20] While walking around, I find different signs of human life: a dog wandering restlessly, the imprints of human steps in the snow, the floating sounds of a radio (with Tina Turner playing through the windows like an ancestral echo).

Encountering the destruction of a human-built environment is shocking at first, and the perception of how wilderness runs unchecked at the very same site is unsettling. While facing these radically deurbanized contexts, I am reminded of Aghdam, a town in Azerbaijan of nearly fifty thousand inhabitants, totally destroyed in the first war of Nagorno-Karabakh.[21] I believe one could feel the same around Pripyat in Ukraine; that area was evacuated in April 1986 because of the high radiation levels. Then, non-human agents took over the area, and the ruined infrastructure now stands as evidence of modern devolution. Practitioners of dark tourism are attracted to this kind of heritage in reverse, characterized by negative forms and an impossible separation of nature and culture that gives rise to a mood of estrangement and unease in the visitor. This is heritage in reverse, excluded from the representations of national history because of its connection to conflict, death, and suffering.[22]

Viivikonna has become popular among bohemians wanting to contemplate the broken dreams of modernity and the spectacle of decay. For decades, the only visitors were thieves coming to remove valuable construction materials such as metal from the existing houses. In more recent years, however, we have seen an increasing number of voyeurs following dark tourism postulates.[23] Perhaps it is the melancholia of decay, of the no more, that draws us to these spaces. What I am doing in Viivikonna, though, is not urban exploration anymore; neither is it rural *flânerie*. Here I am still encountering modern traces yet outside urban areas, in a blind spot that is no longer recognized as contaminated, or as anything, because it does not appear on the map.

This exploration in a left-behind place resonates with the journey into "the Zone" represented in the film *Stalker* (1979). The fraught area depicted by Andrei Tarkovsky is a capricious place with its own laws. The characters who arrive here on a phantasmagoric pilgrimage stumble up against extraterrestrial matter and encounter danger and deception, seemingly produced by the place itself. By scavenging the zone, humans put themselves at risk, not in search of some treasure but to find themselves. In other words, it is the contemplative power of the place that inspires the foray, inviting retrospection.[24] Under the dark sun, it is hard to figure out what is imagined and what is perceived, and the liminal experience appears as quasi-magical. No wonder the Zone has acquired a mythological significance for wayfarers of dangerous leisure, the late modern pilgrims.[25]

Both death and birth are associated with liminal landscapes, as well as an intense contact with the surroundings. Tarkovsky's postapocalyptic film is based on Arkady and Boris Strugatsky's *Roadside Picnic*, a novel set in the aftermath of an extraterrestrial event called "the Visitation," in which strange phenomena beyond human comprehension take place.[26] Another relevant book, also turned into a series of films, is *Dune*. This sci-fi novel was published by Frank Herbert in 1965.[27] The story takes place in a faraway galaxy, where we follow Paul Atreides and his family. They govern the desert planet of Arrakis, which contains a highly valuable resource called "spice." Besides enabling space travel, this narcotic brew can extend life for those who ingest it. Hence, the management of this resource appears in the middle not just of politics but also of technology, religion, and ecology. The book might be read as heralding a future in which extractive activities and technocracy define warfare and social relations. But the story can also be taken as a critique of the environmental destruction brought about by colonialism and the infrastructural violence of empires.

Off the Map

In Viivikonna, history has no record of a recent war, plague, or nuclear explosion. The urbanity of the settlement simply vanished as quickly as it came. Remoteness here refers to an existential sense of displacement, and yet, with repeated visits, this town becomes less exotic and frightening. I could even imagine myself living here. Remoteness might have some advantages, after all. For instance, during the COVID-19 pandemic, local people did not need to wear a mask, as there was little contact with the outside world and its affairs. Perhaps I could also contemplate my own vegetables growing in a little garden while listening to the distant sound of the passing train or the firing exercises of NATO armies at the nearby training grounds.[28]

Most often, remoteness is characterized by notions of spatial distance and isolation; the remote, however, can also be inhabited as a space of autonomy, allowing for personal redefinition, evasion, and new kinds of relationality.[29] In some cases, remoteness can thus be experienced as a resource to be used within a wider constellation of power, belonging, and ecological being (something close to the right of opacity). Nevertheless, it is commonly referred to as negative, sensed affectively in the absent presence of something constitutive. In a critique of the idea of remoteness, anthropologist Martin Saxer notes how this trope glosses over long-standing entanglements and situated forms of connectivity, because remoteness is made through historical knots and infrastructural junctures.[30]

Nowadays we encounter settlements such as Viivikonna as residual and excessive, with stubborn, erstwhile roads, and trees growing inside former houses. They are filled with solitude and non-human agencies. These out-of-the-way locations might also evoke nostalgia and fascination after being left behind in the modern race for progress and domination. Some roads are almost gone, and vegetation has taken over the pavement. "These days, nobody uses this road much," states a resident who refuses to give his name. In Viivikonna, cars appear as signs of civilization and habitation. When there are no cars around a building, it means that no one lives there now. The fact that there are no footprints around it means that no one has walked there today, or this week. I go up and down the main street, Rahu (Peace), and come across an orange mailbox on the façade of the former post office. The saying that communism was Soviet power plus electrification comes to mind.

Yet after spending more time here, I can see more infrastructure working, even if somewhat precariously. Water still runs, the electricity works, and heating systems make homes warm, though not in all buildings. Nonetheless, the village is poorly connected with public transport. Only the number 33 bus runs between Sillamäe and Viivikonna four times a day. As there is no grocery store, some of the residents who don't own cars (most of them elderly) take the bus to Sillamäe, eleven kilometers away, and come back by taxi, at a cost of seven euros.[31] Then I see graffiti at the bus stop that reads, *Begi otsyuda*, "Run away from here."

The former school, now in ruins, stands as a symbolically charged building, like a Noah's Ark gone wrong. When a school stops working as planned and the materiality of the building is defeated, disintegration appears as a form of renewal, yet one apart from humans and without the promise of a future. On my first visit, I saw a bunch of kids hanging around the bus stop. They go to the school in Sinimäe (nine kilometers away), because basic services like this have been closed in Viivikonna.[32] Ambulances come here from Sillamäe, but only in case of an emergency.

As we read in chapter 4, people from Kohtla-Järve (another mining town in the region) refer to Viivikonna with sorrow and apprehension as an example of the dis-urbanization that could happen to them if they do not take preventive measures. There are also those who say that this place is cursed. During World War II, there were several concentration camps in the area, built by both the Nazi army (with Jews forced to work in the mines) and the Soviet army (with German POWs made to rebuild the settlements and work in the mines too).

I keep walking and encountering mundane signs of life, such as small gardens with vegetable patches, a greenhouse, a snowman in the yard, homemade heating systems behind semi-inhabited houses, and so on. They are all traces of affirmative actions, of world-making gestures. Not long ago, journalist Liina Hallik published an interview with a family who had decided to move to Viivikonna while everybody else was leaving. She begins her article with these words: "I arrived in Viivikonna with certain prejudices. A ghost town. A former mining town. Extinct. Broken. Terrifying. Empty streets loom before my eyes, and crows are ominously cawing. It is as if dark-blue clouds are floating in the sky to confirm the foreknowledge. Driving into the infamous ghost town, we are greeted by cheerful wooden figurines and a romantic well with a cake in the middle of a carefully mowed lawn."[33]

She then tells the story of Valentina and Nikolai, who had moved to Viivikonna twenty-four years earlier. "When normal people started moving out of the town, we came here. We left the apartment in Sillamäe to my daughter. She got married and had children," says Valentina. Years later, their daughter also moved to Viivikonna, buying the house next door to her parents. Real estate is cheap and plentiful in the village. In some cases, not going anywhere might turn into an act of endurance and a form of temporal agency.[34] Most of the inhabitants stay, however, because they don't have anywhere better to go, as Dasha—a local resident—explains: "Originally, we didn't have money to buy an apartment somewhere else, so we stayed. Then, you get used to the idea, and carry on living."

Phenomena such as the decline of infrastructure, population decrease, and the vanishing of basic services have been related to localized notions of emptiness and remoteness.[35] Here, not only does real estate have little value, but also moving to this dead end is seen by some as a punishment or forced retreat. For instance, Jelena, from Sillamäe, says that Viivikonna is for those who barely work, for pensioners and drunkards. "When someone is not able to pay for rent and utilities here, then they are sent to Viivikonna." *And how do they make a living there?* "I don't know; still, they find money to buy alcohol." Alas, Valentina remarks, "the situation in Sirgala is more desperate. The apartments there are in worse condition, some without electricity, heating, and water. And still, every year, there is someone who moves back to Viivikonna. You won't see that happening in Sirgala."

How to Represent Decline

Off-the-map towns such as Viivikonna might appear remote to us, but they stand at the core of the Soviet project—not the consequence of its failure but one of its achievements. In this town, drained ecologies were produced after prolonged and systematic harm; yet something other than decline may well be manifesting itself in the aftermath of Soviet modernity. The challenge facing the ethnographer is how to make such liminal and phantasmagoric reality analytically accessible to the senses. These kinds of radically abandoned sites elude straightforward representations, displaying a combination of appropriations and significations, which might range from playgrounds for the young to refuges for human marginals and non-human agents. Nevertheless, it is not enough to document how energy infrastructure can be retrofitted; we also need to account for the fact that their construction had its own decline inscribed in it and eventually entailed the disposal of a place. Indeed, when does an infrastructure cease to be so?

Different touristic interventions have been designed to give new uses to postindustrial remnants in the region. For instance, in 2013 a family adventure resort was opened in Kiviõli, using the artificial landscape of a former oil shale quarry for a ski slope, snowboarding park, and snow-tubing run. In addition, Aidu Water World opened for boating, so one can navigate the canals produced by mining activity by canoe, raft, dragon boat, kayak, or motorboat. Then, in Mäetaguse, the municipality allocated financial compensation provided by the state for the pollution caused in the locality to renovate the ruins of a former manor house into a spa hotel. In any case, accounts of decline and remoteness must include attention to local reckonings. Most often, descriptions of places in decline present their sacrifice as necessary for a bigger goal, while in other cases, these narratives focus on how a new use springs up when the old one comes to an end.

Etymologically, "decline" comes from the Latin *declinare*, and refers to the gradual loss of an ability, a weakening, a bending downwards, to degenerating and sinking into an inferior condition, or at least to a reduction of activity. In Ida-Virumaa, decline is expressed in the encounter with remains of abandoned infrastructure, emptiness, and loss, all illustrating setbacks, ambivalences, and absences that are hard to verbalize. In collaboration with the Estonian Mining Museum, I curated the exhibition "Life in Decline" (June 17–October 3, 2021) at the former Kohtla mining site. For this project, I invited ten Estonian artists to represent decline in its multiple facets while paying attention to the side effects of modern extractive industries in the eastern part of the country. "Life in Decline" was designed to make perceptible the multiplicity of devaluations that followed the collapse of the USSR. Nevertheless, the exhibition took place not in the main areas of the Estonian Mining Museum (which was being renovated at the time with support from the EU) but in the former administrative building and boiler rooms.

Decline was approached as a specific socio-ecological condition, one that can also be ordinary and normal, revealing complex continuations. An example of this phenomenon was *Sore*, by Sandra Kosorotova. For her installation, Sandra transplanted some weeds she found among the mining debris into the museum premises, using trash cans to grow them. She also dyed a textile with local plants, which was then displayed in the laundry room of the mine. Sandra started her research by asking, "What plants actually grow in exhausted ecologies?" Then she developed a genealogy of what a weed is, overcoming modern ideas of how nature and culture should interact.

Paradoxically, a type of flower that we find relatively often on tailings hills, quarry areas, and ash plateaus is one of the prettiest—orchids. These precious plants grow in arid soils because of their great affinity for calcium compounds.[36] Another plant growing in the area is the weed *Bunis orientalis*. It was brought to Europe during the Crimean War (1853–1856) by Russian soldiers, who added it to their horses' feed. Since it was first noticed in Rakvere, the weed was given the folk name "carrion from Rakvere" (*Rakvere raibe*). According to a decree issued in 1939, the plant should be destroyed if encountered, as it is considered invasive. Nevertheless, these weeds thrive where no other plants can survive and can act as a natural dressing for wounds on the land.

As noted by Sandra, the weeds present at the site heal and feed the soil, for instance, by shielding it from sunlight, their roots giving structure to the earth; by drawing up nutrients that allow other plants to grow on the surface; by trapping fallen leaves and other organic matter, which is then dragged underground by earthworms; and finally, by decomposing into humus once they die. Despite their binding contribution, however, weeds are often associated with a lack of care and control, the term thus referring to a plant that is not wanted in human-controlled settings. That is the reason why the word "weed" is applied pejoratively to species that are undesirable in a particular place but manage to survive even in harsh environments. In this sense, the term has also been applied to humans. Indeed, because of her Russian background, the artist has also felt like a "rootless weed," made to feel unwelcome as a descendant of "occupiers."

Another of the installations displayed in the exhibition was *Geofractions*, by John Grzinich. This project gives a sensory experience of the processes and infrastructure of oil shale extraction that are often hidden from the public. While we have grown familiar with the visual language of mined landscapes, rarely have we been able to immerse ourselves in extractive processes through the auditory. During our time in Kohtla-Nõmme, John spoke of unexpected surfacing reactions and "the iceberg effect of land processing," by which he meant that we can see only a small part of the whole industrial intervention.

The one-hundred-minute-long piece represented one minute for every year since the mining industry was founded here. The installation was based on a scale model made in the shape of this region. The symbolic wooden surface rested on a base of sonic shakers, which produced vibrations from underneath and made the earth on the top jump. As part of the public program of the exhibition, John also gave a performance envisioning a possible reduction of 99 percent of the industrial activity in the region. It was a rather dystopian experience, not only because of the content but also because of the "contribution" to the event of a flock of birds, which lived under the roof. They started to sing with such gusto that it was not possible to distinguish clearly between what John had recorded and what the birds performed, in a sort of jam session. Days later, one of the birds was found dead in front of his installation, as if in culmination of the dystopian tale.

Another example from this exhibition is *The Work of Time* by Anne Rudanovski. In the archive of the Kohtla mine and in a telecommunications room, Anne prepared an installation using the measurement technologies of Soviet engineers. These obsolete devices were wrapped in pages torn out of old industrial manuals in Estonian and Russian. Still, a sharp eye could read the instructions, study the drawings, and follow the mining calculations on the wrinkled surfaces. "All this archival material has a strong meaning precisely because of not having meaning anymore," Anne commented while installing her work. By wrapping old mining tools in paper, she wanted to make them ready to be sent elsewhere, as in a rite of initiation. Some packages were incomprehensibly festive; others evoked a sense of holiness, or just seemed to be abandoned. But who was actually the dispatcher of all this? And why does the obsolete create such unrest in us? When asked what inspired her installation, Anne surprisingly mentioned reading Carl Jung, and specifically his reflections on how the old might block the way for the new.

In the very last room of the archives, under the window and on a sun-drenched table, one could find a rather large industrial artifact wrapped in paper and tied with cords. It had a tubular tail wound into a ring, the end of which was bound to the unknown, resembling a snake curled in a ring. Tools, skills, and ideology were assembled in these books. Forty years ago, it would not have been possible to transform them into art as Anne did, but nowadays, one can do almost anything with documents of this kind, which are paper, mere material awaiting intervention or discarding. The archive itself has been deserted. For instance, nobody seems to care about the statistics showing how things went on in the mine back in the late 1980s. Yet, if paying attention, we can note that the archive shows a complex cohabitation of books in Estonian (locally produced) and Russian (sent from various cities of the USSR). For me, the keys to the archive gave access to a sort of secret knowledge and a specific know-how, materializing disappearing skills and ideas, which we might miss or regret later. On one occasion,

FIGURE 6.5.   *Viivikonna Passages* by Jevgeni Zolotko.

while I was revising documents in the archive with Etti Kagarov, the director of
the museum, we found old statistics on what was happening in the mine in the
period of late socialism. She then commented, "In the eighties, it was rather clear
that everything was going to collapse."

Another iteration of this idea is found in *Viivikonna Passages*. This installation by Jevgeni Zolotko was nicely embedded within the things left behind in the
director's office, in the medical clinic, and in the miners' apartments. Black-and-
white photographs displayed in funerary showcases and oral memories of the
few remaining residents were heard as an echo. Visitors described it as "a ghostly
experience" reflecting "an anxious state of affairs."

"Life in Decline" also examined the disintegrative consequences of decline
as it leads to a dismantling of other aspects of society (not simply economic and
demographic, but also including the imaginary). As decline is rarely the last word,
this phenomenon generates specific socio-ecological configurations in the present and unfolds in the effect it has on those who stay. My research in the district
started with fieldwork on the demolition of half-empty apartment houses and
the subsequent relocation of residents following the pilot project promoted by
the Estonian Ministry of Finance (see chapter 4). That research has been documented by artist Laura Kuusk. For ten months, Laura had been visiting the region
with me to explore the empty apartment buildings and meet municipal officials.
All of this knowledge was indeed valuable for producing her contribution to the
exhibition: *Vacant*. In Laura's photo series, local apartments for sale were presented by a choreographic real estate agent. This gesture produced an effect of
estrangement, causing the familiar to be perceived as unfamiliar.

For decades, eastern Estonia has been presented as hard to understand,
referred to as "excessive" or "unsolvable." In the national media, it is most often

FIGURE 6.6.   *Rescue Plan* by Varvara & Mar.

represented in relation to pollution and in need of being taken care of. In the exhibition, we also tried to represent the consequences of this issue. For instance, the art installation *Rescue Plan*, by Varvara & Mar, reflected on the sense of regional disposability and the limits of top-down rescue plans, which have been considered by the local population not just as unhelpful but even as a burden. As the artists tried to show, solutions to local problems are most often prescribed by alien experts. The installation consisted of two elements: a lifebuoy meant to float yet appearing as half-sunk in a pond (created after decades of mining activity) and a red chair similar to those used by lifeguards in their observation posts (here representing both authority and responsibility). On the chair, and as if it were graffiti, the artists had written comments about the region found in the media and on social networks, such as "Money to me, waste to you," "Oil shale fairy tale," "Kohtla-Järve stinks," "This is the Estonian Donbas," "Become an entrepreneur," and so on.

The site-specific installation allowed visitors to visualize the government's failure to deploy working rescue strategies, but also the negative representations associated with the region, where the local population was affected by recurrent accusations and disappointed hopes. These issues can indeed be upsetting to some, to the point where the work was vandalized twice: First, the lifeguard chair was broken and the pieces were thrown into the pond; then a month later, the lifebuoy was stolen. In the meantime, I had to come twice from Tallinn to make sure that the "interactive" installation was repaired. On one of these occasions, K., a colleague from the capital, mentioned, "That area is populated by Russians; they are quite aggressive."

Experiences of decline and remoteness dominate the horizons of Viivikonna. They provide both a specific structure of feeling and an embodied experience, echoing the fragility of the things we construct, the care that our vulnerable world needs, and the need to think about limits and ends. Nowadays, global flows only pass by this settlement—on a train carrying oil shale that does not stop here anymore. Nevertheless, a lot of things have been going on since the lights of extractivism were turned off, holding on to life in these ecologically and socially exhausted contexts. For instance, some residents have stayed, refusing the end simply by being there. Unexpected non-human actors and new ways of living have also been appearing in the meantime. Viivikonna lost its urbanity, but the de-modernization did not mean a return to "pre-modern" forms of living nor to a past ecological state. It is rather an improvised future that has to go through the ecological and social harm of both Soviet and capitalist modernity, thus still engaging with present endings. In this sense, Viivikonna is not simply the remnant of something that is gone but also the seeds of something that could become. And it is repair and reproduction that make that kind of passage possible, enabling as yet undetermined futures.

Socialist modernization was a chapter of a longer, global episode called modernity, itself showing beginnings and endings. Nevertheless, the downfall of this settlement was not a post mortem act of justice against the Soviet regime but a human retreat due to economic withdrawal and lack of social reproduction. Endings certainly generate anxiety, especially when things do not disappear properly. Rather than seeing ending as a rupture, this chapter discusses it as a durable, material process, sedimented in the infrastructures, objects, and practices that haunt everyday life. Indeed, there can be many instances and kinds of endings. And this concept does not do the explaining job itself, but it needs to be explained and empirically contextualized.

A key question, then, is: How can a sustainable order be created out of this postindustrial nothingness? Perhaps, I think, the death of urbanity and subsequent de-modernization processes can also be a preserver in some ways and not just a destroyer. At least human retreat makes room for improvised ways of thriving and new ecological reemergences. After all, modern decomposition and unmaking might be crucial to regeneration—or maybe not, and the exhaustion of resources only brings further stress and exhaustion, rendering lives less than livable.

A GARAGE WITH A VIEW

Any cultural representation of a borderland is a way of negotiating power and acting upon territory. For instance, we can see the frontier between Russia and the EU from the air—from the viewpoint of a drone—or through the eyes of Mikhail Bulgakov's Margarita.[1] We could also follow the wild geese during their migration, like Nils Holgerssons did in his wonderful adventures as described by Selma Lagerlöf.[2] But this chapter, sadly, is not based on any of these experiences from a height. Instead, it happens on the water, on a boat ride around the Kulgu reservoir. Ethnographically, I explore the liminal kind of relations found in this amphibious geography by describing a series of gatherings in the so-called Narva Venice and the nearby allotment gardens. As the research shows, not only are things repaired in the garages of Narva but people's position in the world, too. And not only are vegetables growing in the nearby dachas but also a non-regulated form of relationship between people and with the territory there.

Since the first garages and allotment gardens appeared there in the 1960s, the Kulgu area of Narva has been a space for tinkering, escapism, and an inverted form of normality. It is in this sense that I refer to Kulgu as an extopia, a liminal zone where one is thrown out of the ordinary. In Soviet culture, both garages and dachas were places for disconnection, for individual enterprise, and for testing other forms of being in the world. Their proliferation was related to ways of dealing with the system's shortcomings and abuses without an open confrontation. Still, they are spaces of ambiguity, endurance, and open possibilities, where the alienation and dispossession of time in urban populations is compensated if not healed. The availability of garages and dachas also makes possible some free-time

FIGURE 7.1.   Aerial view of the Kulgu area. Photo: Maa Amet, 2024.

activities, relating oneself to nature and to institutions. These gray interstices, however, are located not outside the state and family but at their margins, built as a calculated removal from institutions. They thus have social repercussions, establishing alternative forms of relation and complex intensities of invisibility.

Historical Context

As it was a front line in 1944, Narva was virtually destroyed in the fighting. After the war, the city was reconstructed according to Soviet principles and repopulated with workers from all corners of the USSR. The urban planning was developed alongside the expansion of energy infrastructures and heavy industries, while strict control over the form and meaning of the built environment was deployed. In the late 1950s, garages and allotment gardens began to be distributed to factory workers to address chronic food shortages and to provide a space for organized free time for men and women. In this sense, these spaces were taken as a gift publicly bestowed by the Soviet state, yet one that had to be physically worked out.[3] Urban garages indeed became a key element within Soviet culture—a place for repairing, storing, and socializing, where the individual was in control and could create a sphere of activity that was felt as independent of the state.[4] Thus, spaces of escapism such as garages and dachas enabled multiple compensations and explorations in a rigidly planned society; hence, the use of these shadow areas was not just about austerity but about a surplus of living as well, a way to have a break from your public self, to get out of yourself for a while.

After Estonia regained its independence, the reality of Narva was one of de-industrialization, unemployment, a transnational border, and also one of ethnicity, with the Narvitians becoming an "other" in the new country. On the Estonian border with Russia, Narva is characterized by an abundance of connections and historical signification. From its Danish foundation and its membership in the Hanseatic League, the city appears as a center out there. Narva has gone through radical ruptures, with identity crises and rebuilding being constitutive of its life history. For decades Narvitians have been recalibrating what their position in and relation to Estonia might be. Currently, it is the third-largest city in Estonia, with a population of 53,000 inhabitants as of 2024 (in 1989 the population was 83,000.) After the breakup of the Soviet Union, the city was consigned to the national fringes, being severely affected by neglect, disinvestment, and the reemergence of a geopolitical frontier. Indeed, we could argue that the city of Narva is the functional border of Germany.

Before coordinating the EU's Just Transition Mechanism in Estonia (see chapter 2), Ivan Sergejev was the chief architect of Narva between 2016 and 2020. As he put it, part of his work was to deal with the fear of changes among local people after negative alterations such as the closure of the Kreenholm textile factory (where thousands of families worked) and the imposition of a heavy geopolitical border. This fear of changes while desperately needing them is manifested in a negative emotional state, mistrust, and stress, he noted. Sergejev explains that there have been problems in communication with the rest of the country, "mostly due to using different languages, but also different interpretations of history and all that." As a result, "in Narva, many people feel misunderstood."

A large part of the Kulgu area belongs to an oil shale–based power plant located nearby (Balti Elektrijaam), and many of the garages still exist in a status that is not always clearly legal. This power plant is one of the two biggest oil shale–fired power stations in the world; the other one is also located in Narva. Aleksandr Jefimov, board member of the Kulgu cooperative (a boat garage union), explains that these waterfront garages were built "to enable workers at the power plant to rest, fish, and spend their time freely."[5] Petro, who is one of those workers, insists on the need to legalize the actual state of affairs. He complains that users will not be motivated to invest in the place until the legal situation is resolved, nor can they pass on the garages to their kin as part of their inheritance.

In present-day Narva, there are two kinds of garage areas: one is continental, traditionally coexisting with cars and buildings, while the other is amphibious, consisting of canal-side structures.[6] The official inception of Narva Venice was on May 13, 1969, when the executive committee of the City Council of Workers' Deputies allocated a plot of land for boat garages (decision number 134). Back then, a "you can stay for now" form of occupation took hold, and in some cases, such occupation has lasted for more than sixty years. The actual number of users varies depending on the source. The cooperative counts 242 members, while those who spend time here say that there are over six hundred people actively making use of the garages. To buy an officially registered and legalized garage, one has to pay at least three thousand euros. A garage with a more uncertain status might be up for grabs for half the price.

Still, fishing remains integral to life in the area. Interestingly, locals talk of going "to the sea" (*na morye*) when referring to the reservoir. Many complain, however, that there are fewer fish every year, like Vassily, who has two garages—one for fishing supplies and another for hanging out; he spends the whole summer here to be closer to nature: "What is there to do in my apartment?" Or like Alexandr, who claims: "You can hardly fish here anymore. Nature is already half-broken. They don't give it time to recover."

Modern humans have profoundly altered the flux of rivers, directly intervening in changing water circuits and sedimentary transport through extensive dredging, dikes, and construction projects.[7] For more than 150 years, the Narva River has been pushed via infrastructure into diverse circuits that support human life and economic activity nearby. For instance, Narva's hydropower fed the Kreenholm textile industry, which operated between 1856 and 2010, employing more than ten thousand workers in the 1970s. The reservoir was created by Soviet engineers in the 1950s, inundating the village of Kulgu, where there used to be a brickmaking factory. "You can crash into the remains of the settlement, if you don't know where they are located," warns Dmitri, who has a sensor on his boat that tells him what's below, including the shoal size and the number of fish.

The Narva River was tamed by a 206-meter-long and nine-meter-high overflow dam featuring eleven locks. In addition to the system of dikes, channels, locks, pumps, and pipes, engineers constructed an earth dam on each side, with a total length of more than 1.5 kilometers. The strip of land hosting the garages is embedded within the border area and depends to a high degree on the wider hydraulic system; thus, it endures the near-constant danger of flooding and geopolitical tension.[8] The dam is partly located in Estonian territory (40 out of the basin's total 191 square kilometers), but it is managed by a Russian state-owned energy company. Indeed, there have been discussions in the Estonian media about the possibility of Russia unilaterally refusing to provide cooling water to the energy plants.

In a book about local heritage, Madis Tuuder and Karin Paulus note that because of the shallow depth (an average of 1.8 meters) and the water draining out of the power plants, the reservoir warms up excessively, causing an overgrowth of plants.[9] In 1971 a plan was designed to divert part of the water back to the old riverbed in order to reduce the negative environmental impact, but it was never implemented. After the collapse of the Soviet Union, with the control line running across the reservoir and two oppositional countries on either side, the means to mitigate or reduce the extent of the damage seem increasingly out of reach.

Water is an element that challenges territorial limits and the strict demarcation of borders. The actual standing of this frontier shows how infrastructural circumstances make the connection of borders to their territory more complex. This transnational frontier (between civilizational absolutes) is highly surveilled, as it prevents the infiltration of other humans into our territory. Nonetheless, the drawing of a line (evoking two sides) on voluminous elements like water and the cutting apart of hybrid entities such as a lake, a forest, or energy infrastructure might indeed create ambiguities and exceptions. For instance, birds and seeds constantly crisscross the Kulgu area.

Despite the proximity of the geopolitical border and its corresponding legal, military, and administrative constraints, trans-location processes continue along and across the reservoir. In some cases, the itineraries of animals and placements

FIGURE 7.2. Aerial view of the confluence of multiple rivers in Kulgu around 1930. Estonian National Archive.

FIGURE 7.3.   Kulgu Port in 1929. Photo: Karl Akel. Estonian National Archive.

of plants might shift by thousands of kilometers.[10] Another element crossing the border is waste, since the energy plants still use the reservoir for their cooling and cleaning circuits.[11] This can create complicated inter-state negotiations, as opposing nations grapple with how to effectively manage these border zones.

Garage Life

Dmitri complains about the artists. He has a fine terrace in front of his two garages, encircled by a small wooden fence, "so the artists are not there making it dirty. They start taking photos of you, sit in front of your garage, they might even enter to check what you're doing inside. And this is private territory: private in the sense of ownership, but also as a realm. It is for me and my friends. These artists don't come here to spend time, but to observe, to look at you." In turn, Dmitri comes to Kulgu "to spend time," or in Russian, *provodit' vremya*. This expression refers to the experience of being at ease in time and without finality. In Kulgu, a liminal temporal unfolding and bonding is correlated with spatial seclusion; indeed, the important thing is not where you come from or what your official job is but what you do when you are here. "It is almost like in a dacha: you're doing things in nature, and the water makes you feel calm," insists Dmitri.

For more than sixty years, this area of garages has been referred to as Kulgu, but increasing numbers of people are starting to call it the "Narva Venice." The rebranding is attributed by the garage users to the activity of "the artists," whether connected to NART (Narva Art Residency, founded in 2015 on the property of the former Kreenholm factory) or to the Station Narva music festival (running since 2018). Both cultural initiatives involve organized guided tours for non-local visitors, making visible the peculiar setting formed by the amphibious garages. Anthropologist Kevin Molloy took part in one of the cultural programs, yet in his case, he spent several weeks living at the site. Kevin felt well received and at ease in Kulgu, and he downplays the narratives of tension between users and visitors. "I was told there might be some language barriers and distrust, but after going to the sauna and drinking with locals, everything was very easy." C., in turn, noted the tension and suspicion of local residents toward the artists "because they felt watched like animals in the zoo, and also due to false promises of being consulted about the design of the cultural program."

Igor kindly shows me his two garages, one for hanging out and the other for his boat and repair tools. He works as a welder and has built a metal dock with a bench on it. During the winter season he has been coming to Kulgu "to prepare things for the spring." In one of the garages, piles of things, tools, and materials

FIGURE 7.4. Alexandr feeding the swans. Photo: Francisco Martínez, 2023.

with no evident usefulness accumulate. The other one reminds me of how philosopher Gaston Bachelard described a garage: a half-box resembling a nest.[12] A hoarding nest to be precise, since it is packed with various Orthodox icons on the wall, next to six industrial helmets, a microwave oven, a bed, water tanks, cleaning products, clothes, and broken furniture of different sizes.

Overall, Kulgu has a seasonal occupancy; the garage owners mostly come here during the summer. But there are also those who live in Kulgu all year, like Alexandr. Fifteen years ago he sold his apartment and moved into a garage, which is delightfully styled. We not only discover tools and materials, however, but also abundant ornaments, from plastic flowers to religious symbols and representations referring to domestic animals such as dogs and cats, bucolic landscapes, and cultural figures such as Vladimir Vysotsky and Putin. Ultimately, this is a space that helps tenants navigate the contradictions of modern social relations and national identity. "I decorate my garage just as you decorate your apartment," says Alexandr, who explains that he is "freer" here: "In the city, it is just different." His friend Kolja comes to visit "to warm up" his brain, Kolja says. "But you cannot warm up what is empty," Alexandr jokingly replies.

I walk along the canal and meet Vadym. His garage is kept in strict order: tools there, materials here. Then, in a second garage, he has a proper living space. Vadym is painting his boat parsimoniously. "I come here every weekend to rest," he says. Though what I see is that you are working, I note. "Working is what I do during the week; what I do here is for me, so I don't consider it work." As in the dacha gardens, working for oneself and not for the state was an important incentive for people during the Soviet period. Yet, whereas gardening has typically been considered a more feminine occupation, the garage remains firmly a male territory. There is one exception, though: a garden constructed on an artificial terrace in front of a garage (on a southwestern corner). Some informants referred to it as strange, not because it's on the water but because it is kept by an elderly woman who, once her husband died, decided to take over the garage and invite her friends along for gardening. They are indeed the only women who spend time here. "They don't mingle with us. They mostly come on workdays," Vladimir tells me. And Dmitri adds that "these babushkas are an exception. Like Estonian speakers. I don't know of any Estonian speakers around either."

"Here, women are not needed," remarks Vladimir with a wry smile on his face. Similarly, Dmitri jokingly says, "Women here mostly bother you." They are both garage residents and often hang out together. Vladimir and Dmitri are not exactly friends, but they care for each other as garage users. In English, the term "friend" refers to freedom, in German to joy (*Freude*), and in Spanish to love (*amigo*). In Russian, however, the word is *drug*, which relates to "the other" (*drugoi*) It is our kind of other, however, different from the other that is felt from afar, which is addressed differently (*inoi*).[13]

"A sofa, a TV, a fridge; all that is a must. Also a *mangal* [barbecue] or a microwave, to prepare food," says Dmitri. He has all that living equipment in one of the garages, while the tools and the boat are stored in the other. Vladimir, in turn, has managed to create a sort of garage-mansion, connecting three garages together so he can host friends and spaciously enjoy mundane liberties. "Sometimes we just watch TV together. Other times, like last night, we drink a bit of whisky, beer, and rum. You should have joined us yesterday," says Vladimir while pointing at Ivan, who states that he likes to come "because here no one controls me."

Dmitri has a ten-year-old son and enjoys doing things with him in Kulgu. He inherited one of these two garages from his father and would like to pass them on to his son. The use of garages thus can contribute to anchoring family relations and establish a sense of continuation. Dmitri agreed to give me a boat ride around Kulgu. For an hour and a half we passed through the canals, visiting other corners of the reservoir, looking at the forest, and contemplating the ash hill generated by oil shale processing. It forms a plateau covering eight hundred hectares, produced by 230 million tons of residual ash, from which electricity had been generated in the power plants. (About three miles from the Russian border, there is a new power plant worth over 600 million euros, which mixes oil shale with wood chips to produce electricity.)

On the way back, I asked Dmitri to pass closer to the border with Russia, demarcated on the water by a series of yellow buoys, which indicate the beginning of the buffer zone between the two countries. When we were a hundred meters away, our engine broke down, so Dmitri had to repair it on the water. The operation took a few minutes, and he tried to keep things calm in the meantime: "Don't worry, the wind blows from that side. And in the worst case, I can always call the rescue patrol." Indeed, we had had to register our excursion in advance to be able to sail in this area. Less than ten minutes after our floating standstill, and after Dmitri had already repaired the engine, a patrol sailed past the yellow buoys in a performance making visible where the frontier lies. Less than a year later, on May 23, 2024, Russian border guards removed twenty-four buoys demarcating shipping lanes from the Narva River, thus threatening to redraw the shared borders between the two countries.[14] The incident, carried out in the dark of night, came after the Kremlin's move to unilaterally extend Russia's maritime boundary in the Baltic Sea.

Once back on shore, I strolled around the canals and suddenly heard someone screaming at me in English: "Go out, go out!" I could not see who it was or from where. As it turned out, a middle-aged man had heard me walking around and recognized me as an *artist* from behind the door. Surprised by his angry reaction,

FIGURE 7.5.   Riding in the boat with Dmitri. Photo: Francisco Martínez, 2023.

I stood in front of the garage where he was lying on a deckchair. Then I asked (in Russian) what the matter was. The man simply replied that this was a private space and that I should go away. A similar scene occurred with a different resident a month later. He was putting his tools in order and reminded me as I passed by that this was a private space. The retreat to the garages could be taken as a way of defending the individual thresholds of privacy while operating as a catalyst for another kind of social relation. Spending time here is experienced as an escape from structure, back into a world where things are not planned.

Extopia

Kulgu is at the margins of the city yet neither marginal nor irrelevant. Indeed, liminal places are often found at the fringes of normative spots, but still, how they matter to local sociality is central—by hosting the carnivalesque and hybrid.[15] Secluded within the borderland between the EU and Russia, Kulgu is an eccentric site. It combines material bricolage and legal shadows with geopolitical attention and ecological insularity; it is thus the kind of place that we anthropologists like—those that enact other forms of relating to nature, things, and the state; those that produce a particular sociality through both the exclusion of outsiders and the inclusion of insiders. Rows of garages lining the canals form a charming area with do-it-yourself architecture built of various materials. The garage tenants creatively face the challenge to utilize the space to the maximum while remaining within the officially demarcated limits.

Spaces of ambiguity like Kulgu are ordinarily used by locals as sites of retreat, beyond the logic of politics, utility, or even reason. Perhaps it is because these gray areas are characterized by a more benign "private publicness" than in the city.[16] Garages and dachas are interstices for doing things differently, a space of liminal relations not always easy to interpret, partly because the users themselves do not always know what they are seeking. Kulgu thus allows us to study the plurality of relationships that exist in place beneath the masks of order and cohesion. Here, one is exposed to the possibility of other ways of life, precisely because of its secluded standing. Hanging out in Kulgu also blurs the prevailing separation between culture and nature.[17]

Garages and dachas can be considered a spatial ornament through which we experience a compensatory withdrawal from urban life. On this matter, Simmel noted that there are things that cannot emerge "in the presence of full publicity," which is why "a second world alongside the manifest world," the one of secrecy, "produces an immense enlargement of life." In such a mechanism of bonding, the content of the secret is not important; indeed, the hideout may even be empty, but it is the availability of the shadow space that matters.[18]

Nevertheless, the ecology of agencies found in Kulgu is not limited to human activity and the hundreds of makeshift garages. For instance, we can hear a concert of frogs, accompanying drips, and the permanent drone of the high-voltage electrical wires. We can watch the flight of birds and find feral trails, mouse droppings, and fungi. There is also bacterial activity happening under the radar of human detectability. This is a liminal zone, inhabited by threshold beings, and where dominant discourses and social codes are often reversed. [19]

Overall, borders suggest separations but also intersections, deploying a particular relation between fixity and contingency.[20] In turn, Kulgu is fluid, hot, and thrown to the exterior world, as an extopia.[21] In his attempt to understand the kind of spaces set apart from the norms of public life, Michel Foucault described heterotopias as worlds within worlds, mirroring and yet upsetting what is outside.[22] Extopias such as Kulgu, however, do not necessarily mirror central activities; rather, they operate in the interstices between different solid somethings, providing an enduring dislocation. The very prefix "ex-" refers to a condition of being off, away, or without an indicated value or right. "Ex-" names someone who has formerly held a specified position, but it can also be a hybrid space in the shadows, where one can integrate conflicting cultural codes.²³ Transgressive qualities are recurrently attributed to these interstitial spaces, edges of structured social life where a particular comradeship breaks away from beneath.²⁴

Kulgu is characterized by warm, horizontal relations among those active at the site. The act of withdrawing yourself from the ordinary alongside other strangers confers privileges of status in the alternative reality while drawing boundaries between the inside and the outside, thus making it harder for those in power to exert control.²⁵ Besides changes in the quality of time, and by way of compensation, "the initiands acquire a special kind of freedom," as Victor Turner notes.²⁶ Yet living on the borderland is difficult; it generates a permanent antagonism, as well as a particular symbolic world and material culture. Being from the border means being on the edge. Thus, by conviction and choice, voluntarily, or irremediably, it demands an instinctive identification of the end of our possibilities.

Borders serve to homogenize societies internally, argued anthropologist Fredrik Barth in a classic study. They are drawn to create clarity and separations, which lend meaning to identity and a sense of membership.²⁷ Borders also serve to designate the nation-state as entitled to a territory (including aquatic and subterranean spaces), yet they are zones where both difference and contact are intensified. Nevertheless, the value of any given location is partly dependent on its connections to and separations from other places. The ways of being located on a border are thus multiple and relative.²⁸

Frontiers themselves might appear and disappear, as well as age and mutate along with their respective societies. In some cases, the border might be hidden or non-existing physically or legally anymore, and yet its effect might still persist or reverberate.²⁹ All in all, a frontier does not simply demarcate an area geopolitically; it also produces a particular connectivity and a semblance of order in practice.³⁰ Hence, it is worth paying attention to both the material and the discursive life of borders and, overall, to the nuances of being positioned in a borderland.³¹

Kulgovites

Peeter Tambu, chief architect of Narva, notes that there are also mental borderlands, not just the geopolitical kind: "Whenever I'm leaving Narva, it seems to me that the border is somewhere near Jõhvi or Kohtla-Järve. . . . It is another world."³² This city makes evident to some degree the polycentricity of Estonian society, being at the intersection of various global flows.³³ And in the margin of this trans-systemic border, we find Kulgu. This area also includes a gardening cooperative made up of hundreds of dachas. I walk there with Yevgenia, helping her to carry bags, as she is ninety years old. She remembers when the gardens were laid out, "with a lot of work," right after the creation of the reservoir in 1961.

Originally, the term "dacha" referred to places for the upper class to take a break from city life. In the nineteenth century, Russian aristocrats, artists, and intellectuals spent time there to find inspiration and enjoy forms of leisure in contact with nature. After the Bolshevik revolution in 1917, the dachas were nationalized (as were all other private property and means of production) and used by leading communists. After World War II, however, the dacha culture found a new life. As an example, in 1946 the journal *More Oil Shale!* (*Rohkem Põlevkivi!*) called upon Soviet citizens to increase food production in suburban gardens: "Because of limited opportunities as a consequence of the war, there are still some difficulties in providing for our labor force. . . . In the first place, extra land is given to invalids of the Patriotic War and families left orphaned. In the second place come exemplary workers, who without violating work discipline have constantly provided a large production."[34]

Back then, settlements such as Narva and Sillamäe were entirely rebuilt around the development of new state factories and followed modern paradigms of urban planning. As thousands of people relocated to panel-built housing, and in the context of a shortage economy, municipal authorities allocated garden land to the workers, hoping that they would be able to grow their own food there. People also began to use these peri-urban locations for recreation and to rest from industrial labor. At first, city authorities tried to organize the space through planning and by providing running water and electricity, yet the infrastructure was never developed until the end, and the lines drawn on paper to divide the plots soon became obsolete, at least in Kulgu.

Around Narva, there are over ten thousand allotment gardens distributed among fifty gardening cooperatives of various sizes. The plots are usually six hundred square meters each and host a small, self-constructed summerhouse (officially up to forty square meters, yet tenants deal with these limits inventively). Geographer Tarmo Pikner has been studying the use of dachas in the region for over a decade.[35] He notes that in Narva, the amount of space occupied by allotment gardens is larger than the total of all the green areas within the city. From the point of view of institutions, however, the dachas are more a gray zone than a green area. They exist partly outside the gaze of state authorities and urban plans, acquiring a structural invisibility—no longer classified and not yet classified at the same time.[36] Their gray status contributes to accommodating the informality in the system, since the practices taking place there may eventually be translated into city planning as a result of institutional porosity.[37] Hence, dachas do not stand apart from municipal or state institutions but are rather otherwise connected with them.

In her dissertation on homemaking practices in Narva, anthropologist Jaanika Kingumets pays special attention to how allotment gardens are intrinsically entangled with local households, "intertwined yet also clearly distinguishable."[38] In addition to discussing different routines and rhythms, she observes that bus timetables change when the garden plots are in active use. She further notes that reliable public transport to the dachas is particularly important for elderly residents, who might eventually complain if they feel that bus fares are too expensive, the routes do not adjust so they can reach more distant dacha areas, or the frequency of service is not increased between April and October.

In another study, this one of allotment gardens in Scotland, geographer Caitlin DeSilvey notes that ambivalence pervades the practices taking place there, highlighting the linkage between formal and informal activities.[39] In Kulgu, for instance, some boat garages have been turned into summer cottages, and the reservoir has been incrementally drained in order to increase the surface area of the allotments. Construction is often done with leftovers and available materials, following bricoleur-like aesthetics and self-taught skills. Yet life in a dacha is not always easy or peaceful. Common complications are the limited access to safe drinking water, the need to deal with floods from time to time, and the lack of a proper sewage system.

In a study of the role of dachas in the political life of Belarusian people, sociologist Ronan Hervouet argues that dacha culture in post-Soviet countries has nothing in common with the countryside second home in western Europe.[40] In his view, a dacha is a place where social status is remade and people can recover from the alienation, demoralization, and exhaustion caused by a dictatorial system. Also, anthropologist Melissa Caldwell has conducted research on dacha culture in the outskirts of Moscow. As she notes, going to the allotment garden is foremost a form of being connected to nature, and the spiritual side of this lifestyle can be historically related to Russian culture. There are also political nuances, such as being part of a totalitarian communist regime, which made working in the dacha particularly fulfilling because "these were activities that one did for oneself, not for the state."[41] Gender roles, too, are important, to the point where Caldwell describes dachas as a "feminized site of problem-solving."[42] In the allotment gardens that she visited, men were responsible for tasks such as construction, barbecuing, and gardening, while women were mostly dedicated to food preparation, canning, cleaning, and child tending. All in all, dacha practices are central to Russian social life, Caldwell concludes, as they shape how people live "at the personal, community, and even national levels."[43]

There are not always fences between dachas, which indicates a sense of trust. Nevertheless, agreed-upon separations are valid as long as the neighbors get along well, and boundaries nevertheless do not often coincide with official entries in the registers. In this regard, Pikner observes the contrast between visible demarcations of property and the verbal narratives of users, which often emphasize that "this land is mine."[44] In turn, Kingumets foregrounds that allotment gardens are in the making over a long period of time—therefore displaying a wide range of hardly matching yet creatively patchworked styles.[45] This form of vernacular architecture expresses not only the changing aesthetics, values, and standards of living, but also traces of past forays into improvement, depending on the material opportunities available.

"That Is How Sputnik Was Built"

In the allotment gardens, the earth is dug as in the mines, albeit with a shovel, in order to plant, water, and maintain the vegetable patch. Ornamental flower beds and ordered rows of growing vegetables indicate human agency, while nonhuman interventions often remain invisible to us. As there is no ultimate guarantee of a harvest, nor its yield, farming introduces a bit of uncertainty in gardeners' lives. Nevertheless, when talking to gardeners, I find they mostly emphasize that the flavors are more genuine, and they are able to avoid buying anything from a grocery store. For instance, Ljuda, sunburned from working on her plot in Kulgu, repeats that "from June to September, we don't have to buy any food in the shop. We grow it here. We eat our own vegetables." Nevertheless, I see only cucumbers, potatoes, and cabbages growing and realize that I wouldn't be able to stand such a diet for very long.

The term "dacha" itself may come from the Russian verb *davat'*, meaning "giving," indicating that something has been given.[46] The largest horticultural cooperative in Estonia is Sputnik, located two kilometers from Sillamäe. These allotment gardens have a heavy seasonal use; nonetheless, over one hundred people are officially registered in Sputnik as living there all year long. And this is not the only dacha area near Sillamäe, where two out of three local residents say they have a cottage. Prices might vary, but not long ago one of the plots was sold for 150 euros and another for 300 euros. That was an exception, as some might also pay thousands of euros for dachas in good condition. Plots can be inhabited and passed on throughout generations. Since the 1990s, most of the allotment gardens are privately owned; the common infrastructure, however, is managed in partnership.[47]

Irina Ivanova is the head of the cooperative. We meet in her office, where she invites me for an assortment of *zakuski* (snacks) and gives me a jar of recently made *adjika* (a sauce made from tomatoes, garlic, and peppers). "Overall, people are positive, but they only think about their allotment. We are just three people dealing with 1,145 plots, doing all the coordination work," she laments. The territory was arranged by the municipality of Sillamäe during reconstruction of the city. Beneath, there is a layer of concrete, so the gardeners have to bring in topsoil from elsewhere for their plots each season.

When thinking of sputniks, I remember a novel by Haruki Murakami that conveys the suffering of unrequited love.[48] And of course the earth-orbiting satellites launched by the Soviet Union in the 1950s come to mind. In Russian, however, the term actually means travel companion. "Sputnik has become a historical practice, which appeared after the great patriotic war. Then, things were truly difficult. Nowadays, people just want to get out of their apartments for a while. They spend five months indoors, during the winter, so they need to get out. And here we value the food we grow," explains Alexandr at the entrance to the cooperative.

Boris is nicely arranging his garden and looks at me suspiciously when I walk by. He is cleaning the *mangal* grill and pruning some dry leaves from the plants. His family will visit him later today to celebrate his grandchild's birthday. "The dacha is always a good place for gathering the family," Boris states. At some point during the summer, extended family members who are dispersed across different locations (countries, in many cases) come together here. Hence, dachas contribute to connecting generations, maintaining kinship relations.[49] Nevertheless, there might be disagreements regarding the main purpose of the allotment too. While older generations mainly use the allotments to produce supplementary food, and are willing to dedicate many hours and much hard work to that aim, leisure activities seem to be preferred by the younger generations, who come here with bags of food and drinks from local supermarkets. They treat the garden as a private space that is meant for barbecues, relaxation, and recreation with friends, rather than for physical effort and production of goods.

In spring, at the start of the season, people in Sillamäe seem to be interested only in dacha-related matters. Intriguingly, they go *on* the allotment, instead of *to* the allotment (*na/v sadu*), which is grammatically incorrect (in Russian) but also has the connotation of spending a floating time on a liminal territory. There, one might see dozens of people digging holes, keeping plants clear of weeds, cutting branches, fixing greenhouses, planting flowers and then watering and fertilizing them with care, and finally gathering and preserving.

Every year, work in the dacha conditions when the holidays are scheduled and the savings required to start the seasonal activity. "During the weekends and in the summer vacation, you will find me in Sputnik," says Nadezhda. "Here, we grow food for the body and for the mind." People also spend holidays (formerly important in Soviet times) such as the first or ninth of May here. "There are no parades anymore, but if you want to see some celebration, then you have to go to Sputnik, not in public, but in private with close ones," says Jelena, the director

FIGURE 7.6. Scene from Sputnik. Photo: Francisco Martínez, 2023.

of the Sillamäe Museum. While preparing our exhibition there, I asked her if I could leave some construction materials and old furniture outdoors (in front of the museum) for a night. Jelena wisely told me not to and explained that Sputnik relies on gleaning practices: "Our people are good. If you ask for help, they will help you, but don't leave anything outdoors because it will disappear. That is how Sputnik was built."

"The city takes energy from you; the allotment gives it back. How? Because of contact with the soil." The reasons are rather obvious to Natalia. Still, from Sputnik one can hear the cars passing on the highway. Nonetheless, each of the individuals has their own motivation, as well as a will to work, skills, and taste. Natalia's dacha has a heating system in the greenhouses. Across this dacha, I see a self-made blacksmith workshop; that allotment over there has a barn for drying fish; and on the corner, I find a goose farm. I walk a bit farther and meet another Jelena, who is standing hunched over on a ridge. She tells me: "Vegetables here are tastier. I don't need to go to a shop to buy anything. Also, I can be barefoot and in my underwear, just as I wish." Indeed, I often found people wearing only underwear or swimsuits while working in the garden. Spending time there relates to a tinkering form of agency and an inventive way of building.[50] In this sense, a dacha or a garage is not just a place but a particular way of standing in the world.

Both dachas and garages have a price, but their ownership and valuation often have more to do with embodied practices of care and a compensatory surplus of living than with investment and capitalist notions of property. That is why Tatyana says that she comes to Kulgu to "support beauty," adding: "You get your fingers dirty while listening to the birds. . . . I feel rested once I have done all the work in the garden."[51] Hence, dachas and garages, as particular kinds of hideouts, aim not to replace the real but to expand it. And in doing so, they contribute to creating social reality.

This chapter has contributed to discussions about spaces of escapism through ethnographic engagement with two particular kinds of extopias. Still, I felt the need to experiment with nonverbal forms of representation in order to foreground how places on the margin enable threshold relations among occupants; therefore, I created the artwork *Liquid Shadows at the Border* with photographer Riina Varol. For the installation, we colored the photos taken in Kulgu by Enas Amerkhanov between 1972 and 1987. The result of this collaboration is a series of Byzantine collages inspired by the liminal standing and bonding gestures among garage users. Our decision to aesthetically intervene in the photos was intended to add an iconic condensation of meanings with auratic colors. Complementing

FIGURE 7.7. *Liquid Shadows on the Border* series. Photo: Francisco Martínez, 2023.

the series, we also included a representation of the amphibious structure of the area made with shells, a non-human shelter that reminds us of the half-box shape of garages.[52] Perhaps in doing this I became an artist myself, one of those disliked by garage users. Yet instead of taking new photos and invading the private space of garage users to extract meaning from them, I engaged with preexisting representations made by one of them and tried to communicate in the vernacular language of the extopia: Russian.

The garages around the reservoir provide an escape from the prosaic solidity of the ordinary.[53] They create a shadow space that is experienced simultaneously as both sacred and banal. What people do there might differ somewhat, but the motivations for spending time in the garages are similar among the people I met in Kulgu: to enjoy a break from the normal, to search for quality time that is not ordered by the authorities, to be engaged in tinkering, to be surrounded by nature, and to do something just for oneself and without a boss. The result is a surplus of living at the margins of the ordinary realm, which plays a compensatory role but also modifies how the world is experienced at large.

Dachas and garages provide a supplement to the alienation of modern normality through an escape to a quasi-countryside.[54] Overall, places on the normative margins allow us other ways of relating to nature, individuals, and institutions such as family or the state, testing the elastic adhesive of social relations and hosting the carnivalesque. In Kulgu, users can do things other than what they do in the city, perform various under-the-radar activities, and spend time at ease. Despite producing gender-distinctive worldviews, both garages and dachas are places for disconnecting, for individual enterprise, and for testing other ways of standing on this planet. They are eccentric territories, whereby one can experience new kinds of relationality.

Nevertheless, these shadow spaces are not simply a source of disorder but rather a space of compensation for a series of difficult factors, which might range from the alienation and boredom of city life to subsistence farming, the will to do something with your hands and put your fingers in the soil, to be on your own for a while, or simply to prepare your own shashlik and host your relatives for a day. In this sense, garages and cottages are not marginal to institutions but intrinsically entangled with them—affording complex accommodations and refusals that allow locals to move on with living. Indeed, garages and cottages are not simply messy areas but spaces of alternative order and classification, which allow the experience of separation without disconnection from the household, community, or state.

CRYPTO-COLONIALISM

Ida-Virumaa is a location where people continue living; hence the importance of looking at this region as a place of present inhabitation and of studying how the existing infrastructure has been incorporated into the contemporary. Research on such areas in decline tends to focus, however, on their relationships with the past rather than on the practices through which such spaces are made and remade toward the future. Likewise, post-socialist infrastructure has mostly been attended to by accounting for its resistance to change.[1] Thus, the actual possibilities of redesign and interconnection within global capitalism deserve further empirical detail.

One example is the production and distribution of energy occurring in relation to cryptomining. This seemingly non-material activity updates the existing energo-political reentanglements and displays a novel combination of financial exchange and technological secrecy in nested systems of extraction. Still, cryptomining is always localized within specific geographical and historical contexts; it affects actual people and becomes integral to local industrial and natural landscapes, even if securitized and barely accessible. Nonetheless, it is not simply about the politics of energy and water use, nor about the multiplication of sacrificed areas of our planet; rather it foregrounds the complex, not always clear relationship between public services and goods and private capital (of transnational tech corporations).

This chapter examines how digital networks and the exchange of cryptocurrencies rely on the situated infrastructure of electricity supply. It shows how the pattern of rescaling territories (while dis-embedding infrastructure from its social context) has become an intrinsic part of paving virtual information highways and financial exchange. Even though the production and distribution of energy are based in specific places, the cryptomining activity appears particularly disentangled from the respective localities, scaling it instead as a global and virtual technological zone by combining corporate secrecy and local invisibility.[2]

This is indeed not a unique phenomenon, as noted by anthropologist Asta Vonderau in a study of how a number of Nordic municipalities refer to cold air as a resource that can be used to attract global IT corporations and data center development.[3] She describes how some regions compete with one another to cut taxes for tech corporations under the promise of bringing jobs. That is not the case in Estonia, however. Ida-Virumaa is always the preferred location for cryptomining, data centers, mineral processing, and "green energy" because of the infrastructural, demographic, and economic climate of the region, not simply on account of the local ecology.

In eastern Estonia, cryptomining corporations are bringing novel uses to Soviet infrastructure originally designed for oil shale extraction and processing. New infrastructures are also being built concurrently for energy production in this same region. According to Mattias Kaiv, head of media relations for Enefit Parks, the company's new plant in Narva was "developed as the most preferred choice among clients with an extensive need for energy." The location allows Enefit "to offer electricity that is cheaper in terms of the network fee," and this provides "a significant competitive advantage to production plants," complemented by "a perimeter with enhanced security and surveillance."[4]

Of a similar opinion is Hermes Brambat, a founding member of the Estonian Cryptographic Association, who states that this new infrastructure is "in the immediate vicinity of electricity and generators, and we can very easily deliver that energy. As setting up a network for such consumption is very expensive, it would be more difficult to do it elsewhere."[5] Brambat's company, Nordcoin Mining, installed a container (with 240 processors already in operation) in the middle of the area of the projected VKG pulp mill (see chapter 2).

A factory for the production of wind generators is also being built in the Kohtla-Järve industrial park, using a new technology patented by a Ukrainian entrepreneur who previously created one of the world's largest companies dealing with cryptocurrencies.[6] The factory will produce over three thousand wind generators a year and occupy nearly seventeen thousand square meters. It has been funded by investors from Argentina, Georgia, Ukraine, Cyprus, Finland, and Belarus at a total sum of 5.9 million euros. Nevertheless, public money has also been allocated to start production, and the joint venture of KreDex and Enterprise Estonia (EAS) is supporting the project with 2.6 million euros from the Just Transition Fund. (In 2023, the EU allocated 354 million euros to diversify the region's economy.) According to Nikolai Grebenkine, a member of the board of Freen, "the investments will help create at least thirteen new jobs in the region." Other relevant projects are the Purtse hybrid wind and solar park, a facility that comprises five turbines and 49,000 solar panels; the Aidu wind park, featuring seventeen turbines; and the Estonia mine solar park, built on a twenty-seven-meter-high structure made from oil shale ash. These three new projects will provide energy for approximately one-sixth of the total households in the country.

One of the main potential clients of the Enefit park, however, did not survive to see it completed. Burfa Tech, an information technology company owned by Ivan Turõgin and Sergei Potapenko, built a data processing center worth 10 million euros. It was meant to provide cloud computing, graphic rendering, artificial intelligence, and machine learning services to customers around the world. With an average electrical consumption of thirty gigawatt hours per year, the Burfa Narva Center was in turn one of the largest electricity consumers in Estonia. As Turõgin told a local newspaper: "The location of the chosen data center gives us some competitive advantages—firstly, being near the protected area of Balti Elektrijaama ensures high security, which is one of the main conditions for our customers, and at the same time we get significant savings on electricity prices."[7] The founders of Burfa Tech, Turõgin and Potapenko, were well known in the region for their charity supporting the activity of the Ida-Viru Central Hospital (they donated an ultrasound lung scanner worth forty thousand euros needed for the diagnosis of coronavirus), and the soccer club Jõhvi FC Phoenix, which displayed the company's logo on the club's shirt. In the autumn of 2022, however, Turõgin and Potapenko were arrested following accusations of fraud and money laundering.[8]

The increasing industrial demand for energy, the geopolitical need to cut existing infrastructural connections with Russia, and the aim of reducing the country's oil shale dependency have created the motivation to complement the mining activities with a nuclear industry—which, nonetheless, remains located in the same region. In 2024, the Estonian parliament passed a resolution supporting the adoption of nuclear energy in the country. Viru-Nigula (near Kunda) and Aa (in Lüganuse) were being considered as potential locations. Fermi Energia, the managing company, explained that this area had been selected because of its industrial heritage, specifically its suitable logistics, the presence of a workforce with industrial experience, and the availability of cooling water in the Aidu quarry and the disused Kohtla, Sompa, and Viru mines, as well as strong power grids, areas that are not densely populated, and the absence of nature reserves.[9] Fermi Energia CEO Kalev Kallemets promises about two hundred employees around the two nuclear reactors and energy for 1,354,286 households, which will allow Estonia to become a net exporter of electricity. The 4.74 terawatt-hours power plant is also expected to generate twelve tons of radioactive waste a year, though it had yet to be decided where the spent fuel would be deposited.

Depoliticized Infrastructure

An infrastructure is a mediator between state and citizen, thus an important site of political kinship.[10] This can be seen in the high expectations around the EU-funded "green transition," though "transition" itself is a depoliticizing term which downplays the turmoil and uncertainty caused by the restructuring of the production and distribution of energy, presenting a rather convoluted process as instead gentle, gradual, and consensual.[11] Hence, the energy model is being changed in the sense of rapidly disconnecting from Russia, but there is no degrowth of consumption planned, nor are the underlying structures and regional hierarchies within Estonia being challenged. Indeed, efforts to replace fossil energy with a green alternative have concentrated most of country's wind turbines and solar panels in eastern Estonia, which will also be the site of the new nuclear plant. Indeed, what this region is experiencing is an expansion of the electrical grid and a reproduction of some of the colonial logic that had severe effects on the environment and that has given shape to its particular sociality and ecology over the last century.

Another example is the construction of a "superfactory" in Narva meant to produce neodymium magnets, which are primarily used in the manufacturing of electric vehicles and wind turbines. Aivar Virunen, production manager of NPM, has called electricity the main resource the plant needs; hence the company is seeking cheap energy, since the magnet factory would become Estonia's largest consumer once it started operating in late 2025. Originally, NPM had promised jobs in order to attract public support, but what it will actually bring is massive energy consumption. Paradoxically, companies such as NPM promote a narrative of environmental concern while proposing themselves as the appropriate industry to manage natural resources and energy production, thus combining sustainable discourses with global neoliberal practices. They largely demand limited resources such as water, electricity, and access to the existing infrastructure, therefore having direct implications for both the natural environment and the people living there. Where value is extracted from, however, and where profit is allocated rarely coincide. On the contrary, such corporations often buy renewable energy certificates that allow them to negate their local impacts despite running on oil shale–powered energy infrastructures.

In the Soviet era, extraction was associated with progress and moderniza-tion, which allowed officials to cast opponents as anti-progress. Nowadays, those questioning the impact of data centers, electric batteries, and green energy infra-structure in specific localities are similarly labeled as anti-sustainability. Once a problem is identified as simply economic or technocratic, it is then abstracted and dis-embedded from its social context, thus away from the realm of people and not subject to deliberation and contestation.[12] Nevertheless, depoliticization is a process related to concrete ideas and decisions made by specific agents.[13] Indeed, the production of invisibility is a function of power relations, as if some infrastructural projects were nonexistent. Hence, uncovering these practices of invisibilization is a relevant field intervention, making the energy infrastructure at stake visible in order to call attention to its social and ecological harm.[14]

In matters of technical content, such as oil shale extraction and processing, the privatization of the sector in Estonia was accompanied by institutional depolitici-zation and the transferring of decision-making and responsibility to technocratic bodies whose work appears opaque and far from public scrutiny. In other cases, and as we saw in chapter 4, the depoliticization happens by framing local issues as non-problems. Still, what is invisible to those in the center is highly visible to others at the margins, so what matters here, what is at stake, is how the invisibility of energy production and consumption in Ida-Virumaa is politically mobilized (as a statecraft tool) and who actually profits from it.

Indeed, one problematic issue is that residents do not seem to benefit directly from the green energy, rare earth materials processing, and cryptomining activ-ity, as the money produced does not improve local well-being, nor do the direct tax revenues tend to remain within the municipality, invested in communities that are already deprived. As a result, the green, digital futures of both private corporations and the Estonian state become instead a form of energy gentrifica-tion.[15] Furthermore, the employment numbers generated by this kind of industry are rather limited despite the original promises, and once the energy production rates can no longer be increased, at least not at competitive prices, the private corporations demand public support to do so or simply relocate to another global periphery.

Certainly, more cryptomining in the region does not lead to more transpar-ency or necessarily to an increase in well-being; quite the opposite, it can be understood as a masked recolonialism. In 2002, anthropologist Michael Herzfeld coined the term "crypto-colonialism," though at that time, it had nothing to do with cryptocurrencies.[16] He presented crypto-colonialism as a practice that limits certain areas' access to the dominant advantages of modernity. As described by Herzfeld, the political independence of countries such as Greece and Thailand was gained at the cost of economic dependence, and their national culture was refashioned to suit foreign models. As a result, these areas operate as buffer zones between the already colonized lands and those yet to be tamed.

In Estonia, discourses of e-governance and e-residency have been an important part of national statecraft and policy. The successful rhetoric of digital sovereignty and the new socio-technical imaginaries contributed to underscore the state's affiliation with the Western camp and the collective identity.[17] See, for instance, the nationwide digitization, branded by the government as e-Estonia, which has been intrinsic to the goal of integrating the country into the Euro-Atlantic community and distancing itself from its Soviet past and the Russian state.[18] The country's first information policy strategy indeed framed digitization as supporting "the integration of Estonia into the family of developed nations."[19]

The e-residency created a new kind of borderless economic space, allowing people worldwide to access the country's services without needing to be physically present. Estonian e-residency is a paradigmatic example of unbounded transnational exchange occurring digitally, beyond physical frontiers. Likewise, this country was a pioneer in the adoption of blockchain for administrative uses, building a program that offers non–Estonian citizens services such as digital signature of documents and establishing and administering a company online.

Digital technologies and the correlated strategic infrastructure are thus used to bolster sovereign power.[20] Yet as transparency initiatives proliferate to advance with the digital statecraft of the Estonian nation, these technocratic mechanisms are generative of further mistrust and suspicion over what might be hidden. Also, the development of both a transparent e-state and digital entrepreneurship has failed to resolve another problem of invisibility in the country: nearly 5 percent of the Estonian population still has "undetermined citizenship," a status that complicates getting a job and does not grant the right to vote in national elections. Furthermore, novel forms of governance and sociotechnical development came along with the deployment of new energy infrastructure in Ida-Virumaa. Indeed, discrepancies between where and how energy is produced and the eco-digital nationhood imaginary have been noted.[21]

A Parallel World, Which Is Not Far Off

The abbreviation "crypto" comes from "encryption," defined as the process of changing electronic information into a secret code using cutting-edge algorithms and mathematical concepts. But cryptography has ancient roots. For example, in Egypt, around 1900 BC, we can find inscriptions with codes, transposition, and substitution of hieroglyphic symbols. Cryptography is a branch of mathematics that develops techniques to encrypt communication in order to prevent others from capturing or deciphering our codes.

Crypto technologies might appear opaque, and we might not know how cryptography actually works, but we may use them nevertheless in our quotidian activities on the Internet, from email and e-commerce to electronic identity authentication. And in point of fact, many of the technologies we use on a daily basis in the digital age are not just helpful but intrinsically linked to specific ways of organizing power.[22] Also of resisting authority and avoiding state monitoring; for instance, cryptocoins are used to pay for the espionage activities against NATO soldiers in the Baltic region, as acknowledged in a private conversation by an official deployed there.

Cryptominers are those who add new blocks to a computational chain and monitor each new transaction, articulating a distributed verification system. Thus, a decentralized network of computers keeps a blockchain constantly running and authenticates its transactions. The movement of digital money is ensured through a digital ledger or database, which does not need the approval of centralized financial institutions to execute each transaction. Thus, cryptominers code an exit from politics, allowing a virtual sense of community to exist through encryption. These seemingly non-material networks nonetheless have a spatial resonance, as they rely on the situated infrastructure of electricity supply. For instance, cryptocurrency companies in Estonia can consume up to 1 percent of the country's electricity, an immense demand that raises questions about the industry's supposed decentralization, sustainability, and greenhouse gas emissions, as well as its supposed non-materiality and carbon footprint.[23] In short, even virtual activities such as cryptomining are emplaced somewhere, and our digital presence has a geologic past and future.

Nonetheless, users of cryptocurrencies often have their own sense of historicity, seemingly apart from those of nations and states.[24] After several attempts to create a cryptocurrency (eCash, B-money, Bit Gold, and Hashcash), the Bitcoin peer-to-peer electronic cash system emerged as an alternative in reaction to the global financial crisis of 2007–8. In 2008, an anonymous individual using the pseudonym "Satoshi Nakamoto" published a document often referred to as "the Bitcoin white paper." It proposed to create a virtual representation of hard cash, arguing that this new form of digital money would allow online payments between two parties "without going through a financial institution." Nakamoto also outlined a series of principles such as durability, divisibility, portability, intrinsic value, and scarcity, as well as basic features, including the analogical, extractive metaphor of mining, to describe the incentive system behind the blockchain.[25]

But why are some cryptocurrencies "mined" instead of "farmed" or "coined"? Users mine Bitcoins with powerful hardware, and this expenditure of computational energy is rewarded with new coins "extracted" from the digital bedrock.[26] As the number of users grows, the value per coin increases, which in turn attracts more users, generating a positive feedback loop. Yet because of the increasingly intense competition among miners, it has become correspondingly difficult for individuals to win a full block reward. From the original grassroots, antiestablishment ethos of the movement, cryptocurrencies have been embraced by transnational corporations, financial institutions, and large-scale mining farms. Likewise, the high valuation of cryptocurrencies has precipitated a flood of capital-intensive miners with advanced computing power, pushing small-scale individuals to the margins of the system.[27]

Originally arranged to enhance collaborative frameworks of economic organization and articulate horizontal structures, blockchain models appeared as a revolt against the broken promises of neoliberal capitalism. Technologies such as Bitcoin, however, have not reduced the centralizing power of the state or of large corporations. Quite the opposite, they have contributed to a technocratic centralization in decision-making and to an oligopolistic market structure. That is the conclusion of science and technology studies scholars Primavera De Filippi and Benjamin Loveluck.[28] As a result, a market-driven approach to social relations and natural resources has been imposed over the initial horizontal ethos, a model not based on reciprocity and exchange but rather a capitalocentric one of financial transactions and a voracious appetite for energy.

This activity is also caught in webs of capital circulation and accumulation, following the financial reasoning of late (postindustrial?) modernity, in which flows of energy and power reinforce each other toward profit. Nevertheless, the connection between energy infrastructures, digital culture, and secrecy is still relatively unknown, as there are no comprehensive data on the locations of cryptomining activities, even as they spread globally.[29]

Proponents of blockchain say that this technology can improve transparency and protect users from fraud. Alas, cryptominers' fear of the activity of hackers and cryptobros has only increased, along with safety measures among holders.[30] Additionally, trust is placed in the collective ability to review and evaluate transactions, and open-source algorithmic codes stand at the center of these operations, supported by a strong belief by users in participative techno-optimism. The working algorithms of the leading tech corporations remain secret, however, and the human force behind the operations remains invisible.

In the world of cryptocurrencies, transactions exist outside the management of a central authority (in some cases leading to their use in criminal activities), but the value of money and the capacity for exchange still require public trust. Traditionally, this sense of trust has been created by banks, which keep our money safe while allowing us to use it as we need it. By contrast, in the case of cryptocurrencies, trust is created by the constant growth in the number of users, the encryption capacity of the mathematical algorithm, and the digital addresses of users (codes in the form of long strings of numbers and letters).

Mining networks also compensate for the risk inherent in cryptocurrencies by means of rituals of recognition, and those practicing computational accounting are rewarded with cryptocoins. These digital currencies are, however, not money per se but an exclusive right to send data privately in a financial space that is presented as public. This is reminiscent of Simmel's description of how secret societies operate: the contribution of concealment to social organization does not rely on the content of the secret but rather depends on the rules governing the telling of it (as well as who gets to tell it).[31] At first, the healthy functioning of a network relies on the wisdom of crowds, related to the collective monitoring of the blockchain that allows further mining. The online dataset, however, can also be experienced as opaque and autonomous to users. Thus, both the secret societies of Simmel and the world of cryptocurrencies provide freedom from the hegemonic vision but do not articulate an organized alternative unaffected by issues of power and secrecy.

Investments in cryptocurrencies are based on speculation, thus made at the boundary between knowledge and non-knowledge. As a result, cryptomining transforms individuals into calculative, entrepreneurial investors. In some cases, that might generate the same sentiment of alienation that Simmel described with regard to how money turned into a goal in itself, despite being created as a means. In the same way that money does, cryptocoins institute complex relationships, not just between people and things but among people themselves. As a result, the world is objectified as if it were created and measured through monetary connections.

At this writing, Bitcoin remains by far the most valuable cryptocurrency. Nonetheless, it is much more than a financial asset or a technology. Many of its followers claim to have formed a "digital nation." Some others define it as an "ecosystem" or "a culture." Still, this is a rapidly changing field, and the situation might be different by the time this book is published. Indeed, profits are made not only by those engaged in mining (a smaller and smaller cohort every year) but also by speculative investors (particularly younger generations disenchanted with traditional financial instruments) and those who gain passive returns by "staking" their holdings to help secure the network. Hence, further empirical research is required about how energopolitical entanglements persist in the present and the way infrastructures inhabit a whole spectrum of visibilities, from opacity to spectacle.

This chapter has attempted to contribute to new discussions about the territorial organization of cryptocurrencies, green energy, and data storages. An attentive study of their sited activities reveals how old dynamics or patterns of inclusion and exclusion continue to take place in our digitally global world through renewed socio-technical arrangements. Since energy is the cryptominers' direct connection with the material realm, the study of electricity consumption can be approached as the door to investigating opaque digital geographies. Electricity, however, is invisible itself (hidden in high-voltage cables); we do not see the electric flux flowing through our devices, or the financial profits from cryptomining activities, but the environmental damage and the related public investment that accompany digital platforms have an impact on the everyday life of the residents living where the energy is produced.

Cryptocurrencies constitute a parallel world in which the borders between the virtual and the physical, money and collecting, and transparency and opacity are rather blurred but the costs are visible and unequally distributed. What people in Ida-Virumaa see is that the flows and networks of cryptomining are not just in flux but also grounded and often path-dependent. Digital layers, along with energy infrastructure, compound global geometries of power, with their own centers and peripheries relying on legacies of economic imbalances, political invisibility, and colonial relations. In the case of eastern Estonia, this opaque industry displays a continuity with the extractive activities historically present in the region, the asymmetric integration within global capitalism, and the widespread secrecy and alienation. As a result, Ida-Virumaa has the best climate for technological innovation: already polluted, with an oversized energy infrastructure ("industrial heritage"), demographically half-empty and populated by disempowered people afraid of unemployment, while remaining semi-peripheral in geopolitical and financial terms.

CONCLUSION
An Outside Inside

We know so little about the world underneath—low and in the shadows. When you step into a basement, bunker, or mining excavation, you seem to have just landed from another planet. The gesture of descending into the cold and wet regions of the earth relates to a tradition of revelation, wonder, and rebirth, allowing us to look at the world from another inside.[1] That is why the subterranean is associated with creativity, non-judgment, and preservation. And that is why totalitarian authorities recurrently attempt to remove or transform those dark corners into spaces to light.

Underground areas have been a hotbed of myths, burials, and stories for millennia. Since antiquity, shadow spaces have hosted cults of initiation, resistance movements, experimental events, and the storing of what is deemed confidential. People need shadow spaces in which to keep certain things in the dark—things that should not be visible or cannot be said, things that might gain a different value through the work of time, things concealed underground so we can present a clean picture elsewhere or in front of others.

Many things can disappear behind the curtains, back in the lair, under the bed, locked in a drawer, or between the pages of this book. Then, some kind of Aladdin has to come and open the mouth of the cave with his magic command, "Open sesame!" Stories of human journeys into darkness are as old as cave painting and literature itself. Few of them present happy endings, however. On old Babylonian cuneiform tablets, the dark infernal regions are typically referred to as subterranean. For the Maya, caves were the entrances to the underworld. In the Epic of Gilgamesh and in the myth of Orpheus, the underworld appears as a shadowy reality of life on earth, the realm of twisted dreams from which it is impossible to escape.

A hideout is a space where treasures are deposited alongside secrets and refusal. There, we can deploy oblique glances toward power and the normative culture, thinking beyond the dominant channel of recognition. A hideout operates as a device for deviation and disappearance, connecting us to deeper existential questions. Knowing how to hide certainly has its payoffs. Indeed, the function of a hideout is not only to conceal but also to afford an opportunity to think and transform yourself. It is in this vein, perhaps, that both Søren Kierkegaard and Henry David Thoreau noted that those who do not have a proper place to hide are incapable of enjoying a good life.[2] Both safety and well-being relate to the mastering of shades, accountability, and the very terms of our public persona. This book points in that direction, foregrounding the idea that hiding is also an attempt to enact another order to the world, even if temporary or illusory.

Anthropologists have been advocating for a reclamation of secrecy and deviation as holding a transformative potential—from shamans to ghosts, tricksters, jokers, coyotes and parasites, figures of epistemic subversion, those existing at the margin, in the cracks. Indeed, we have traditionally attended to different forms of concealment and liminal practices in order to access alternative notions of personhood and worlds of relation. Nevertheless, there seems to be a renewed fascination with concealment and places at the margin that matter but cannot be comprehended to the end. Corners, hideouts, and other shadow spaces provide a necessary flexibility to ordering and defining processes. But what is the intrigue behind current acts of disappearing? And why do they raise so many red flags in our society?

Hideouts are sites for ambiguity and non-aligned knowledge, where the quality of being open to more than one interpretation is preserved. They make possible a purposeful uncertainty of meaning, allowing us to reckon with the limits of relationality and visibility. While not found, we can test multiple sides of the self and redesign how we are in the world. Hideouts might be considered intervals that both separate and connect, generating diverse notions of relationality across time and space. In this way, hiding reveals the reversibility of the outside and the inside. After all, to withdraw oneself socially is just another way of relating to the same whole.

As humans often want to hoard some things only for themselves, people build closets, basements, and pockets. These devices encourage opacity and deception but also facilitate the transmission of knowledge and complex engagement with time and exchange. We just have to check inside the respective pockets. Little treasures, big lies, evidence of desires and hopes—they can all disappear within us, along with car keys, credit cards, purses, house keys, workplace ID cards, and smartphones. The things we carry with us on a daily basis reveal many of the complex intricacies of our lives, creating a personal cosmos in miniature hidden in our pockets.[3]

Secrets and shadows make us human. In certain contexts, they are a natural resource for those precariously positioned in the present, operating as ligaments or suturing points within too tightly arranged public spheres. Concealment is indeed an effective social tool for managing complicated relations and forms of belonging—not in direct or open opposition to the dominant expressions of power but in some sense converging with them (hence, not antisocial but playing a compensatory role to public interactions). Likewise, the gesture of refusing to yield an account of ourselves or to reveal a secret potentially redistributes what can be perceived in public. That is why Simmel referred to secrecy as "one of the greatest accomplishments of humanity. . . . [S]ecrecy procures enormous extension of life, because with publicity many sorts of purposes could never arrive at realization."[4] Nonetheless, he indicated that the modern progress and evolution in social organization would cause secrecy to disappear in favor of relations of confidentiality (closer to science and the credit economy). Still, situated forms of secrecy and opacity remain essential to the functioning of systems, even today. And for certain individuals or groups, concealment and illegibility are a necessary protective device in the effort to avoid oppression or pain.[5]

Secrecy is not just about concealment; it also aims at opening up alternative forms of relationship and discussion. In this way, the skillset of shadows has to do with disrupting someone else's view. We can identify, historically and cross-culturally, different devices facilitating opacity. The most obvious case is, perhaps, the wearing of masks. We can also bring to light the working of a folding screen: by dividing a room, this device gives us the chance to differentiate the whole into separate areas, even if the space does not change as such. The folding screen generates a shadow, a separation inaccessible to the eyes of others which unavoidably triggers our embodied imagination. By doing so, it both hides and brings together, creating an outside inside.[6]

Hideouts allow people, things, and also non-human creatures to disappear or to be illegible while remaining linked. Deploying a sideways glance at institutions and making oneself illegible to the eyes of the state is, indeed, a normal situation. It is a form of refusal toward the symbolic or material elements of dominant configurations and a way of negotiating how power is culturally internalized through structures of feeling.[7] As saying no might have the effect of undermining ongoing policies, relatively powerless groups find shadow spaces and deploy practices of refusal that are often private or actively covert. Expressions of refusal constitute a stoppage in our relation to the state, opening new kinds of infrapolitical spaces, some of them as mundane as a garage, a basement, or an allotment garden. For this reason, the understanding of everyday life as a field of refusal expands the possible forms of resistance while limiting those of domination.

The Other Estonians

This ethnography has attempted to capture the structure of feeling in Ida-Virumaa over thirty years after the Soviet collapse by speaking from the region and by speaking to its residents. In doing so, I have learned about the nation's dominion over ordinary domains established by prioritizing monolingualism, affirming cultural supremacy, and making claims to historical and political discontinuity. People such as Katja, Semjon, Dmitri, and Jelena have been living for decades on borderlines within the nation-state. In the context of Estonia, they are second-class citizens in a country that privileges and values ethnic Estonians only.[8] Nonetheless, these people have a strong identification with their respective localities, to the territory where they bring a cultural shift by creating their own community-bonding activities and narratives of continuity, despite the fact that their efforts are not free from self-defeat, frustrations, contradictions, and uncertainty.[9]

Different demographic, geopolitical, historical, ethnic, and economic factors make eastern Estonia a critical zone of translation and divergence. The long history of mining and the radical political shifts over the last century left the region in a state of environmental, infrastructural, and social estrangement, with mine shafts underground, abandoned Soviet facilities, outmigration, stench, as well as a population that does not meet expectations about what it means to be a citizen of Estonia. Hence, this book renders Ida-Virumaa as a socio-ecological lab but also as the shadow reflection of Estonian identity and the success story of the country as a transparent, digital, European republic nicely integrated within global capital flows. Indeed, Ida-Virumaa stands as a blind spot in Estonia, and the people of this region are trapped in their status as a problem in the current nation-state, being in need of integration before they can become equal members of the community.[10] They are the other Estonians, a part of the country that is demanded to existentially adapt to the normative rest. Indeed, despite doing research in Eastern Estonia for a decade, I have never met anything resembling "the Russian minority," but a variety of groups of people with diverse ethnic, economic, and cultural backgrounds and differently positioned in relation to the state and official institutions.

The Soviet idea of progress, built around the exploitation of natural resources and military power, attracted a large number of young Soviet citizens who moved here as workers and stayed. Nowadays, they are regarded as remnants of the Communist past, unable to find their place in independent Estonia and often being asked to "go home" in ordinary settings such as a café. After the Russian attack on Ukraine, identity politics got more tense and the population management tighter too.[11] Nowadays, the agency of the domestic others is officially deployed in security-related frames that foreground an incomplete belonging. Citizenship laws, language requirements, and fears of Moscow's influence turn the presence of the Russian-speaking population into a geopolitical "problem."

In March 2025, the Estonian Parliament (Riigikogu) voted in favor of amending the Constitution to revoke the right of any third country nationals to vote in local elections. The stateless persons living in the country, those holding gray passports, will also be affected. They are officially addressed as a threat to national security even though there is no pro-Russian political party in Estonia and the few cultural and civic organizations active in Ida-Virumaa are rather critical to Putin's regime and the military invasion of Ukraine (with the exception of the Russian Orthodox Church). Hence, it is not simply language that turns the other Estonians into a minority, but also how these groups of people are framed within the actual nation-state. Accordingly, one of the novelties introduced by this ethnography has been to approach the residents of Ida-Virumaa as just Estonians, instead of referring to them as a minority (a term never used by the people I met in the region).

Historically, states have worked toward the placement of people, tying political subjects to fixed identity categories and locations.[12] In the case of Ida-Virumaa since 1991, these processes seemed to be directed toward unbinding people and territory while unmaking the institutions that had been working until then. In turn, the residents of this region faced the need to come to terms with the void left by the reconfiguration of mining activity (also a question of identity), by the restructuring of industrial activities, and by the dismantling of state-supported services. All of these radical changes, along with ethnic divisions, produced a sense of a loss of social coordinates, especially among those who had found their identity within the old collective. Eventually, the asymmetric integration of this region within the global circulation of energy commodities, its place as an *other* in the actual nation-state, the industrial extraction of natural resources, the historical relocation of entire communities, and military destruction have contributed to the spread of these negative feelings.

The legacies of extractivist colonialism are certainly an impossible inheritance, not simply unsettled but ultimately uncontainable, and they continue to shape horizons of expectation in the region. But the book does not simply pay attention to the enduring effects of extractivism and how infrastructure from the past is hard to fit into the present; it is above all concerned with the local population and their relation with the territory. This ethnography has therefore studied different forms of refusal of prescribed affiliations through a series of shadow spaces and relations of secrecy. The research delved into the ways in which ordinary activities of concealment and opacity practiced by the region's present-day population constitute particular forms of sociality and how these give us insight into political alterity and things that do not disappear properly. In Ida-Virumaa, secrecy and illegibility are partly rooted in the dramatic events of the twentieth century and the colonization that extractivist activities demand, but they are also mobilized to cope with the sense of an emptied-out future, cultural loss, and incomplete belonging in the present.

The performative disengagement among locals does not entail belief in something else or comfort in the position of disbelief; rather, it manifests the refusal to occupy the subject position offered to them, displaying an opaque agency in a frame of reference that they feel as alien and unfair. In certain contexts, hiding can be a form of defiance of authority, where individuals or communities choose to conceal their true selves or resist visibility to protect themselves. The void felt among Russian speakers and their refusal to accept national representations or engage with state institutions are not merely the results of fantasies of imperial greatness. Today, these feelings are enduring effects of state marginalization and resource extractivism, which have left elements of the population with a pervasive sense of worthlessness and homelessness.

Concealment has indeed important political dimensions, influencing how people interact with their realities. It can represent opacity in the negotiation of power dynamics as well as function as a symbolic act in different cultures. For this reason, there was a need to think through the relations between people, infrastructure, and the territory to understand how secrets remain co-constitutive of the social order and contribute in particular ways to the accommodation of cultural differences. In Ida-Virumaa, where people are simultaneously estranged from this place and attached to it, secrecy also becomes synonymous with illegibility, as a subjective indication of unwillingness to be represented (holding multiple internal positions at once), and as a form of withdrawal while remaining not totally outside society or relations.[13] Here, cultural hybridity is not just publicly performed or mimicked but rather kept in the dark, away from the eyes of others. Eventually this gesture questions seeing Estonian society as monolithic and always consensual.[14] By emphasizing the kinds of relationalities constitutive of and constituted by secrecy, this ethnography has demonstrated that social order is something that needs to be constantly produced and stabilized. It has also pointed out that secrecy and refusal operate as affiliative forms of critique, thus working as factors of social organization and the accommodation of difference. But even if these dissonant practices can offer self-assertion and resistance, they often entail little coordination among the dominated social groups.[15]

Identity is never something we find and then retain forever, but rather a dynamic "we" continually work through, sometimes publicly and visibly, and other times silently and in the shadows. Likewise, identity presupposes a sense of location and kinship with others, deeply embedded in historical narratives and cultural practices that shape how individuals relate to their territories and to other groups.[16] Hence, the study of complicated processes of belonging requires a finer recognition of the liminal spaces of negotiation and the disjunctive input of hybrid counter-energies. In doing so, this book contributes to actual discussions of decolonization, being part of a wider exercise of identifying and eventually un-making asymmetric relations and imaginaries, often taken as common sense.[17]

As this book has shown, the gesture of keeping things in the dark plays an important role in the iterative ordering and adjustment of personal identity, family relations, belonging, and wider political and technological transforma-tions. Yet keeping things in the dark is not just a metaphor but a complex process in which people engage to make part of their lived reality opaque. Therefore, this ethnography of secrecy has explored various strategies, such as refusal and concealment, used by individuals marginalized from the national mainstream to navigate sociopolitical change. Secrecy is not tantamount to an absence of relationality or of rationality per se; rather, it is a way of marking difference and ambiguity. Thus, a study of such practices and spaces might uncover complex dynamics of social interaction and identity formation. Indeed, concealment is a political act insofar as it is intended to influence the actions of others and creates new relationalities. Therefore, hideouts are not antisocial but expand the poros-ity of belonging, thus acting as a suture allowing us to be part of relations while simultaneously resisting them.

We keep things in the dark for the purpose of editing the self and ordering social relationships. Nevertheless, and perhaps because refusers often do not explicitly declare their refusal, contemporary forms of opacity have not received the attention they deserve, even though they play a critical role in animating soci-ality and anchoring our identity. Shadow spaces and things that are not in their proper place also create social order; they are constitutive themselves of a par-ticular sociality. This take on the materiality of secrecy and illegibility expands Mary Douglas's ideas about how societies maintain a representational order by denoting what is out of place.[18] For Douglas, thinking about dirt implies both a set of ordered relations and contraventions of them, so elements of divergence are also structurally and symbolically needed for the maintenance of social order. Yet matter that is rejected and referred to as "out of place" can be potentially dan-gerous and question prevailing classifications with its clinging half-identity. As a result, all that contradicts or refuses what frames our seeing has to be eradicated or made invisible.

Where there is a basement, garage, or pocket, there is a system, since any given organization requires some sort of boundary and separation to keep it

operational. By putting something out of sight, societies demarcate the territory where certain people and ideas do not belong—indicating the content of
the possible in an act of power. That classificatory gesture, however, might have
a boomerang effect: when things are oppressively tight and ordered, ambivalence and secrecy then spread socially as a form of compensation. In this way,
a secret is more than a piece of withheld knowledge; it is a surplus of living,
the manifestation of an excess. Similarly, the shadow spaces of our societies can
also be taken as a by-product of the systematic ordering of modernity. Sociologist Zygmunt Bauman has pointed in that direction, describing modernity as an
ideology characterized by the incessant attempt to create meaning and keep the
world categorized, presenting ambivalence as the unavoidable side effect of this
ordering obsession.[19]

This book, however, is not strictly a refusal of modern visibility and planning but rather a critique of it. It focuses on understanding people, places, and
things that are perceived as out of place and time, often relegated to a liminal
corner as disruptions to the social order. In short, we need zones of divergence,
even though they may be culturally challenging and a source of social anxiety.
These insights eventually contradict the claims for celebrating transparency and
placelessness as an emancipatory strategy of empowerment. Social order is still
made and unmade in hideouts such as basements, bunkers, and garages. Shadow
spaces are recursively arranged to favor an illegible presence through the eyes of
those who dominate, thus allowing us to enjoy alternative notions of value and
representation.

The well-being of our communities might depend on the depth and density
of the interstices that facilitate adaptation, areas in which to recursively host all
that cannot be reduced: the visceral, uncanny, and dissonant.[20] Indeed, traditional accounts of the dark side have noted that the form of concealment, the
hideout, is often more important than the content of secrets; in other words, how
the secret is told and managed, and the way in which it takes place and unfolds
through time, makes a difference.[21] Still, the form of concealment requires maintenance. Furthermore, the ever-increasing datafication of everyday life across the
world, with its tracking and mining, is making the decision to hide more complex
(and difficult).[22] That is why in 2014 the EU approved the "right to be forgotten,"
which relies on the legal idea that one can demand the removal of data about oneself that is accessible online as a form of securing one's digital privacy. Here we are
talking of the capacity to keep our autonomy within social networks, as well as
about organizational control and corporations that capitalize on us and develop
algorithms based on our tastes and lifestyles. The bad news, however, is that such
a way of navigating transparency and managing visibility can hardly be the result

of the absence of any work or "inoperosity."[23] Rather, it requires a skillful oscillation between openness and closure, refusal and engagement, concealment and revealing, knowledge and non-knowledge.

The right to be forgotten can be placed alongside the right to opacity and also with the right to fail, since ambivalence and the possibility of tinkering with different faces of the self are constitutive of human freedom. Eventually, practices of secrecy and opacity challenge the institutional shift toward transparency, neoliberal notions of accountability, and the overwhelming digital exposure that have transformed our attentional practices.[24] Accordingly, opacity and secrecy are presented as different ways of sorting out the asymmetries in knowledge, power, and economy.

Ecological Memory

The disposal system of the Auvere power plant involves washing ash away with water, which is stored in a lagoon situated twenty-nine kilometers from the Russian border. The mesmerizing blue color of the lagoon is due to light-reflecting particles of limestone and carbonate deposits from the ash that is produced from burning oil shale in the power plants and is flushed with water into the dump. The blue color is just an alkaline mask, hiding all toxicity beneath. To foreign eyes, the setting may resemble an Estonian Maldives. Ash itself is not dangerous, but the water in these ponds has a high pH (12.5); therefore, prolonged contact with it is corrosive and harmful to health.[25] Thus, this highly alkaline water has to be contained no matter how much it rains or snows. In addition to the closed system of pipes and canals, five workers monitor for leaks 24/7. Despite its potential toxicity, there are no restrictions on access to the pond, say, to bury a set of documents on its shore. Running alongside the blue lagoon, there is an unpaved road that leads to a small dacha area. Enefit, the owner of the energy plant, would prefer to have the road closed, but that is not possible, since it is still used by residents (around fifty in total). Local legend says that they have the most beautiful gardens in Narva, because the ash filters into the ground and makes flowers and vegetables grow bigger.

The oil shale infrastructure is a legacy on which thousands of people depend in the short term, but it restricts their well-being and alternative orders in the medium term. In other words, while opening up new possibilities, this burdensome legacy (and its array of externalities) simultaneously closes, or disenables, others.[26] Mining changed the sociality of eastern Estonia and left behind negative commons, such as polluting industries and contaminated rivers and soils. But it also facilitated phenomena such as institutional mistrust, collective loss, pollution, and dispossession. Eventually, the shadow of oil shale extraction shows that ecological memory is a social and cultural phenomenon, not only an environmental one.

Indeed, mining does not simply signal a series of means to occupy space economically; it is, ultimately, a culture: a represented power on the ground that limits the conditions for the emergence of another order and exceeds the direct consequences of its harmful operations.[27] Our encounter with the underground is based on factors that are not only economic but also sentimental, scenic, and atmospheric.[28] In that sense, we can also study the territory in terms of relationships and affect. For instance, our ecological memory includes the senses of smell, hearing, taste, and touch, not just sight and maps. Our identity indeed happens in the middle of motion, echoes, traces, and smells, which become an agent within the active and passive negotiation of power, memory, and belonging. Nonetheless, the territory affected by mining activities is most often experienced as one of radical alterity, as an alienating agent refusing the human gesture toward connection and not fitting within the existing relational frameworks.[29]

In an extractivist culture, mineralogical and inorganic elements generate relations and processes that have an impact on the social despite being indifferent to its logics.[30] But how to represent this form of ecological memory? I investigated it through the art installation *Greetings from Another Land and Another Time* (Contemporary Art Museum of Estonia, 2019). Along with curator Marika Agu, I gathered a number of postcards from the early twentieth century that represented landscapes soon to be sacrificed to the mining and chemical industries in Ida-Virumaa—a *terra nullius* created by humans at the altar of modernization. Valleys, mills, meadows, pastures, and trails were eliminated to develop an infrastructural grid that lies partly underground (pipes, tunnels, wires). The irreversible destruction of landscapes evidenced the mineral, logistic, and military character of Soviet modernity but also of the Anthropocene overall, presenting resource exploitation as an inevitable element of progress and civilization. We also included postcards from the Soviet era. As technologies of exposure, and through three-dimensional storytelling, they hide some aspects by overexposing others. Their visual language, however, stressed the importance of using nature as a resource, with model cities such as Kohtla-Järve presented as a symbol of progress.[31]

In an extractivist understanding, knowledge of the underground is a means toward perfecting the exploitation of land. But land can be understood and made meaningful in many ways.[32] While explorations of faraway territories were the cornerstone of colonialism and early anthropology, there is a need to unearth the strange and devastated sites of our present, in many cases not that far from where we live. Modern relationships between humans and the world remain largely extractive themselves, but there are other ways of knowing, as many as forms of making relations. Hence, I created an art installation in which nature was called on to do the representational work in a hybrid epistemic gesture. Five documents from the former School Number 1 of Sillamäe were buried for three weeks in the area where the uranium factory used to be (now processing rare earth materials), and another five documents were submerged for a day in the alkaline waters of the poisonous blue lagoon of the Auvere power plant. Cataracts of toxic time began soaking through the documents. The tortured aesthetics were achieved by external elements, such as leaks, rainfall, material interactions, mineral mutations, and bacterial interventions, in addition to the spirit of the place, of course.

The *Territory* art project helped me to implicate the non-relationality of polluted and stigmatized territories in the relationality of the present. This installation is the result of an experimental collaboration with the soil and water of eastern Estonia in an attempt to represent the underground as opaque and refusing human domination, instead of empty, transparent, and available to sociotechnical engineering.[33] The unstable and contingent artistic expression enacted other epistemologies of transience, suspension, and connection through more-than-human aesthetics. Indeed, I did not know what the images would look like once dug up.

FIGURE C.1.   View of the installation *Territory*. Photo: Joosep Kivimäe, 2024.

To practice ethnographic research in the dark underground, however, might challenge our presumed ability to *see* knowledge, since it breaks down the anthropological method of participant observation.[34] Overall, the installation does not necessarily represent the region but makes present its ecological memory—the alienating repercussion of extractivist industries and the vernacular ways of dealing with it. Here, humans and the land have not held hands for over a century; on the contrary, one tried to break the other's arm arrogantly. The result is that landscapes are not on the scale of our embodied perception and recollection, forming a relationship of strangeness older than memory. An impossible inheritance that, nevertheless, continues to shape the horizons of those who live in the region, conditioning, in turn, present and future systemic responses. A way of understanding this dark ecological memory is by studying how the past events of violence and extractivist activities in Ida-Virumaa frame the present responses of the local community, constituting both particular ecological equations and new kinds of relations between people and with the state. In this way, we can talk of a particular ecological memory, a concept that refers to how environmental representations and practices are spread over a given territory and dispersed among its residents.[35]

For me, as social researcher, the issue also has to do with how we generate and share knowledge about people who are linked to one another and to the territory in entangled ways. One way of doing so is to approach ethnographic research as derived not only from social interactions but also from non-human ones. Indeed, we also need to reconsider what our research actually gives back to the world and the learning that this action might entail. This has important methodological implications, and it suggests practicing a more reciprocal relation with the localities and people in the field instead of adopting an extractive attitude toward the world. Extractivism in turn is a practice of taking without depositing, of removing without giving anything back. Édouard Glissant, for instance, criticized the importance of the verb "to grasp" within modern epistemology, as if things were just awaiting human domination.[36] In the act of grasping, the movement of the hands reproduces a gesture of extracting and holding, thus of appropriation. In contrast to extracting, depositing is characterized by additions, mutation, and hybridization, producing border-transgressing materialities in turn. This gesture of letting be is paradoxically similar to the underground processes that have affected the formation of oil shale and uranium, minerals that gave form to the landscape and the sociality of this region in the last century through their extraction and industrialization.

This book summons readers to think about the heterogeneity of place-making practices in a liminal corner of the world, extending an invitation for further

cross-disciplinary dialogue on topics that are not often connected, such as mining, transparency, and reified notions of the nation-state. It thus expands how we
locate culture, politics, and infrastructure, connecting spatial separation with the
question of belonging and social order. Ethnographic considerations of our way
of standing on a given territory provide insights about the performative character
of our sense of place, the way sentiments of belonging and inclusion have material resonances, and the need for localizing some kind of order in space and time.

Still, secrecy and opacity unfold over places, within situated relations and
infrastructure, in some cases upsetting modern planning, state oversight, and
the calculative technopolitics of visibility.[37] The study of basements, garages,
holes, dachas, and bunkers underlined the importance of sites where opacity and
secrecy find space, away from the eyes of others, and therefore away from institutional sight and control. These shadow spaces are useful for presenting oneself
to others. When you dramatize your own identity in order to be part of social
relationships, as Goffman said, you need certain tools or spaces for it. There is,
indeed, a certain theatricality in the use of basements, garages, and dachas, as
if it were a performance; but that does not make the effect, the surplus, any less
real. Reality arises from interactions, not from essences; that's why social order is
intrinsically vulnerable.

Secrecy and opacity are part of these ordinary practices wherein cultural differences are embedded. This curbed position vis-à-vis institutions and the state
is not necessarily adversarial, however, but rather oblique. Therefore, strategies
of opacity and secrecy are part of a functional adaptation: they help preserve different sides of the self in a context of precarity and enable individuals to anchor
themselves to the whole on their own terms. As we have seen throughout this
book, secrecy is about inventive ways of relating to a whole, and the hidden and
disguise are associated with refusal and the denial of legibility. What this research
demonstrates, however, is that territories remain important as a cultural process
and as a way of arranging social relations. In other words, sociality emerges not
only from within the relations among individuals, or between individuals and
institutions, but also contingently out of topological representations.

This book has thus shown that places continue to play an important organizing role in our relationships. It explains how practices of concealment and illegibility unfold in a particular kind of topology seeking to bypass the state and its
institutions in ways that are about not struggle but opacity. Part of our public life
is deposited in these opaque contact zones, with multiple incorporations, gatherings, and attachments that happen in a not always conscious way. By looking
at how shadow spaces are enacted and their role in the articulation of belonging
and cultural distinction, we can better understand how people make room for
alternative regimes of visibility and the multiple instances of social adaptation

at large. In their opacity, shadow spaces favor an illegible presence in the eyes of those who dominate. Therefore, I conclude that (1) in our overwhelmingly digital world, concealment still needs a place; (2) secrecy is not external to society but constitutive of social relations; (3) transparency does not make secrets disappear altogether; rather, it demands new hideouts.

Now what remains is to invent a protocol for ending things nicely, an art of closure for what has been harmful while lasting years and years.

Knock, knock. "Close sesame!"

Acknowledgments

Throughout the process of preparing this ethnography, I have worked in seven different academic institutions. Academic life can be easy but also not. Writing a book like this required time, dedication, and a certain level of obsession as well as the generosity of many people, who compensate for the spiritual stinginess of many others.

During my research, I collaborated with three Estonian artists—Viktor Gurov, Anna Škodenko, and Darja Popolitova—on several exhibitions. To prepare the artworks, we visited various places in the region together, observing the invisible, all the while making connections between personal biographies and collective discourses. This kind of expanded ethnography had two epistemic implications, one outward and another inward. The outward one suggests that collaborations in the field do not have to be limited to the level of practice but can also promote a shared analytical outcome, such as, for instance, an art installation. The inward implication, in turn, is that experimental collaborations might involve not remaining an anthropologist in some of the stages of the research, borrowing epistemic positions and leaving behind disciplinary frames when necessary.

Likewise, another important part of the research was also performed with two urbanists: Keiti Kljavin and Andra Aaloe. Perhaps because they work on the margins of academia, their insights were always refreshing. Without them, this book would not have been the same, or perhaps even possible. *Aitäh!* More people have supported my waka journey along the way. Special thanks to Siobhan Kattago and Patrick Laviolette, supervisors forever, still giving advice about how to remain in the game. Also to Tomás S. Criado and Adolfo Estalella, engaged companions in discussion on anthropological issues and much more. To Pablo Zerm, whose sharp feedback always makes a difference. And to my Estonian *güey* Dirk Lloyd.

Indeed, kindness must be recognized, and Semjon Krasulin was very generous in helping me in the field when possible; the same goes for Jelena Antusheva, Dmitri Bolotov, Dmitri Fedotkin, Ekaterina Grafova, Svetlana Ivanova, Andrei Mitkovets, Meelis Muhu, and Jelena Mutonen. At the risk of omitting some names, special thanks are also due to Ieva Astahovska, Eeva Berglund, Alex Bieth, Mar Canet, Salva Cayuela, Mike Cole, Nuno Correia, Max Dade, Tomás Errázuriz, Sarah Green, Igors Gubenko, Guy Julier, Liisa Kaljula, Eerika

Koskinen-Koivisto, Pille Kruus, Eléonore de Montesquiou, Liene Ozoliņa, Gabor Szirko, and Jonas Tinius.

Noblesse oblige, my gratitude to Giorgi Cheishvili, Alina Jašina-Schäfer, Katie Kilroy-Marac, and Kiven Strohm for writing a noble endorsement. Also to the brilliant team at Cornell University Press, whose accurate work made this book much better. And, of course, to my Spanish family for being so warm and supportive.

Research for this publication was financially supported by the European Union: first, by my project "EUROREPAIR: Europeanisation Through Repair" (MOBERC30) at Tallinn University; and second by the WasteMatters project (ERC grant number 101043572), led by Olli Pyyhtinen at Tampere University. In its late stages, it was also supported by the Ramón y Cajal Research Excellence Program of the Spanish State, hosted by the University of Murcia.

Notes

PREFACE

1. Simmel also noted the growing fluidization of the social experience and the multiplication of fragmented spaces with a strong symbolic character. Georg Simmel, "The Sociology of Sociability," *American Journal of Sociology* 55 (1949): 254–61.

2. Erving Goffman, *The Presentation of Self in Everyday Life* (1959; Penguin, 1990).

3. Forming a sense of privacy that allows communities to share and preserve secrets. See Édouard Glissant, *Poetics of Relation* (University of Michigan Press, 1997), 191.

4. Victor Turner, *The Ritual Process: Structure and Anti-structure* (Aldine, 1969), 95.

5. H. G. Wells, *The Invisible Man* (1897; Bantam, 1983).

6. Ralph Ellison, *Invisible Man* (Random House, 1952), 3.

7. Erving Goffman, *Stigma: Notes on the Management of Spoiled Identity* (Simon & Schuster, 1963), 148–49, 138.

8. Fyodor Dostoyevsky, *Notes from Underground* (1864; Vintage, 1994).

9. Santiago Alba Rico, *Catorce palabras para después del capitalismo* (Contexto, 2023), 53.

10. Carl Jung, *The Red Book* (W. W. Norton, 2009).

11. J. M. Barrie, *Peter Pan* (1911; Penguin, 2004).

12. Adelbert von Chamisso, *La maravillosa historia de Peter Schlemihl* (1814; Nordica, 2013).

13. Hans Christian Andersen, *"La sombra" y otros cuentos* (Alianza, 2001).

14. For the tale, see Tim Horvath, "The Discipline of Shadows," *Conjunctions* 53 (2009): 293–311. And anthropologist Tomás S. Criado has turned this fictional idea into reality. For more information about the department, see https://umbrology.org.

15. Plato's allegory of the cave is in book 7 of *The Republic*.

16. But was the cave a cage or a stage, asks philosopher Siobhan Kattago. Perhaps the people inside the cave had freely chosen the fate of gazing solely at the opposite wall, since semblance and idols (simulacra) are more comfortable and entertaining to watch than the painful sun. Siobhan Kattago, "All the World's a Stage . . . or a Cage," in *Playgrounds and Battlefields*, ed. Francisco Martínez and Klemen Slabina (Tallinn University Press, 2014), 65–84.

17. Different scholars have noted how privacy is in dire need of protection. For instance, see B. Herlo et al., eds., *Practicing Sovereignty* (Transcript, 2021); and R. Kelomees, V. Guljajeva, and O. Laas, eds., *The Meaning of Creativity in the Age of AI* (Estonian Academy of Arts, 2022). Additionally, the lockdown and confinement brought by COVID-19 drew attention to new problems of visibility. Interestingly, during the quarantine we discovered that our homes were more transparent and virtually stretchable than ever before. See F. Martínez, E. Berglund, and A. Estalella, "Anthropology of/at/from Home: Introduction," *Entanglements* 3 (2020): 39–43; and T. Khalvashi and N. Aivazishvili-Gehne, "The Pandemic (Day)dreams," *Entanglements* 4 (2021): 207–13.

18. To know more about how to deal with invisible forces that are capable of tracking our moves even when we are sleeping, see V. Peacock, "Writing Opacity: Going Beyond Pseudonyms with Spirit Portraiture," *Political and Legal Anthropology Review* 47 (2024): 90–97.

19. Matias Serra Bradford, "La tentación de no volver," *Oropel* 2023, accessed March 2024, https://revistaoropel.cl/index.php/2023/08/02/la-tentacion-de-no-volver-por-matias-serra-bradford/.

20. Visibility and attention are presented as a currency and also as a resource that can be optimized, hence made stretchable and plastic. For example, media theorist Yves Citton proposes that instead of asking what we should be attentive to, we might also try to explore what to do with our attention, thus taking attention as a form of action rather than a property. See Yves Citton, *For an Ecology of Attention* (Polity, 2017); also M. Pedersen, K. Albris, and N. Seaver, "The Political Economy of Attention," *Annual Review of Anthropology* 50 (2021): 309–25.

21. R. Sansi and M. Strathern, "Art and Anthropology After Relations," *HAU: Journal of Ethnographic Theory* 6 (2016): 425–39.

22. Svetlana Boym, *The Off-Modern* (Bloomsbury, 2017).

23. Carole McGranahan, "Theorizing Refusal: An Introduction," and "Refusal and the Gift of Citizenship," *Cultural Anthropology* 31, no. 3 (2016): 319–25 and 334–41.

INTRODUCTION

1. A plaque bore the inscription "There is a message [inside] from the residents of the city of Kohtla-Järve to be opened in 2046. It was buried during a citywide rally of workers on the 25th anniversary of the city. 26.VI.1971," written in both Estonian and Russian.

2. Longer versions of the message include wording such as "A historical milestone—25 years—is for us the outcome of the past and the beginning of the work ahead. In the name of V. I. Lenin, and following the call of the Communists, we create socialism with our own hands, and our work is the basis for the transition to the complete victory of Communism. Of those present here, only the youngest will survive until the centenary of the city," and "Those who started the construction work—of both socialism and our city—will see it for centuries. But it doesn't mean that we won't see the future. Because we see it now and, in its name, we work, live, and breathe! But what does it mean to see tomorrow today? . . . For 25 years, the city has grown; it has become what you can see partly in the photo in the attached issue of today's city newspaper. . . . For the sake of this, we wish great happiness to future generations and say: 'A new day is coming, a new work is beginning.'" For more, see T. Linnard, *Dva Nepyushikh* [The Two Sober Ones] (Retro Järve, 2002), accessed July 2023. Artist Anna Škodenko also engaged with the hidden message in her installation *The Past of the Future*, staging different encounters with the capsule in the exhibition "Keeping Things in the Dark Again" (EKA Gallery, 2023). While the forms resonate with the chimneys that characterize the cityscape of the region, the very way that she crafted the diorama—a trompe l'oeil sort of device—seems to claim that we may know the past the way we know animals.

3. Walter Youngquist, "Oil Shale," in *WEC Survey of Energy Resources,* World Energy Council, 2001, accessed February 2024, https://www.worldenergy.org/assets/downloads/PUB_Survey-of-Energy-Resources_2001_WEC.pdf

4. Roy Wagner, *The Invention of Culture* (University of Chicago Press, 1981).

5. Marcel Mauss, *The Gift* (1925; W. W. Norton, 1967).

6. Susan L. Star, "The Ethnography of Infrastructure," *American Behavioral Scientist* 43 (1999): 377–91; Brian Larkin, "The Politics and Poetics of Infrastructure," *Annual Review of Anthropology* 42 (2013): 327–43.

7. Oil shale generates 57 percent of the country's electrical power through the combustion of the burning stone. Five oil shale mines remain in operation: three are open-pit mines and two are underground mines. Indeed, the oil shale industry contributes almost 5 percent of the GDP of Estonia. Likewise, 61.7 percent of waste in Estonia is generated by

mining and energy production activities. Eastern Estonia has the lowest life expectancy at birth, highest at-risk-of-poverty rate, highest early mortality rate, above average mortality due to external causes, and the highest incidence rate of hepatitis, tuberculosis, and sexually transmitted diseases in the country. See the overview of health and well-being, 2021, https://tai.ee/sites/default/files/2021-03/134985843965_4_Ida-Viru_county_over view_ENG.pdf, accessed February 2024.

8. The factory was designed by the German engineering company Julius Pintsch AG.

9. Namely, Estländische Steinöl (German), New Consolidated Gold Fields (British), and Estländska oljeskifferkonsortiet (Swedish).

10. Märt Raud, *Põlevkivi ja põlevkivi-tööstus Eestis* [Oil Shale and the Oil Shale Industry in Estonia] (Riigi Põlevkivi-tööstuse kirjastus, 1925); *A/S Esimene Eesti Põlevkivitööstus endine Riigi Põlevkivitööstus, Tagasivaade tööstuse tegevusele ja saavutustele tööstuse XX aastapäeva puhul 25.XI.1938* [A/S Esimene Eesti Põlevkivitööstus, Previously Riigi Põlevkivitööstus: A Retrospective on Activity and Achievements on the Occasion of the Twentieth Anniversary of the Industry, 25.XI.1938] (Esimene Eesti Põlevkivitööstuse kirjastus, 1938); H. Martinson, *Khimiya v Estonii v period burzhuaznoy vlasti* [Chemistry in Estonia During the Bourgeois Regime] (Akademiya nauk ESSR, 1987); Rurik Holmberg, "Survival of the Unfit: Path Dependence and the Estonian Oil Shale Industry" (PhD diss., Linköping University, 2008).

11. Among those who were sent to Siberia, see the case of Märt Raud, who was the director of the Estonian State Oil Shale Industry (Riigi Põlevkivitööstus in Estonian), or that of Karl Luts, who was the director of the chemical laboratory of that organization; or the Estonian Swede Mathias Westerblom, director of the Sillamäe factory. See *Eesti Entsüklopeedia,* vol. 14, accessed July 2024, http://entsyklopeedia.ee/artikkel/esimene_eesti_põlevkivitööstus2; and T. Kirss, E. Kõresaar, and M. Lauristin, eds., *She Who Remembers Survives* (Tartu University Press, 2004).

12. David Vseviov, "Kirde-Eesti urbaanse anomaalia kujunemine ning struktuur pärast Teist maailmasõda" [The Formation and Structure of the Urban Anomaly of Northeastern Estonia After the Second World War] (PhD diss., Tallinn Pedagogical University, 2002).

13. Olaf Mertelsmann, "Ida-Virumaale sisserändamise põhjused pärast teist maailamsõda" [The Reasons for Immigration in the Ida-Virumaa Region after the Second World War], *Ajalooline Ajakiri. The Estonian Historical Journal* 119 (2007), 51–74.

14. Olaf Mertelsmann, "Was There Stalinist Industrialization in the Baltic Republics? Estonia—an Example," in *The Sovietization of the Baltic States, 1940–1956,* ed. Olaf Mertelsmann (Kleio, 2003), 151–70.

15. A. Raukas, "Past pollution and Its Remediation in Estonia," *Baltica* 17 (2004): 71–78.

16. Mertelsmann, *Sovietization of the Baltic States.*

17. Jaak Valge, "Riikliku põlevkivitööstuse majandustingimused ja–tulemused 1920. Ja 1930. aastatel" [The Economic Conditions and Performance of the State Oil Shale Industry in the 1920s and 1930s], *Akadeemia* 8–9 (1995): 1712–40.

18. The life of Osvald Tooming demonstrates well the complexities and suffering in this part of the world during the twentieth century. For instance, the articles he published in newspapers at the time resulted in his arrest by both the Nazis and the Soviets. He also worked as a clerk at the Ubja oil shale mine and published novels about both mining and prison life. See Osvald Tooming and Peeter Tooming, *Maantee kutsub* [Highway Attracts] (Ida-Viru County Government, 1993).

19. Lembit Lauri, *Unrecorded History: Thirteen Interviews with Fellow Estonians* (Tallinn: Perioodika, 1988), 40.

20. The British gang-based television series is set in Birmingham in the aftermath of the First World War.

21. Only fifty-seven of them came from Estonian owners, while Baltic Germans owned most of the rest.

22. Historian Alexander Etkind uses this concept to describe how the Russian state colonized its own people within its own borders. Alexander Etkind, *Internal Colonization: Russia's Imperial Experience* (Polity, 2011).

23. This book is an ethnography of the northeastern part of Estonia, thus not including the municipality of Alutaguse—the southern part of the region, which includes interesting corners and parallel worlds such as the Orthodox Kuremäe Monastery. Ida-Virumaa refers to a broader territory that includes more than just the industrial and Russian-speaking northeast. Nonetheless, in this corner of the country, there are also locations that this book does not cover in detail, such as the new administrative center, Jõhvi (hosting the second-largest prison in the country), or Toila and Oru Park (where the presidential summerhouse used to be). Overall, I use the term "northeast" when referring to a geographical area and "eastern" when referring to a political and cultural reality within Estonia, mentally separated but still part of the country.

24. Aleksandr studied art and design in Moscow, and in 1994 he played a key role in the creation of the Sillamäe Museum, where he worked until his death in 2021.

25. Michael Herzfeld, *Cultural Intimacy: Social Poetics in the Nation-State* (Routledge, 2005).

26. In some cases I was also received as a harbinger, a stranger who foreshadows something to come and might in turn enhance the locals' sense of belonging. One who does not belong to the community but is here among us nonetheless, arriving today and staying tomorrow, opening up a change or initiating an activity. See Georg Simmel, "The Stranger," in Wolff, *The Sociology of Georg Simmel* (Glencoe: The Free Press), 402–8.

27. "Also, I am interested in the surface of words and the performative mixing of established linguistic rules," Darja added, while describing her ideas about giving voice to a mineral. Interview by the Estonian Centre for Contemporary Art in its newsletter, June 2021, https://cca.ee/ajakiri/sel-nadalal-kaevandusmuuseumis-avatakse-naitus-kohanemine-kahanemisega.

28. In the second film of the series, Katja talks with her friend Sasha in the kitchen, disclosing that they always have to consider carefully what to say or not, even with friends.

29. B. Grant, *In the Soviet House of Culture* (Princeton University Press, 1995).

30. Erving Goffman, *Stigma: Notes on the Management of Spoiled Identity* (Simon & Schuster, 1963).

31. See Statistics Estonia 2021, accessed September 2023.

32. E. Balibar, *Politics and the Other Scene* (Verso, 2002).

33. The expression "my negri" (we're "niggers") refers to a sense of non-respectability. It combines the current status of lacking citizenship with a sense of ethnic inferiority; yet this "blackness" also signifies an inferiority vis-à-vis the supposedly superior Estoniaphones, who represent wealth, power, and cultural capital. Other colleagues have also noted the use of this term in their research, for example, E. Kesküla, "Mining Postsocialism: Work, Class, and Ethnicity in an Estonian Mine" (PhD diss., Goldsmiths, University of London, 2012).

34. For example, the "Sign Me Up for Military Service" project (winner of the award for Best Service Design Project in Estonia in 2022), led by Helelyn Tammsaar in cooperation with the Defense Forces of Estonia.

35. Performances of ambiguity show that a simple dichotomy of dominant and subaltern might be analytically limited, if not shallow. For more on postcolonial discussions of post-socialist issues, see Gayatri Chakravorty Spivak, "Can the Subaltern Speak?," in *Marxism and the Interpretation of Culture*, ed. Cary Nelson and Lawrence Grossberg (University of Illinois Press, 1988), 271–313; S. A. Oushakine, "Postcolonial Estrangements: Claiming a Space Between Stalin and Hitler," in *Rites of Place*, ed. J. Buckler and E. D.

Johnson (Northwestern University Press, 2013), 285–314; and L. A. Kaljund, "Orientalism Against Empire: The Paradox of Postcoloniality in Estonia," *Anthropological Quarterly* 91 (2018): 749–70.

36. See the coverage by, for instance, Deutsche Welle, https://www.dw.com/en/estonia-launches-own-russian-language-tv-channel/a-18747088.

37. For more on this discussion, see A. Herbert and B. Gigantino, "The Poverty of Cultural History: Decolonization, Race, and Politics in Post-socialist Studies," *Lefteast* (2024), https://lefteast.org/the-poverty-of-cultural-history-decolonization-race-and-politics-in-post-socialist-studies/.

38. Epp Annus, *Soviet Postcolonial Studies* (Routledge, 2018), 125.

39. Helena Jerman, *The Hidden Minority* (Berghahn, 2025).

40. Through discourse analysis, I studied the key terms used by the Estonian media during the 2010s to refer to Ida-Virumaa, identifying "potential," "pollution," "residues," "ruination," "problems," and "injustice" as significant ones. See, for instance, the journals *ERR* and *Delfi*, nos. 1 and 2.

41. "Keskkonnahoidu mõjutavad maksud Eestis 2021" [Taxes Affecting Environmental Protection in Estonia in 2021], report of the Foresight Centre think tank, accessed July 2024, https://www.riigikogu.ee/wpcms/wp-content/uploads/2021/09/2021_maksustruktuur_keskkond_luhiraport.pdf.

42. Besides acknowledging the pleasure of keeping a secret and the power that such a gesture gives, Simmel also noted the difficult consequences that revealing the "wrong" thing at the "wrong" place to the "wrong" people can have. Georg Simmel, "The Sociology of Secrecy and of Secret Societies," *American Journal of Sociology* 11 (1906): 441–98.

43. Thus revealing hope for something better. See Carole McGranahan, "Theorizing Refusal: An Introduction," and "Refusal and the Gift of Citizenship," *Cultural Anthropology* 31, no. 3 (2016): 319–25 and 334–41; also E. Weiss, "Refusal as Act, Refusal as Abstention," *Cultural Anthropology* 31, no. 3 (2016): 351–58.

44. James Scott, *Domination and the Arts of Resistance* (New Haven: Yale University Press, 1990); James Scott, *Seeing Like a State* (New Haven: Yale University Press, 1998).

45. Bhabha posits cultural hybridity as an in-between area where the cutting edge of translation occurs. In postcolonial critiques, hybridity is described as an epistemological construct that refers to the effects of colonialism on Indigenous people—those of assimilation—but also to subversion, mimicry, and camouflage. Bhabha opened up a space beyond the traditional dichotomies and polarities of "East" and "West," "self" and "other," "master" and "slave" by paying attention to emancipatory practices of reappropriation and translation. More generally, hybridity has been used to refer to a partial construction, a lack of determinacy, and to a process of synthesizing. Bhabha built the concept on Mikhail Bakhtin's notion of the "intentional hybrid." See M. M. Bakhtin, *The Dialogic Imagination* (University of Texas Press, 1981); and Homi K. Bhabha, *The Location of Culture* (Routledge, 1994).

46. N. Ssorin-Chaikov, "The Black Box: Notes on the Anthropology of the Enemy," *Inner Asia* 10 (2008): 37–63.

47. Kharkhordin also argues that subjectivity in the Soviet Union was produced by and in the collective, as the collective sets the public stage for outward manifestation and the individual was defined by our role within the community. Oleg Kharkhordin, *The Collective and the Individual in Russia* (University of California Press, 1999).

48. Erving Goffman, *The Presentation of Self in Everyday Life* (1959; Penguin, 1990).

49. Another example of this is the use of the Russian term *pokazukha* (putting on a show, in other words, a hollow spectacle or window dressing), which presumes that the "true" reality lies behind the Potemkin façade. This understanding of social interaction is thus closer to Scott's ideas on the hidden script and masked feelings emerging from

the frustration of the weak than to Goffman's postulate that every social act is unavoidably a presentation of self. In Russian studies, *pokazukha* is described as a performance of the achievement of objectives for a preexisting audience and a brief period of time. For instance, István Sántha and Tatiana Safonova describe how the Soviet power was showcased by building Houses of Culture, which exemplified a top-down understanding of culture. Also, in an ethnography of urban survival in stagnation-era Leningrad, Finn Sivert Nielsen noted a general split of life into private and public that spread into the city space as well. To understand that gap, Nielsen contraposed two concepts, the *prospekt* (avenue) as a place that represents civilization and authoritative power and is well taken care of, and the *dvor* (courtyard), the place where people actually live and interact, because such domains remain ungoverned and hidden from the foreigner—"a society outside society." Nielsen concluded that after the fall of the Soviet system, the private-public balance started to change; the role of the open spaces and the courtyards had thus to be reinterpreted. István Sántha and Tatiana Safonova, "Pokazukha in the House of Culture: The Pattern of Behavior in Kurumkan, Eastern Buriatiia," in *Reconstructing the House of Culture*, ed. B. Donahoe and J. O. Habeck (Berghahn, 2011), 75–96; Finn Sivert Nielsen, *Glaz buri* (Aleteja, 2004), accessed July 2023, available in English as "The Eye of the Whirlwind" in *AnthroBase*, https://www.anthrobase.com/Txt/N/Nielsen_F_S_03.htm.

50. Michael Taussig, *Defacement: Public Secrecy and the Labor of the Negative* (Stanford University Press, 1999).

51. Geographers David Bissell, Mitch Rose, and Paul Harrison have also studied negative topographies such as voids, fissures, cracks, corners, and dead ends. As the authors put it, positive spaces are defined by essential characteristics inherent to them, while negative ones are rather designated in relation to something else. Negative spaces, however, do not simply produce disruptions or facilitate a removal from society, nor are they a dead zone of imagination; shadow spaces also generate an inventive setting, frame experimental relationships, and trigger multiple interpretations. David Bissell, Mitch Rose, and Paul Harrison, eds., *Negative Geographies* (University of Nebraska Press, 2021).

52. Victor Turner also reminds us that threshold people have nothing: "no status, insignia, secular clothing, rank, kinship position, nothing to demarcate them structurally from their fellows." Victor Turner, *The Forest of Symbols* (Cornell University Press, 1967), 98.

53. As noted by Turner, a corner connotes a transitional space that might eventually become "a center out there" through rites of passage. Victor Turner, "The Centre Out There: Pilgrims' Goal," *History of Religions* 12, no. 3 (1973): 191–230.

54. For instance, in Spanish it can be divided into two terms—*esquina* (corner) and *rincón* (hideout, retreat). In French there is also *coin* and *angle*, while the German *Ecke* is frequently used for orientation and has a strong geographical connotation. In ordinary English uses, a corner is a point of convergence where two surfaces or lines intersect, forming an angle. Thus, it is an edge or a place where people meet for a particular purpose. This term is also applied to address an extremity, meaning a certain area hosting the extraneous, weird, or embarrassing.

55. In the classic *Street Corner Society*, sociologist William Foote Whyte described the formation of the "corner boys" (a street gang) during the Great Depression. He shifted the traditional emphasis, however, from disorder to the process of social reorganization. Whyte contraposed the self-segregation of young Italian American men in Boston with the social integration among college boys to argue that the problem was not any intrinsic disorder of the corner boys but their eventual failure to fit into the patterns of society at large. Thus, the fact that the corner boys had no regular employment, engaged in racketeering, and spent hardly any time at home was simultaneously a mirror of social problems and a

way of coping with them. William Foote Whyte, *Street Corner Society* (University of Chicago Press, 1943). In another classic, sociologist Elijah Anderson investigated the kinds of interactions happening on a corner in a black ghetto in Chicago. Outdoors at a liquor store and bar there, some of the men were drinking from paper cups, others from bottles, and there were also those begging for money. In the eyes of the outside world, these guys were just hanging out, talking, laughing, or eventually arguing; but as Anderson outlined, social status emerges within those kinds of places too. Alas, status depended on the identity that other groups were willing to grant. For instance, being "a winehead" was better than being "an outsider" or "a hoodlum" but worse than being "a regular." People might move within and between categories and gain status by their ability to perform particular unwritten values in the eyes of others. This generated eventual discrepancies between how the men who frequented the corner saw themselves and how they were seen by others. Anderson further suggests that the status processes he observed on the ghetto corner were not limited to lower-class Blacks but might also occur within other groups. This issue has since been investigated in other contexts, for instance, in relation to life in North American suburbia. Elijah Anderson, *A Place on the Corner* (University of Chicago Press, 2003).

56. Gaston Bachelard, *The Poetics of Space* (1958; Penguin, 2014), 155.

57. Dead ends are closer to what activist Val Plumwood called "shadow places," related to withdrawal and referring to disregarded areas of economic and ecological support. These are sites of extraction and production that provide for a clean, comfortable living elsewhere. Val Plumwood, "Shadow Places and the Politics of Dwelling," *Australian Humanities Review* 44 (2008): 139–50.

58. Transparency thus works to "demolish the unlit chambers" and "eliminate the shadowy areas of society." Patches of darkness expose the relativity of the universalizing values of the center, revealing how identities are also made with shadow figures and what is rendered anomalous. In *Discipline and Punish*, Foucault also foregrounded that "visibility is a trap," which summons surveillance, demands constant accountability, and provokes voyeurism. Michel Foucault, "The Eye of Power," in *Power/Knowledge: Selected Interviews and Other Writings* (Pantheon, 1980), 153–54. Michel Foucault, *Discipline and Punish* (Vintage, 1977), 200.

59. F. Woods, "Ilya Kabakov and the Shadows of Modernism," *Artefact: Journal of the Irish Association of Art Historians* (2008), http://www.acw.ie/images/uploads/Ilya_Kabakov_and_the_shadows_of_modernism.pdf.

60. Epitomizing this phenomenon is Le Corbusier's suggestion of imposing a "law of whitening" (*loi du blanchiment*) to favor purity and cleanliness in our physical surroundings. See Le Corbusier, "Salon d'automne," *L'Esprit Nouveau* 19 (1923); also Anthony Vidler, *The Architectural Uncanny* (MIT Press, 1994).

61. Producing a scorching hypervisibilization of the other and their knowledge in terms of the normalizing gaze. Rhys Dafydd Jones, James Robinson, and Jennifer Turner, eds., *The Politics of Hiding, Invisibility, and Silence* (Routledge, 2015).

62. See R. Morris, "Intimacy and Corruption in Thailand's Age of Transparency," in *Off Stage, On Display*, ed. A. Shryock (Stanford University Press, 2004), 225–43; and S. Tidey, "Corruption and Adherence to Rules in the Construction Sector: Reading the 'Bidding Books,'" *American Anthropologist* 115 (2013): 188–202.

63. Walter Benjamin, "Experience and Poverty" (1933), in *Walter Benjamin: Selected Writings*, vol. 2, ed. Michael W. Jennings (Belknap Press of Harvard University Press, 1999), 731–36.

64. Historian Daniel Jütte also notes that traditional Japanese houses do not feature glass windows but rather use screens made of light-colored paper. Daniel Jütte, *Transparency* (Yale University Press, 2023).

65. H. West and T. Sanders, *Transparency and Conspiracy* (Duke University Press, 2003).

66. C. Hood and D. Heald, *Transparency: The Key to Better Governance* (Oxford University Press, 2006); A. Sharma, "State Transparency After the Neoliberal Turn: The Politics, Limits, and Paradoxes of India's Right to Information Law," *PoLAR* 36 (2013): 308–25.

67. An example of this is Marilyn Strathern's research on audit practices within British higher education, accounting of the contingent practices through which transparency is culturally produced. Accordingly, she shows the schism between transparency as an ideal and as a culturally produced relation. M. Strathern, "The Tyranny of Transparency," *British Educational Research Journal* 26, no. 3 (2000): 309–21. Additionally, Cris Shore and Susan Wright have noted how audit culture stresses accountability and ranking, which undermines autonomy and has unanticipated and dysfunctional consequences. Cris Shore and Susan Wright, "Audit Culture Revisited: Rankings, Ratings, and the Reassembling of Society," *Current Anthropology* 56 (2015): 421–44.

68. For instance, in his study of urban life, Simmel foregrounded that to see and be seen is the basis for social interaction. Georg Simmel, "Sociology of the Senses," In *Simmel on Culture*, ed. D. Frisby and M. Featherstone (Sage, 1997), 109–19.

69. In this vein, cultural theorist Clare Birchall poses transparency as a political form of relating and suggests further questioning who is transparent, about what, and how in a contextual way. In order to preserve diversity, acknowledge the value of knowledge that has been rendered irrelevant, and resist new forms of power, she argues, we need to decouple secrecy and transparency as an oppositional binary. In conclusion, Birchall proposes radical secrecy as a way of interrupting the current uses and abuses of transparency and observes how the explosion of accountability models and regimes of exposure have, paradoxically, contributed to amplifying distrust toward institutions alongside new claims for increasing the security within both states and private organizations. Birchall investigated the technical assumptions about the principles frequently opposed to transparency, namely, secrecy, inefficiency, and corruption. To deal with them, she distinguishes among three masking practices: secrecy, by keeping certain information from becoming public; privacy, a dimension of the self that is free from intrusion; and opacity, which denotes a position of illegibility. She also outlines other forms of tactical defiance (concerning datafication), such as, for instance, the practice of digital experiments, the refusal to move too quickly toward revelation, and the exercise of representing the unrepresentable. Clare Birchall, *Radical Secrecy* (University of Minnesota Press, 2021).

70. J. Niewöhner, "Co-laborative Anthropology: Crafting Reflexivities Experimentally," in *Etnologinen tulkinta ja analyysi*, ed. J. Jouhki and T. Steel (Ethnos, 2016), 81–125.

71. I am talking about the *where, how,* and *by whom* of my fieldwork and analysis, exceeding what is understood as observation and participation in anthropology. M. von Oswald and J. Tinius, eds., *Across Anthropology: Troubling Colonial Legacies, Museums, and the Curatorial* (Leuven University Press, 2020); H. Spriggs, "From Basement to Debasement? A Probing Response to Opacity," *Etnográfica* 28 (2023): 305–9; and M. T. Weiss, "Etnografiar lo subterráneo: Notas e inspiraciones sobre el texto de Francisco Martínez," *Etnográfica* 28 (2023): 298–99.

72. Instead of a distant cultural critique or a representational practice, anthropologists Tomás Criado and Adolfo Estalella have proposed composing different tales with the field (not only about it) through inventive devices of relationality, situated arrangements that allow us to pay attention to the multiple materialities, spatialities, and agencies of the ethnographic encounter. Tomás S. Criado and Adolfo Estalella, eds., *An Ethnographic Inventory* (Routledge, 2023); Francisco Martínez, *Ethnographic Experiments with Artists, Designers, and Boundary Objects* (UCL Press, 2021); and K. Strohm, "The Sensible Life of

Return: Collaborative Experiments in Art and Anthropology in Palestine/Israel, *American Anthropologist* 121 (2019): 243–55.

73. See M. Taussig, *I Swear I Saw This: Drawings in Fieldwork Notebooks, Namely My Own* (University of Chicago Press, 2011); and M. D. Frederiksen, *An Anthropology of Nothing in Particular* (Zero Books, 2018).

74. In Jacques Rancière's view of politics, public exclusion and inclusion revolve around what is seen and what can be said about social matters, as well as who is found, when, and how. Hence, politics relate to the question of who has the ability to speak and see. J. Rancière, *The Politics of Aesthetics* (Continuum, 2004).

1. KEEPING THINGS IN THE DARK

1. Francisco Martínez, "Store It in a Cool Place: Basements as Social Machines," *Home Cultures* 24 (2024): 1–16.

2. Arseny also collects films from the 1960s in two boxes so he can directly see what was "the real *byt*' of that time." The Russian term *byt*' encompasses the English terms "daily life," "domesticity," "lifestyle," or "way of life." Victor Buchli, *An Archaeology of Socialism* (Berg, 1999), 23.

3. Walter Benjamin, *The Arcades Project* (Belknap Press of Harvard University Press, 1999), 4.

4. By *sarai*, Dima refers to an outdoor (not underground) basement, a sort of aboveground depot. The word originally derives from the Persian, meaning a palace, and has also been used to designate the capital of the Golden Horde, as well as a resting place for caravans along the Silk Road. In Russian, there are two words that refer to underground structures, *pogreb* (cellar) and *podval* (basement).

5. L. Suchman, "Affiliative Objects," *Organisation* 12 (2005): 379–99; B. Callén and D. López, "Intimate with Your Junk! A Waste Management Experiment for a Material World," *Sociological Review Monographs* 67 (2019): 318–39.

6. Francisco Martínez, "Gifts in the Dark, or How Far Can We Stretch an Old Library?," *Ethnologia Europaea* (forthcoming).

7. M. Bell, "The Ghosts of Place," *Theory and Society* 26, no. 6 (1997): 813–36.

8. J.-S. Marcoux, "The 'Casser Maison' Ritual: Constructing the Self by Emptying the Home," *Journal of Material Culture* 6 (2001): 213–35.

9. Mauss proclaimed gift exchange "a total social fact" because of the synthetic power of this gesture to create social communities, based on the materialization of reciprocity. As Annette Weiner noted, however, while extending Mauss's argument, there are things that gain value by not circulating inside the market. See Marcel Mauss, *The Gift* (1925; W. W. Norton, 1967); and Annette Weiner, *Inalienable Possessions: The Paradox of Keeping-While-Giving* (University of California Press, 1992).

10. Here I revise Claude Lévi-Strauss's suggestion that myths are important because they exemplify the way in which communities think. Claude Lévi-Strauss, *Le cru et le cuit* (Pion, 1964).

11. Michael Herzfeld, "The Performance of Secrecy: Domesticity and Privacy in Public Spaces," *Semiotica* 175 (2009): 135–62.

12. P. Korosec-Serfaty, "The Home from Attic to Cellar," *Journal of Environmental Psychology* 4 (1984): 303–21.

13. Francisco Martínez, "Narva as Method: Urban Inventories and the Mutation of the Postsocialist City," *Anthropological Journal of European Cultures* 29 (2020): 67–92.

14. R. Vetik and J. Helemäe, *The Russian Second Generation in Tallinn and Kohtla-Järve* (Amsterdam University Press, 2011).

15. S. Newell, "Uncontained Accumulation: Hidden Heterotopias of Storage and Spill-age," *History and Anthropology* 29 (2018): 37–41.

16. This led Bachelard to foreground the ex-centric symbolism of cellars, as these kinds of storage spaces oppose the rational verticality of the house. He claimed that in a cellar, the rationalization of fears "is less rapid and less clear; also, it is never definitive," as "darkness prevails both day and night." Gaston Bachelard, *The Poetics of Space* (1958; Penguin, 2014), 40; see also R. Coser, "Insulation from Observability and Types of Social Conformity," *American Sociological Review* 6 (1961): 28–39.

17. Freud would refer to it as *unheimlich,* or uncanny, a hidden place of familiar unfa-miliarity. Different schools of psychoanalysis study how the subject might emerge in what is hidden—in the secret, in some cases—conditioning our personality traits more than what is exposed: the mask and the ornament.

18. K. Kilroy-Marac, "Becoming with Things," *Home Cultures* 24 (2024): 1–8.

19. As noted by Bhabha, the private and the public can become part of each other through storing. Homi K. Bhabha, "The World and the Home," *Social Text* 31/32 (1992): 141–53.

20. O. Shevchenko, "'In Case of Fire Emergency': Consumption, Security and the Meaning of Durables in a Transforming Society," *Journal of Consumer Culture* 2 (2002): 147–70; S. A. Oushakine, "'Against the Cult of Things': On Soviet Productivism, Storage Economy, and Commodities with No Destination," *Russian Review* 73 (2014): 198–236.

21. Kevin Hetherington, "Secondhandedness: Consumption, Disposal, and Absent Presence," *Environment and Planning D: Society and Space* 22 (2004): 157–73.

22. A kulak was a prosperous peasant who became a landowner, a class that was later persecuted by the Soviets.

23. Martínez, "Narva as Method."

24. Édouard Glissant, *Poetics of Relation* (University of Michigan Press, 1997), 190.

25. S. Pinedo-Padoch, "Time After Death: Material Afterlives in the Work of Estate Administration," *Journal of Material Culture* 27 (2022): 432–49.

26. The installation was first exhibited in the show *Decolonial Ecologies,* curated by Ieva Astakhovska at the Riga Art Space, 2022.

27. As a result, a melancholic question to which there is no answer is felt, as if the past does not give up on the present entirely while sparking moments of awakening. See R. Storr, "An Interview with Ilya Kabakov," *Art in America* 83 (1995): 66; and F. Woods, "Ilya Kabakov and the Shadows of Modernism," *Artefact: Journal of the Irish Association of Art Historians* (Winter 2008), http://www.acw.ie/images/uploads/Ilya_Kabakov_and_ the_shadows_of_modernism.pdf.

28. Ordinary objects are inherently aesthetic and rather silent, since they tend to remain below the radar of normative surveillance. See Daniel Miller, *Material Culture and Mass Consumption* (Blackwell, 1987).

29. Inspired by the work of writer George Perec, Viktor developed an inventory to interpret the visual narratives (such as different codes, numeration, stencils, fumage, and existentialist messages) seen there: "a tag; a date, a dark-green paint bucket stain; the initials H.K.; the letter ж; a faded yellow spray line; the spray-painted letters g and b; an arrow; a drawing with skull and bones; the name of a famous electronic band, the name of a famous rap artist from the 1990s; a green, yellow, gold, light-blue, and dark-red spray-painted surface; Nirvana." See G. Perec, *Species of Spaces and Other Pieces* (Penguin, 2008), 34.

30. In the background of the installation, the song "The Land of Sannikov" (1974) played. "There is only a moment, between past and future, this moment is called life," sang Anna with her father, reinforcing the experience of intimacy traditionally found in these underground spaces.

31. The dystopian description is inspired by the OneState of Yevgeny Zamyatin's *We*. The novel is narrated by D-503, an engineer building a spacecraft for the totalitarian regime that controls the earth. This transparent society is built on the principles of uniformity, mechanization, and mathematical precision. Accordingly, people wear uniforms and are assigned a number that serves as their name; ordinary activities such as sleep, exercise, eating, and sex are monitored by the OneState. Yet we gradually see cracks in the glass paradise through the eyes of D-503, who discovers his own irrationality and meets the secret resistance force living in the underground. E. Zamiatin, *Nosotros* (1921; Akal, 2008).

32. For more on the idea of an ethnographic not-yet, see Francisco Martínez, Lili Di Puppo, and Martin Demant Frederiksen, eds., *Peripheral Methodologies: Unlearning, Not-knowing and Ethnographic Limits* (Routledge, 2021).

33. K. Kilroy-Marac, *An Impossible Inheritance: Postcolonial Psychiatry and the Work of Memory in a West African Clinic* (University of California Press, 2019).

34. For Dmitry Fedotkin's TV report of May 5, 2023, see https://rus.err.ee/1608969187/v-muzee-sillamjaje-otkrylas-vystavka-sovremennogo-iskusstva-vewi-v-temnote.

35. Personal communication, May 7, 2023; my translation from Russian.

36. Personal communication, May 9, 2023; my translation from Russian.

37. Y. Ashikhmin, review of *Decolonial Ecologies*, *Sillamäeski Vestnik*, May 11, 2023.

2. A WOUND THAT GIVES OFF A DARK LIGHT

1. The production of shale oil began in 1921, and oil shale was first used to generate electrical power in 1924. The old mines are located near the towns of Jõhvi, Kohtla-Järve, and Kukruse (1921–1967), Kiviõli (1922–1987), Käva (1924–1972), Kohtla (1937–1999), Mine Number 2 (1949–1973), and Mine Number 4 (1953–1975). There is also an underground mine near Kunda in Ubja, which was in operation between 1926 and 1959. See I. Valgma and T. Kattel, "Low Depth Mining in Estonian Oil Shale Deposit—Abbau von Ölschiefer in Estland," Kolloquium: Schacht, Strecke und Tunnel, TU Freiberg, 2005; and J. Vassiljev et al., *Põlevkivi altkaevandatud alade varingute uuring*, Final Report, KIK project no. 11735, 2018.

2. Ingo Valgma, a Taltech engineer, was the person behind the digitalization.

3. J. Chu, "When Infrastructures Attack: The Workings of Disrepair in China," *American Ethnologist* 14 (2014): 351–67; Francisco Martínez, "What's in a Hole? Voids Out of Place and Politics Below the State in Georgia," in *Repair, Brokenness, Breakthrough*, ed. Francisco Martínez and Patrick Laviolette (Berghahn, 2019), 121–44.

4. James C. Scott, *Seeing Like a State* (Yale University Press, 1998).

5. L. Bennett, "Assets Under Attack: Metal Theft, the Built Environment and the Dark Side of the Global Recycling Market," *Environmental Law and Management* 20 (2008): 176–83.

6. T. Richardson and G. Weszkalnys, "Introduction: Resource Materialities," *Anthropological Quarterly* 87 (2014): 5–30.

7. For more on the topic, see Č. Brković et al., "Europes," in *Anthropology in Europe*, ed. J. Tošić, S. Strasser, and A. Lems (Berghahn, in press).

8. See ERR's coverage of VKG's choice of the Ida-Viru County pulp mill location. "VKG Picks Ida-Viru County Pulp Mill Location," ERR, June 18, 2023, https://news.err.ee/1609010813/vkg-picks-ida-viru-county-pulp-mill-location.

9. A plant in Ahtme was closed in 2013 after the application of EU environmental regulations.

10. Andra Aaloe, "The Power of Stench," *Maja* 118 (2024): 6–19.

11. The plant consists of two factories processing 280 tons of oil shale per hour and an old one processing 140 tons per hour, alongside six energy blocks.

12. Rurik Holmberg, "Survival of the Unfit: Path Dependence and the Estonian Oil Shale Industry" (PhD diss., Linköping University, 2008), 427; J. Aleksandrov, "85 Years of Oil Shale Processing in Estonia," *Oil Shale* 26, no. 4 (2009): 540–43.

13. The experience of disgust contributes to the daily organization of modern societies, since our ordinary forms of sensory approximation are constitutive of both bonds and separations. Georg Simmel, *Sociología* (Alianza, 1986), 687.

14. Hence the need to discuss with them the impact of the new policy and seek economic alternatives. As we shall see in chapter 3, Ivan Sergejev is the former head architect of Narva and a person who has been proactive in raising a new discourse about eastern Estonia and novel connections within the region and beyond.

15. See *Müürileht*'s special issue on Ida-Virumaa (2021), https://www.muurileht.ee/francisco-martinez-ida-virumaa-kui-elav-laboratoorium/.

16. Martínez, "What's in a Hole?"

17. Dace Dzenovska, "Emptiness and Its Futures: Staying and Leaving as Tactics of Life in Latvia," *Focaal* 80 (2018): 16–29; Dace Dzenovska, "Emptiness: Capitalism Without People in the Latvian Countryside," *American Ethnologist* 47 (2020): 10–26.

18. Finished in 1930, the novel was not published in the Soviet Union until 1987 on account of censorship. Andrei Platonov, *The Foundation Pit* (New York Review Books, 2007), 127. For a literary study of the book, see T. Lane, "A Groundless Foundation Pit," *Ulbandus Review* 14 (2012): 61–75.

19. Lewis Mumford, *Technics and Civilization* (Harcourt, Brace, 1934), 69–70, 178.

20. All in all, she concludes that "the underground may be an enduring archetype, but it is not a theme beyond time and society." Rosalind Williams, *Notes on the Underground* (MIT Press, 1990), 65, 3 (referring to the displacement of the organic environment by a technological one), 11.

21. Tiiu Jaago, " 'It Was All Just as I Thought and Felt': One Woman's World in the Context of 20th Century Events," in *She Who Remembers Survives*, ed. T. Kirss, E. Kõresaar, and M. Lauristin (Tartu University Press, 2004), 144–65. See also Tiiu Jaago, A. Printsmann, and H. Palang, "Kohtla-Järve: One Place, Different Stories," in *Place and Location*, vol. 6, ed. E. Näripea, V. Sarapik, and J. Tomberg (Estonian Academy of Arts, 2008), 285–303; and A. Printsmann, "Public and Private Shaping of a Soviet Mining City: Contested History?," *European Countryside* 2 (2010): 132–50.

22. Olaf Mertelsmann, ed., *The Sovietization of the Baltic States: 1940–1956* (Kleio, 2003), 14.

23. In letters from the time, residents complain about the loss of a sense of private property and responsibility for their surroundings.

24. Marju Lauristin, "Social Contradictions Shadowing Estonia's Success Story," *Demokratizatsiya* 11 (2003): 601–16, quotation at 610.

25. The first association of veteran miners, called Prometheus, was created in 1971 with celebratory pomp. In her ethnography, Kesküla describes how work was at the center of their moral universe, as well as the "social contract" forged between a paternalistic socialist state and the worker. As a result, ideas about what it means to be a miner, of a certain social order, and of a collective identity were strongly related. See Eeva Kesküla, "Mining Postsocialism: Work, Class and Ethnicity in an Estonian Mine" (PhD diss., Goldsmiths University of London, 2012).

26. According to Humphrey, the unmaking of the Soviet economy created conditions of dispossession and deprivation for many, who were simultaneously disowned and excluded from collective belonging. Caroline Humphrey, *The Unmaking of Soviet Life* (Cornell University Press, 2002).

27. Between 1920 and 1924, the cement industry in Kunda consumed 60 percent of all oil shale mined in Estonia. H. Martinson, *Khimiya v Estonii v period burzhuaznoy vlasti* [Chemistry in Estonia During the Bourgeois Regime] (Akademiya nauk ESSR, 1987).

28. Holmberg, "Survival of the Unfit."

29. Ivar Rooks, *Esimesest Eesti põlevkivitööstusest Kiviterini, 1938–1998: Mälestused ja faktid* [From the First Estonian Oil Shale Industry to Kiviter, 1938–1998: Reminiscence and Facts] (Ivar Rooks, 2004).

30. Looking beyond those tales of progress and ruination allows us to bring visibility to how things are remade and redesigned to last even in places that have been decommissioned from above, as noted by geographer Leila Dawney in a study of maintenance practices in the Soviet *atomgrad* of Visaginas, Lithuania. Leila Dawney, "Decommissioned Places: Ruins, Endurance and Care at the End of the First Nuclear Age," *Transactions of the Institute of British Geographers* 45 (2020): 33–49.

31. M. Leavitt Cohn, "Convivial Decay: Entangled Lifetimes in a Geriatric Infrastructure," *Proceedings of the 19th ACM Conference on Computer-Supported Cooperative Work & Social Computing* (2016): 1511–23.

32. N. Marres, *Material Participation* (Palgrave Macmillan, 2012).

33. James C. Scott, *Weapons of the Weak* (Yale University Press, 1985).

34. J. Rancíere, *Politics and Aesthetics* (Continuum, 2006).

35. J. E. Orr, *Talking About Machines* (Cornell University Press, 1996); J. Denis and D. Pontille, "Material Ordering and the Care of Things," *Science, Technology & Human Values* 40 (2015): 338–67; Francisco Martínez, "Time to Fix: Repair Heuristics in Estonia and Portugal," *Etnográfica* 27 (2023), 601–17.

36. Christopher Henke and Benjamin Sims, *Repairing Infrastructures* (MIT Press, 2020).

37. Francisco Martínez, "Politics of Recuperation. An Introduction," in *Politics of Recuperation in Post-crisis Portugal* (Bloomsbury, 2020), 1–36.

38. S. Ureta, "Normalizing Transantiago: On the Challenges (and Limits) of Repairing Infrastructures," *Social Studies of Science* 44 (2014): 368–92.

39. Scott, *Seeing Like a State.*

40. See C. Pussetti, *Makeover Me* (Berghahn, in press).

41. For critical views on eco-friendly design practices, see T. Fry, *Design Futuring* (Berg, 2009); E. Shove, "The Shadowy Side of Innovation: Unmaking and Sustainability," *Technology Analysis and Strategic Management* 24 (2012): 345–62; C. Tonkinwise, "'I prefer not to': Anti-progressive Designing," in *Undesign*, ed. G. Coombs, A. McNamara, and G. Sade (Routledge, 2019), 74–84; E. Berglund, "Small Mutinies in the Comfortable Slot: The New Environmentalism as Repair," in Martínez and Laviolette, *Repair, Breakage, Breakthrough*, 228–44; and K. Lindström and Å. Ståhl, "Un/making the Plastic Straw: Designerly Inquiries into Disposability," *Design and Culture* 15 (2023): 393–415.

42. V. Liblik and A. Ratsep, "Impact of Oil Shale Mining and Mine Closures on Hydrological Conditions of North-East Estonian Rivers," *Oil Shale* 21 (2004): 137–48.

43. Paul Virilio, "The Primal Accident," in *The Politics of Everyday Fear*, ed. B. Massumi (University of Minnesota Press, 1993), 210–18.

44. See J. Armstrong, "On the Possibility of a Spectral Ethnography," *Cultural Studies ↔ Critical Methodologies* 10 (2010): 243–50; and J. Gribbin and M. Gribbin, *Companion to the Cosmos* (Little, Brown, 1996).

45. Rancíere, *Politics and Aesthetics.*

46. David Bissell, Mitch Rose, and Paul Harrison, eds., *Negative Geographies* (University of Nebraska Press, 2021).

47. G. Moshenska, "Curated Ruins and the Endurance of Conflict Heritage," *Conservation and Management of Archaeological Sites* 17 (2015): 77–90; C. DeSilvey, *Curated Decay* (University of Minnesota Press, 2017).

48. The main difference between the Kohtla-Järve and Kiviõli formations, nonetheless, is not the materials that constitute them (after combustion or chemical processing, about half of the total mass becomes waste) but how the transportation of ashes was originally carried out. In Kiviõli (where the first hill reached over one hundred meters in height), the transportation of waste used to be done by horses, later replaced with cableway transportation. Today, the semicoke is transported by truck. See A. Toomik and V. Liblik, "Oil Shale Mining and Processing: Impact on Landscapes in North-East Estonia," *Landscape and Urban Planning* 41, no. 3–4 (1998): 285–92; and T. Pae, A. Luud, and M. Sepp, "Artificial Mountains in North-East Estonia: Monumental Dumps of Ash and Semi-coke," *Oil Shale* 22 (2005): 333–43.

49. Männi is also the sculptor of the Lenin monument that at this writing was still standing in the courtyard of Narva Castle. See Linnard, *Dva Nepyushikh* [The Two Sober Ones] (Retro Järve, 2002).

3. NEW HIDEOUTS FOR AN OLD FEAR

1. See Facebook post covered by the Internet journal Delfi, May 7, 2024, https://rus.delfi.ee/statja/120291163/s-7-po-9-maya-v-rayonah-sinimyae-i-sirgala-mozhno-budet-uslyshat-vzryvy-pochemu.

2. E. Domanska, "The Material Presence of the Past," *History and Theory* 45 (2006): 337–48; C. DeSilvey, "Salvage Memory: Constellating Material Histories on a Hardscrabble Homestead," *Cultural Geographies* 14 (2007): 401–24; S. Kattago, *Encountering the Past Within the Present* (Routledge, 2019); S. De Nardi, "The Materiality of Conflict Memory: Reflections from Contemporary Italy," *Journal of Material Culture* 25 (2020): 447–61.

3. Viktoria Robinson, "Blagodarim vseh neravnodushnyh ljudej, kto segodnja prisoedinilsja k nashemu obshhemu delu!" The Virtual Museum of Sillamäe Facebook group, May 10, 2024, https://www.facebook.com/groups/550010012295751/.

4. A. Storm, "When We Have Left the Nuclear Territories," in *Deterritorializing the Future*, ed. R. Harrison and C. Sterling (Open Humanities Press, 2020), 318–45.

5. In total, between 1948 and 1990, nearly 100,000 tons of uranium and over 1,300 tons of enriched uranium, used in 70,000 nuclear weapons, were produced at the Sillamäe site, making it the third-largest producer in the Soviet bloc.

6. C. K. Rofer and T. Kaasik, eds., *Turning a Problem into a Resource: Remediation and Waste Management at the Sillamäe Site, Estonia* (Springer, 2000).

7. Tarmo Pikner, "Environmental Futures and Urbanity Entangled in Nuclear Legacies in the Baltic Sea Coastal Towns of Paldiski and Sillamäe," in *Spatial Futures*, ed. LaToya E. Eaves, Heidi J. Nast, and Alex G. Papadopoulos (Palgrave Macmillan, 2024), 375–414.

8. E. Rindzevičiūtė, "Nuclear Power as Cultural Heritage in Russia," *Slavic Review* 80 (2021): 839–62; V. Ialenti, *Deep Time Reckoning* (MIT Press, 2020); Francisco Martínez, "How Final Is Final? The Construction of Finality in the Onkalo Spent Nuclear Fuel Repository," *Anthropological Theory* (forthcoming).

9. Andrew Suttaford, "A Soviet Brigadoon: The Strange History of Estonia's Sillamäe," *National Review,* January 13, 2013,.

10. For more on the topic, see H. Hiiop and R. Treufeldt, "Difficult Stories of a Difficult Legacy: Research, Problems, and Solutions in Conserving Art from Within the Soviet Armed Forces," paper delivered at 12th Baltic States Triennial Conservators' Meeting, Vilnius, 2022.

11. A war is a rather ephemeral intervention with enduring cultural and ecological consequences and led by an antisocial logic. See A. González Ruibal, *Tierra arrasada* (Crítica, 2023).

12. J. Reno, *Military Waste: The Unexpected Consequences of Permanent War Readiness* (University of California Press, 2020).

13. David Henig, "Iron in the Soil: Living with Military Waste in Bosnia-Herzegovina," *Anthropology Today* 29 (2012): 21–23; David Henig, "Living on the Frontline: Indeterminacy, Value, and Military Waste in Postwar Bosnia-Herzegovina," *Anthropological Quarterly* 92 (2019): 85–110.

14. Reverberation differs from repetition and echo; this phenomenon implies continuity with a certain degree of distortion. Y. Navaro et al., eds., *Reverberations: Violence Across Time and Space* (University of Pennsylvania Press, 2021. See also R. Nixon, *Slow Violence and the Environmentalism of the Poor* (Harvard University Press, 2011); and A. Vorbrugg, "Ethnographies of Slow Violence: Epistemological Alliances in Fieldwork and Narrating Ruins," *EPC: Politics and Space* 40 (2022): 447–62.

15. Alas, the trigger for Seidl's film was the story of Natascha Kampusch, a young woman kidnapped when she was ten years old and locked up by her captor for eight years in the basement of a house in Vienna. This led Seidl to investigate what Austrians hide in their cellars.

16. A. Raukas, ed., *Nõukogude okupatsiooni poolt tekitatud keskkonnakahjud* [Environmental Damages Caused by the Soviet Occupation] (Eesti Entsüklopeediakirjastus, 2006).

17. David Vseviov, "Kirde-Eesti urbaanse anomaalia kujunemine ning struktuur pärast Teist maailmasõda" [The Formation and Structure of the Urban Anomaly of Northeastern Estonia After the Second World War] (PhD diss., Tallinn Pedagogical University, 2002).

18. S. Sultson, "Arisen from Ignoring—Planning of a Secret Soviet Stately Industrial Town, Sillamäe," *Acta Architecturae Naturalis* 6 (2020): 29–43.

19. Quoted in Eléonore de Montesquiou, *Atom Cities: Sillamäe* (Linnagaleriis, 2006), 175.

20. K. Brown, *Plutopia: Nuclear Families, Atomic Cities, and the Great Soviet and American Plutonium Disasters* (Oxford University Press, 2013).

21. The title of his memoir can be translated as both *The Tragedy of Sillamäe* and *Sillamäe Passion*. Andrei Khvostov, *Sillamäeskaya Passionata* (Kite, 2013).

22. Alfidina Orlova, "Kino Rodina," in *Sillamäe, 1946–1989* (self-published, 2005).

23. See M. Dworzecki, *The Jewish Camps in Estonia* (Yad Vashem, 1970); R. Västrik and M. Maripuu, "Vaivara Concentration Camp in 1943–1944," in *Estonian International Commission for the Investigation of Crimes Against Humanity*, ed. T. Hiio, M. Maripuu, and I. Paavle (Inimsusevastaste Kuritegude Uurimise Eesti Sihtasutus, 2006), 719–38; Anton Weiss-Wendt, *Murder Without Hatred: Estonians and the Holocaust* (Syracuse University Press, 2009).

24. On the basis of these testimonies, Burström foregrounds the importance of material objects for the work of memory, showing how the hoard of hidden family possessions was particularly connected with a feeling of homesickness. Mats Burström, "Buried Memories: Wartime Caches and Family History in Estonia," *Archaeologies of Mobility and Movement*, ed. M. C. Beaudry and T. G. Parno (Springer, 2013), 101–11; Mats Burström, "Treasured Memories: An Anecdotal Mapping of Wartime Caches in Estonia," in *Ruin Memories*, ed. B. Olsen and T. Pétursdóttir (Routledge, 2014), 143–61.

25. Sofi Oksanen, *Purge* (Grove Press, 2010).

26. This word comes from the Corsican *macchia*, which originally referred to both a stain and a weed.

27. Their story has been made into a film, *The Endless Trench* (dir. Jon Garaño, Aitor Arregi, and Jose Mari Goenaga, 2019). In this film, we see how Higinio, a Republican,

hides in a hole underneath his house with his wife's help between 1936 and 1969, when the Franco regime approves an amnesty. There is also the documentary *Thirty Years of Obscurity* (dir. Manuel Martín, 2012), inspired by the life of Manuel Cortés, the former mayor of Mijas, Málaga. Scared, and with the help of his wife, Cortés grew old inside a small room behind a closet, because for the Topos, capture essentially meant death.

28. S. Dümpelmann, *Flights of Imagination* (University of Virginia Press, 2014).

29. A. R. E. Taylor, "Future-Proof: Bunkered Data Centres and the Selling of Ultra-secure Cloud Storage," *Journal of the Royal Anthropological Institute* 26 (2021): 76–94; L. Bennett, "The Bunker's After-Life: Cultural Production in the Ruins of the Cold War," *Journal of War & Culture Studies* 13 (2020): 1–10.

30. N. Ssorin-Chaikov, "Hybrid Peace: Ethnographies of War," *Annual Review of Anthropology* 47 (2018): 251–62.

31. See Estonian press agency ERR's coverage of the topic, January 19, 2024.

32. B. Garrett, *Bunker: Building for the End Times* (Penguin, 2020).

33. F. Vidal and N. Dias, eds., *Endangerment, Biodiversity and Culture* (Routledge, 2016).

34. P. Hirst, *Space and Power* (Polity, 2005); L. Bennett, ed., *In the Ruins of the Cold War Bunker* (Rowman & Littlefield, 2017).

35. J. Beck, "Concrete Ambivalence: Inside the Bunker Complex," *Cultural Politics* 7 (2011): 79–102, quotation at 82.

36. Cornelius Holtorf, "Averting Loss Aversion in Cultural Heritage," *International Journal of Heritage Studies* 21 (2015): 405–21.

37. R. Tzalmona, "Traces of the Atlantikwall or the Ruins That Were Built to Last," *Third Text* 25, no. 6 (2011): 775–86.

38. Mads Daugbjerg, "Invasive Materialities: War Bunkers as Disturbing Nodes of Collaboration," *Journal of Material Culture* 28 (2022): 1–19.

39. B. Highmore, "Playgrounds and Bombsites: Post-war Britain's Ruined Landscapes," *Cultural Politics* 9 (2013): 323–36.

40. J. D. Giblin, "Post-conflict Heritage: Symbolic Healing and Cultural Renewal," *International Journal of Heritage Studies* 20 (2014): 500–18.

41. J. E. Tunbridge and G. Ashworth, *Dissonant Heritage* (Wiley, 1996); S. Macdonald, "Undesirable Heritage: Fascist Material Culture and Historical Consciousness in Nuremberg," *International Journal of Heritage Studies* 12 (2006): 9–28.

42. In her account of undetonated bombs found decades after the Second World War in several German cities, ethnologist Regina Bendix highlights "failure" as the term that best describes leftover ordnance and military waste. Failure should, however, appear in plural form, as a series of deficiencies and missteps, given that we are indicating a failed explosion, a wrong location, how this ordnance remained in time, and also a failure of social relationships as the cause of all that has happened from the very beginning. Regina Bendix, "Heritage Out of Control—(B)lasting Bombs," *Allegra* (2022), accessed June 2023, https://allegralaboratory.net/heritageouttacontrol-4-blasting-bombs/.

43. P. Dobraszczyk, C. López Galviz, and B. Garrett, eds., *Global Undergrounds* (Reaktion, 2016).

44. Tamta Khalvashi, "What Else Can We Do with/in Holes?," *Etnográfica* 28 (2024), 285–312.

45. Stories such as the tale of the Hanseatic "golden ship" that sank in the Narva River, along with the fortune hidden by the city judge during the Northern War, or the disappearance of the "famous" tiles of Narva.

46. The bastion's defensive architecture follows the old Italian system: its structure is pentagonal and multilevel; from its front and also from the two wings, it was possible to fire on the enemy with artillery and with muskets.

47. K. B. Gotfredsen, "Enemies of the People: Theorizing Dispossession and Mirroring Conspiracy in the Republic of Georgia," *Focaal* 74 (2016): 42–53; K. Verdery, *My Life as a Spy* (Duke University Press, 2018); F. Mühlfried, "Suspicious Surfaces and Affective Mistrust in the South Caucasus," *Social Analysis* 65 (2021): 1–21.

48. M. Tamm, "In Search of Lost Time: Memory Politics in Estonia, 1991–2011," *Nationalities Papers* 41, no. 4 (2013): 651–74; Francisco Martínez, *Remains of the Soviet Past in Estonia* (UCL Press, 2018).

49. See D. Dzenovska, *The School of Europeanness* (Cornell University Press, 2018); and M. Cole, "Understanding Russophone Estonian Identity Through Popular Culture: An Analysis of Hip-Hop Hit 'Für Oksana,'" *Nationalities Papers* 52 (2024): 1–29.

50. Susan Harding, "Representing Fundamentalism: The Problem of the Repugnant Cultural Other," *Social Research* 58 (1991): 373–93.

51. Sherry Ortner, "Dark Anthropology and Its Others: Theory Since the Eighties," *HAU: Journal of Ethnographic Theory* 6 (2016): 47–73.

52. Sherry Ortner, "Resistance and the Problem of Ethnographic Refusal," *Comparative Studies in Society and History* 37 (1995): 173–93. See also A. McLean and A. Leibing, eds., *The Shadow Side of Fieldwork* (Blackwell, 2007).

53. "When a man hasn't seen war, then he's like a woman who never gave birth—he lives like an idiot. You are always to be seen through." Andrei Platonov, *The Foundation Pit* (New York Review Books, 2007), 18.

54. "Have you served in the army, faggot?!" read one of the comments written in the Russian-speaking media.

55. The monument was erected there on May 9, 1970.

56. Indrek Kiisler, "Minister Hartman on Heritage Status of Sillamäe, Maarjamäe Memorial," ERR November 16, 2022, https://news.err.ee/1608790711/minister-hartman-on-heritage-status-of-sillamae-maarjamae-memorial.

57. May 9 is known as Victory Day in the Russian calendar, as it refers to the Red Army defeat of Nazi Germany.

58. M. Ferme, *The Underneath of Things: Violence, History, and the Everyday in Sierra Leone* (University of California Press, 2001); T. Edensor, "Mundane Hauntings: Commuting Through the Phantasmagoric Working-Class Spaces of Manchester, England," *Cultural Geographies* 15 (2008): 313–33; K. Kilroy-Marac, "Speaking with Revenants: Haunting and the Ethnographic Enterprise," *Ethnography* 15 (2014): 255–76.

4. THE SOCIAL LABORATORY

1. Laboratories are strictly designed to produce the possibility of actions without consequences. A lab combines controlled testing with the epistemic authority and legitimizing rituals of scientists. See H.-J. Rheinberger, *Toward a History of Epistemic Things* (Stanford University Press, 1997); Matthias Gross, *Ignorance and Surprise: Science, Society, and Ecological Design* (MIT Press, 2010); and M. Guggenheim, "Laboratizing and Delaboratizing the World: Changing Sociological Concepts for Places of Knowledge Production," *History of the Human Sciences* 25 (2012): 99–118.

2. See K. Grišakov et al., "Kohtla-Järve ruumilise analüüsi kokkuvõte" [Summary of Spatial Analysis of Kohtla-Järve], Taltech, SPIN Unit, 2020, accessed July 2024, https://planeerimine.blogi.fin.ee/wp-content/uploads/2021/05/Uuringu-kokkuvote_Kohtla-Jarve.pdf.

3. I. Dietzsch, "Perceptions of Decline: Crisis, Shrinking and Disappearance as Narrative Schemas to Describe Social and Cultural Change," *Anuarul Institutului de Istorie George Baritiu* 7 (2009): 7–22; C. Martínez-Fernández et al., "Shrinking Cities: Urban Challenges of Globalization," *International Journal of Urban and Regional Research* 36

(2012): 213–25; K. Pallagst et al., eds., *Shrinking Cities* (Routledge, 2014); A. Haase et al., "Shrinking Cities in Post-socialist Europe: What Can We Learn from Their Analysis for Theory Building Today?," *Geografiska Annaler B* 98 (2016): 305–19.

4. Dace Dzenovska, "Emptiness and Its Futures: Staying and Leaving as Tactics of Life in Latvia," *Focaal* 80 (2018): 16–29.

5. The Kohtla-Järve municipality was not interested in owning more properties, since they involve costs—for maintenance as well as for their potential demolition. Even during the application of the pilot project, local officials have been selling municipally owned apartments at property auctions.

6. On this matter, see X. Cherkaev, *Gleaning for Communism* (Cornell University Press, 2023).

7. Or rootlessness, in the case of Russian speakers. My field experience, however, finds no evidence of that.

8. For more on the procedures, see Francisco Martínez and Keiti Kljavin, "Making Room for the Future? Half-Emptiness and the Ordered Demolition of Soviet Housing in Estonia," *Journal of Baltic Studies* (forthcoming).

9. See A. Corsín Jiménez and A. Estalella, *Free Culture and the City* (Cornell University Press, 2023).

10. As part of the consultation work, dozens of interviews with local politicians and residents were conducted by the Estonian Urban Lab over a year and a half (2020–21). Some of the insights appear in the reports, such as K. Kljavin, J. Pirrus, and M. Derlõš, *Pro-aktiivne Kiviõli linn* [Pro-active Kiviõli] (Linnalabor, 2019).

11. A classic example of this is Whyte's account of the hierarchies and self-perception within street corner society in Boston by taking part in a bowling competition with his informants; see William Foote Whyte, *Street Corner Society* (University of Chicago Press, 1943). Another example is Brian Moeran's fieldwork in a Japanese advertising agency. Moeran took his ethnographic engagement in the organization as an opportunity to gather data about modalities of worldviews and value systems that are unobtainable by other means. Brian Moeran, "From Participant Observation to Observant Participation," in *Organizational Ethnography*, ed. S. Ybema et al. (Sage, 2009), 139–55. In another classic work on this topic, Raymond Gold distinguished four kinds of observation in social research varying by the role of the researchers: the complete participant, the participant-as-observer, the observer-as-participant, and the complete observer. Raymond Gold, "Roles in Sociological Field Observations," *Social Forces* 36, no. 3 (1958): 217–23.

12. Dace Dzenovska, "Emptiness and Order," *Fieldsights,* Society for Cultural Anthropology (2020), accessed June 2023, https://culanth.org/fieldsights/emptiness-and-order; and Felix Ringel, "Post-industrial Times and the Unexpected: Endurance and Sustainability in Germany's Fastest-Shrinking City," *Journal of the Royal Anthropological Institute* 20 (2014): 52–70.

13. Marcel Mauss, *The Gift* (1925; W. W. Norton, 1967); Georges Bataille, *The Accursed Share* (Zone Books, 1991).

14. R. Bryant and D. M. Knight, *The Anthropology of the Future* (Cambridge University Press, 2019); Dace Dzenovska and D. M. Knight, "Emptiness: An Introduction," *Fieldsights*, Society for Cultural Anthropology (2020), accessed June 2023, https://culanth.org/fieldsights/emptiness-an-introduction.

5. INTERIOR EXTERIORITIES

1. A. Stenning and K. Hörschelmann, "History, Geography and Difference in the Post-socialist World: Or, Do We Still Need Post-socialism?," *Antipode* 40 (2008): 312–35.

2. M. Murawski, "Actually-Existing Success: Economics, Aesthetics and the Specificity of (Still-) Socialist Urbanism; A Review Essay," *Comparative Studies in Society and*

History 60 (2017): 907–37; Francisco Martínez, "Narva as Method: Urban Inventories and the Mutation of the Postsocialist City," *Anthropological Journal of European Cultures* 29 (2020): 67–92; D. Light and C. Young, "Reconfiguring Socialist Urban Landscapes: The 'Left-Over' Spaces of State-Socialism in Bucharest," *Human Geographies* 4 (2010): 5–16.

3. Thomas Lahusen, "Decay or Endurance? The Ruins of Socialism," *Slavic Review* 65 (2006): 736–46.

4. In Russian, the term *remont* came originally from French, meaning the provisioning of horses to the cavalry. Nowadays it is used to refer to all kinds of reparative interventions. As revealed by Ekaterina Gerasimova, Sofia Chuikina, and Wladimir Sgibnev, *remont* might be understood as both the expression of a state of permanent unfinishedness and a way of negotiating modernity. Ekaterina Gerasimova and Sofia Chuikina, "The Repair Society," *Russian Studies in History* 48 (2009): 58–74; Wladimir Sgibnev, "Remont: Housing Adaptation as Meaningful Practice of Space Production in Post-Soviet Tajikistan," *Europa Regional* 22 (2015): 53–64.

5. Overall, in the 1990s, domestic changes were deeper and more radical than the accustomed user-generated modifications. For instance, in her study of urban apartment homes in Ukraine, Kateryna Malaia describes how the first post-Soviet decades were accompanied by a near-pathological desire for home improvement. Kateryna Malaia, *Taking the Soviet Union Apart Room by Room* (Cornell University Press, 2023).

6. K. Fehérváry, "American Kitchens, Luxury Bathrooms, and the Search for a 'Normal' Life in Postsocialist Hungary," *Ethnos* 67 (2002): 369–400.

7. See T. Berge, "The Worse, the Better: On Safe Ground in 'the Most Polluted Town on Earth,'" *Anthropological Journal of European Cultures* 21 (2012): 81–102.

8. M. Douglas, *Purity and Danger* (Praeger, 1966); M. Thompson, *Rubbish Theory* (Oxford University Press, 1979).

9. V. Napolitano, "Anthropology and Traces," *Anthropological Theory* 15 (2015): 47–67; M. D. Frederiksen, "In the House of Un-things: Decay and Deferral in a Vacated Bulgarian Home," in *Repair, Brokenness, Breakthrough*, ed. Francisco Martínez and Patrick Laviolette (Berghahn, 2019), 73–86.

10. Rachel Hurdley, *Home, Materiality, Memory and Belonging* (Palgrave, 2013).

11. For instance, in a study conducted in *khrushchëvka* apartments, historian Susan Reid examined how hanging pictures was a way of establishing a sense of continuity and making oneself at home. From her interviews with individuals who had moved to mostly prefabricated apartment blocks in seven cities across the USSR, Reid pointed out the special role played by pictures on the wall in the identity formation of tenants. An example of this are the photos of deceased relatives, which were common in interiors and served to locate a sense of self in place and time, and within social relations. Susan E. Reid, "Picturing the Self and Homeland in the Late Soviet Home," *eSamizdat* 13 (2020): 27–58.

12. Tomás Errázuriz, "Home, a Place Not to Feel," in *Reconstructing Homes*, ed. E. Koskinen-Koivisto et al. (Berghahn, 2024): 54–71. See also H. Giannini, *La reflexión codidiana* (Santiago de Chile Editorial Universitaria, 1987).

13. D. Miller, "Behind Closed Doors," in *Home Possessions*, ed. D. Miller (Berg, 2001), 1–19.

14. Thus enabling a more or less fluid interchange. In his 1909 essay "Bridge and Door," Simmel referred to a doorway as a space of potentiality; on the one side, life flows forth limitlessly, on the other, a separate isolated existence begins. In contrast, a window "goes almost exclusively from inward to outward: it is there for looking out, not for seeing in." Bachelard, in turn, refers to lighted windows as generating a sense of intimacy for external viewers. Georg Simmel, "Bridge and Door," *Theory, Culture & Society* 11 (1994): 5–10, quotation at 8; Gaston Bachelard, *The Poetics of Space* (1958; Penguin, 2014).

15. N. Gregson, *Living with Things* (Sean Kingston, 2007); D. Miller and F. Parrot, "Loss and Material Culture in South London," *Journal of the Royal Anthropological Institute* 15 (2009): 502–19; T. Errázuriz, "When New Is Not Better: The Making of Home Through Holding On to Objects," in Martínez and Laviolette, *Repair, Brokenness, Breakthroughs*; Francisco Martínez and Tomás Errázuriz, "Introduction: With and Without Things," *Home Cultures* 21 (2024): 1–14.

16. For instance, anthropologist Katie Kilroy-Marac has studied psychiatric research on hoarding and the work of so-called professional organizers. As she shows, an excessive passivity toward ordering, or a lack of skill to do so, can be taken as pathological. Katie Kilroy-Marac, "An Order of Distinction (or, How to Tell a Collection from a Hoard)," *Journal of Material Culture* 23 (2018): 20–38.

17. Sophie Woodward, "Clutter in Domestic Spaces: Material Vibrancy, and Competing Moralities," *Sociological Review* 69, no. 6 (2021): 1214–28; A. Kajander and E. Koskinen-Koivisto, "Clutter in Finnish Middle-Class Homes: Three Viewpoints to Affective Practices of Domestic Life," *Home Cultures* 21 (2024): 1–14; O. Löfgren, "Mess: On Domestic Overflows," *Consumption Markets & Culture* 20 (2017): 1–6.

18. "This is a man for whom putting on the second sock would be an entirely separate activity from putting on the first sock." Daniel Miller, *The Comfort of Things* (Polity, 2008), 10.

19. Joseph Brodsky, *Less Than One: Selected Essays* (Farrar, Straus and Giroux, 1986). Historian Yuri Slezkine likened Soviet internationalism to life in a communal apartment, with each nationality apportioned its own room. Then, in the middle of the home, there is "the Russian room," from which the supranational Soviet civilization and enlightenment are disseminated to the other peoples of the empire. Yuri Slezkine, "The USSR as a Communal Apartment, or How a Socialist State Promoted Ethnic Particularism," *Slavic Review* 53 (1994): 414–52.

20. Kitchens strangely symbolized intimacy and openness, activated through the willingness to drink tea or to smoke. See N. Ries, *Russian Talk: Culture and Conversation During Perestroika* (Cornell University Press, 1997); and A. Kurg, "Free Communication: From Soviet Future Cities to Kitchen Conversations," *Journal of Architecture* 24 (2019): 676–98.

21. Roger Bartlett ed., *Land Commune and Peasant Community in Russia* (Palgrave, 1990).

22. Ekaterina Gerasimova, "Public Privacy in the Soviet Communal Apartment," in *Socialist Spaces*, ed. D. Crowley and D. E. Reid (Berg, 2002), 207–30, quotation at 207.

23. Walter Benjamin, "Moskau," *Die Kreatur* 1 (1927): 71–101.

24. Svetlana Boym, *The Off-Modern* (Bloomsbury, 2017), 138.

25. In *The Location of Culture* (Routledge, 1994), Homi K. Bhabha described migration and colonialism as split between authoritative forms that appear original and their enactment through repetition and performative difference. Also, from Baudelaire to Benjamin, modernity has recurrently been compared to a transcendent sense of homelessness. Nevertheless, anthropologist Jeremy Morris claims that the post-socialist condition is slightly different from the colonial one, as it is characterized by uncertainty instead of ambivalence. See Jeremy Morris, *Everyday Post-socialism* (Palgrave Macmillan, 2016).

26. Generally, "hybridity" has been used to refer to a partial construction and to a process of synthesizing, enabling a "spatial politics of inclusion rather than exclusion that initiate new signs of identity and innovative sites of collaboration and contestation." See Bhabha, *The Location of Culture*, 1.

27. Francisco Martínez, *Remains of the Soviet Past in Estonia* (UCL Press, 2018).

28. M. L. Caldwell, "Newness and Loss in Moscow: Rethinking Transformation in the Post-socialist Field," *Journal of the Society for the Anthropology of Europe* 5 (2005): 2–7; D.

Boyer and A. Yurchak, "Post-socialist Studies, Cultures of Parody and American Stiob," *Anthropology News* 49, no. 8 (2008): 9–10.

29. A. González-Ruibal, *An Archaeology of the Contemporary Era* (Routledge, 2019).

30. S. Collier, *Post-Soviet Social* (Princeton University Press, 2011); I. H. Knudsen and M. D. Frederiksen, eds., *Ethnographies of Grey Zones in Eastern Europe* (Anthem, 2015); L. Chelcea and O. Druță, "Zombie Socialism and the Rise of Neoliberalism in Post-socialist Central and Eastern Europe," *Eurasian Geography and Economics* 57, no. 4–5 (2016): 521–44; L. Ozoliņa, *Politics of Waiting* (Manchester University Press, 2019); M. Murawski, *The Palace Complex* (Indiana University Press, 2019); and T. Khalvashi, "A Ride on the Elevator: Infrastructures of Brokenness and Repair in Georgia," in Martínez and Laviolette, *Repair, Brokenness, Breakthrough*, 92–114.

31. O. Shevchenko, "'Between the Holes': Emerging Identities and Hybrid Patterns of Consumption in Post-socialist Russia," *Europe-Asia Studies* 54, no. 6 (2002): 841–66.

32. A. Starosta, "Gardens of Things: The Vicissitudes of Disappearance," *Intermédialités* 10 (2007): 147–63.

33. Dace Dzenovska, "Emptiness: Capitalism Without People in the Latvian Countryside," *American Ethnologist* 47 (2020): 10–26.

34. Specifically, one of the movie theaters, the smaller one, served this purpose.

35. Kino Rodina was finally sold to a real estate entrepreneur in May 2024. According to rumors, he bought the building, which formerly housed the *Sillamäe Herald*, to turn it into a spa hotel and the old cinema as a present for his wife. For a longer description, see Francisco Martínez, "Remaining Without Preservation: The Zombie Standing of Kino Rodina in Estonia," in *Ambivalent Heritage*, ed. T. Äikäs and T. Matila (Bloomsbury, 2024), 203–22.

36. K. Zubovich, *Making Cities Socialist* (Cambridge University Press, 2024).

37. K. Fehérváry, *Politics in Color and Concrete* (Indiana University Press, 2013); Francisco Martínez, "Memory, Don't Speak! Monumental Neglect and Memorial Sacrifice in Contemporary Estonia," *Cultural Geographies* 29 (2022): 63–81.

38. S. Hirt, S. Ferenčuhová, and T. Tuvikene, "Conceptual Forum: The "Post-socialist" City," *Eurasian Geography and Economics* 57, no. 4–5 (2016): 497–520.

39. I. Kiviselg, "The Fairy-Tale Glade of Sillamäe," *Pohjarannik,* July 17, 2021, accessed September 2023, https://sillamae.raamatukogud.ee/?action=136&id=9436.

40. See E. Materka, "Hybridizing Post-socialist Trajectories: An Investigation into the *Biznes* of the U.S. Missile Base in Rędzikowo and Urbanization of Villages in Provincial Poland," *Anthropology of East Europe Review* 30 (2012): 141–83; S. Kattago, "The End of the European Honeymoon? Refugees, Resentment and the Clash of Solidarities," *Anthropological Journal of European Cultures* 26 (2017): 35–52; and Francisco Martínez, "*Que reste-t-il de nos amours?* The Expectations of 1989–1991 Revisited," *Anthropological Journal of European Cultures* 23 (2017): 1–16.

6. LEFT-BEHIND PLACES

1. This chapter partly relies on two essays, Francisco Martínez, "What Used to Be (Viivikonna)," *Emptiness Field Reports,* July 21, 2021, https://emptiness.eu/field-reports/what-used-to-be-viivikonna/; and Francisco Martínez et al., "Far Away, So Close: A Collective Ethnography Around Remoteness," *Entanglements* 4 (2021): 246–83.

2. Anna Storm, *Post-industrial Landscape Scars* (Palgrave Macmillan, 2014); Hugo Reinert, "Sacrifice," *Environmental Humanities* 7 (2015): 255–58.

3. M. L. Pratt, "Modernity and Periphery: Toward a Global and Relational Analysis," in *Beyond Dichotomies*, ed. E. Mudimbe-Boyi (SUNY Press, 2012), 21–47, esp. 35.

4. N. Ssorin-Chaikov, *Two Lenins: A Brief Anthropology of Time* (HAU Books, 2017).

5. Hence, the territory allocated for the settlements decreased from 5,000 to 3,300 hectares, which meant an extra 1,700 hectares for the oil shale mining. Sultson provides demographic calculations: In 1947, 833 people were living in Viivikonna, and 2,041 people in 1957. See Siim Sultson, "Viivikonna—Formation of a Ghost Town Amongst Other East Estonian Oil-Shale Mining and Industrial Towns," *Baltic Journal of Art History* 19 (2020): 157–77.

6. Tanya Richardson and Gisa Weszkalnys, "Resource Materialities," *Anthropological Quarterly* 87, no. 1 (Winter 2014): 5–30.

7. A. Monnin, "The Negative Commons: Between Waste and Ruins," *Études* 9 (2021): 59–68.

8. Brian Larkin, "The Politics and Poetics of Infrastructure," *Annual Review of Anthropology* 42 (2013): 327–43.

9. A. Dunlap, "Wind, Coal, and Copper: The Politics of Land Grabbing, Counterinsurgency, and the Social Engineering of Extraction," *Globalizations* 17 (2020): 661–82.

10. C. Mukerji, "The Political Mobilization of Nature in Seventeenth-Century French Formal Gardens," *Theory and Society* 23 (1994): 651–77; Penny Harvey and Hannah Knox, *Roads: An Anthropology of Infrastructure and Expertise* (Cornell University Press, 2015).

11. Geoffrey Bowker and Susan Leigh Star note that infrastructures are both concrete objects and knowledge objects, while anthropologist Jörg Niewöhner refuses to reduce infrastructure to the status of a mere technical thing and instead presents it as a form of social organization. Geoffrey C. Bowker and Susan Leigh Star, *Sorting Things Out: Classification and Its Consequences* (MIT Press, 1999). Niewöhner has also pointed out that infrastructure is characterized by features such as embeddedness and transparency. Pipes, railroads, and tunnels sediment out and disappear from view, seeping into the background of other social and ecological arrangements, yet becoming visible upon breakdown as we saw in chapter 2. Jörg Niewöhner, "Infrastructures of Society, Anthropology of," in *International Encyclopedia of the Social & Behavioral Sciences*, ed. J. D. Wright (Elsevier, 2015), 119–25.

12. T. Tuvikene, T. W. Sgibnev, and C. Neugebauer, eds., *Post-socialist Urban Infrastructures* (Routledge, 2019).

13. G. Gordillo, *Rubble: The Afterlife of Destruction* (Duke University Press, 2014).

14. P. Högselius, A. Kaijser, and E. van der Vleuten, *Europe's Infrastructure Transition* (Palgrave, 2016).

15. See her study of the Kvartsitnyi settlement in Karelia: Anna Varfolomeeva, "The Nothingness Myth: Creation and Collapse of a Soviet Industrial Settlement," *Focaal* 96 (2023): 16–31.

16. In some cases, capitalism has been parasitically feeding on decommissioned Soviet infrastructure, filling the space left behind by Soviet emptiness. In other cases, the usefulness of this kind of nothingness remains unclear. What is certain is that we cannot turn back the clock to the early nothingness status. See L. Khatchadourian, "Life Extempore: Trials of Ruination in the Twilight Zone of Soviet Industry," *Cultural Anthropology* 37 (2022): 317–48.

17. T. Edensor, "The Ghosts of Industrial Ruins: Ordering and Disordering Memory in Excessive Space," *Environment and Planning D* 25 (2005,): 829–49.

18. P. Dobraszczyk, *Animal Architecture* (Reaktion, 2023).

19. Francisco Martínez and Olli Pyyhtinen, "Garbography: Tracing Waste as Material Data," *Journal of Material Culture* (forthcoming).

20. See Leila Dawney, "Decommissioned Places: Ruins, Endurance and Care at the End of the First Nuclear Age," *Transactions of the Institute of British Geographers* 45 (2020): 33–49; also *Ehituskunst* 61–62, *Small Towns: Non-Growing*, ed. E. Hermann (2022).

21. Aghdam was a casualty of the war fought by Azerbaijan and Armenia over the Karabakh. It was considered the world's largest dead city until the more recent fate of Bakhmut in Ukraine.

22. J. Sather-Wagstaff, *Heritage That Hurts: Tourists in the Memoryscapes of September 11* (Left Coast Press, 2011); S. Thomas et al., "Dark Heritage," in *Encyclopedia of Global Archaeology*, ed. C. Smith (Springer, 2019), 1–11.

23. Some websites labeled Viivikonna a "cool place" and a "ghost town." See, for instance, Nocamerabag, https://nocamerabag.com/blog/viivikonna-ghost-town-estonia, and Off the Beaten Track, https://stepoffthebeatentrack.com/2016/03/15/viivikonna-an-almost-abandoned-village-estonia/.

24. Hartmut Böhme, "Ruinen–Landschaften: Zum Verhältnis von Naturgeschichte und Allegorie in den späten Filmen von Andrej Tarkowskij," in *Natur und Subjekt* (Suhrkamp, 1988), 334 –79.

25. Patrick Laviolette, *Extreme Landscapes of Leisure* (Ashgate, 2011); Patrick Laviolette, "The Neo-flâneur Amongst Irresistible Decay," in *Playgrounds & Battlefields*, ed. Francisco Martínez and K. Slabina (Tallinn University Press, 2014), 243–70; Francisco Martínez and Patrick Laviolette, "Trespass into the Liminal: Urban Exploration in Estonia," *Anthropological Journal of European Cultures* 25 (2017): 1–24.

26. Arkady Strugatsy and Boris Strugatsy, *Roadside Picnic* (Macmillan, 1977).

27. Frank Herbert, *Dune* (Chilton, 1965).

28. In May 2024, the Estonian Ministry of Defense announced that the territory between Viivikonna and Sirgala had been handed over to them and would now be used as a military training ground. See the news coverage from ERR, https://www.err.ee/1609339227/sirgala-harjutusvali-laieneb-suletud-viivikonna-karjaari-arvelt.

29. For more on the topic, see E. Ardener, "Remote Areas: Some Theoretical Considerations," in *Anthropology at Home*, ed. A. Jackson (Tavistock, 1987), 38–54; J. C. Scott, *The Art of Not Being Governed* (Yale University Press, 2009); E. Harms et al., Remote and Edgy: New Takes on Old Anthropological Themes," *HAU Journal of Ethnographic Theory* 4 (2014): 361–81; P. Schweitzer and O. Povoroznyuk, "A Right to Remoteness? A Missing Bridge and Articulations of Indigeneity Along an East Siberian Railroad," *Social Anthropology* 27 (2019): 236–52; and J. Brachet and J. Scheele, "Remoteness Is Power: Disconnection as a Relation in Northern Chad," *Social Anthropology* 27 (2019): 156–71.

30. Martin Saxer, *Places in Knots: Remoteness and Connectivity in the Himalayas and Beyond* (Cornell University Press, 2022).

31. Sillamäe is a former atomic town that has also been losing its population: from 20,104 inhabitants in 1994 to 12,480 inhabitants in 2020.

32. Sinimäe has over three hundred inhabitants and is well known for being the site of an important battle in World War II, the battle of the Tannenberg Line.

33. This discussion is drawn from Liina Hallik, "Varemeis kummituslinn: siin elavad põhiliselt need, kes ei tööta: Ei hakka ka tööle" [Ruined Ghost Town: Mainly People Who Don't Work Live Here. Won't Work Either], *Õhtuleht*, August 21, 2018.

34. Lisa Baraitser, *Enduring Time* (Bloomsbury, 2017).

35. As Dzenovska points out, emptiness refers to a state in which places lose their constitutive elements, such as people, activities, and purpose. Dace Dzenovska, "Emptiness: Capitalism Without People in the Latvian Countryside," *American Ethnologist* 47 (2020): 10–26.

36. See K. Kljavin and A. Aaloe, "Ida-Virumaa mitukümmend nägu" [Several Faces of Eastern Virumaa], *Müürileht* (2021), accessed May 2024, https://www.muurileht.ee/ida-virumaa-mitukummend-nagu/.

7. A GARAGE WITH A VIEW

1. Karl Schlögel opens his book *Moscow 1937* with a midnight flight similar to that of Margarita, in *The Master and Margarita*, dissecting Moscow's cultural and social geography as Bulgakov did. Karl Schlögel, *Moscow 1937* (Polity, 2014).

2. Selma Lagerlöf, *The Wonderful Adventures of Nils* (Sahara, 1907).

3. Stephen Lovell, *Summerfolk: A History of the Dacha, 1710–2000* (Cornell University Press, 2003).

4. Both designer Ernesto Oroza (regarding Cuba) and anthropologist Xenia Cherkaev (regarding the Soviet Union) have shown that tinkering, gleaning, creating things from waste, and breaking objects down into pieces reflected the way socialist economies worked. In his study of garages in Tallinn, geographer Tauri Tuvikene argues that their proliferation was related to their usefulness in dealing with the system's shortcomings. In an ethnography of DIY Soviet culture, however, anthropologist Zinaida Vasilyeva claims that the meaning of the practices taking place therein goes far beyond the context of shortage; instead, she refers to garages as places in which to feel alive and be modern, making possible some hobby activities. Also in this vein, Ekaterina Gerasimova and Sofia Chuikina argued that the practice of repair became a form of creativity and lifestyle, offering Soviet citizens the opportunity to develop their individuality outside the state-controlled sphere. Ernesto Oroza, *RIKIMBILI: Une étude sur la désobéissance technologique et quelques formes de réinvention* (Université de Saint-Étienne, 2009); Tauri Tuvikene, "From Soviet to Post-Soviet with Transformation of the Fragmented Urban Landscape: The Case of Garage Areas in Estonia," *Landscape Research* 35, no. 5 (2010): 509–28; Zinaida Vasilyeva, "From Skills to Selves: Recycling 'Soviet DIY' in Post-Soviet Russia" (PhD diss., University of Neuchatel, 2019); Ekaterina Gerasimova and Sofia Chuikina, "The Repair Society," *Russian Studies in History* 48 (2009): 58–74; Xenia Cherkaev, *Gleaning for Communism* (Cornell University Press, 2023).

5. See media coverage by the Estonian news service, "Narva 'Venice' Dwellers Anxious on Development's Future," June 27, 2021, accessed February 2025, https://news.err.ee/1608259221/ak-narva-venice-dwellers-anxious-on-development-s-future.

6. Elsewhere I proposed an inventory of local relations as a thinking tool to understand the complex intersection of people, scales, and temporalities taking place in Narva, a method that I termed "Narvaology." See Francisco Martínez, "Narva as Method: Urban Inventories and the Mutation of the Postsocialist City," *Anthropological Journal of European Cultures* 29 (2020): 67–92.

7. G. Parrinello and M. Kondolf, "The Social Life of Sediment," *Water History* 13 (2021): 1–12.

8. Nowadays, the reservoir renews itself thirty-five times a year, because in addition to the Narva River, the Pljussa, Pjata, Must, and Boroni Rivers also bring in fresh water. J. Jauhiainen and T. Pikner. "Narva–Ivangorod: Integrating and Disintegrating Transboundary Water Networks and Infrastructure," *Journal of Baltic Studies* 40 (2009) 415–36.

9. Madis Tuuder and Karin Paulus, *Narva: Daatšast paleeni* [Narva: From the Dacha to the Palace] (Narva linnamuuseum, 2020).

10. S. Green, "The Hedgehog from Jordan: Or, How to Locate the Movement of Wild Animals in a Partially Mediterranean Context," in *Locating the Mediterranean*, ed. C. Rommel and J. J. Viscomi (Helsinki University Press, 2022), 199–222.

11. Francisco Martínez and T. Pikner, "The Infrastructural Side Effects of Geopolitics: Fortuitous Socio-Biological Modifications to Three European Borders," *Roadsides* 1 (2019): 18–27.

12. Gaston Bachelard, *The Poetics of Space* (1958; Penguin, 2014).

13. In Russian, *svoi* (our people), *inoi* (another), and *chuzhie* (not-ours). See Svetlana Boym, *The Off-Modern* (Bloomsbury, 2017), 91–92; and A. Yurchak, *Everything Was Forever, Until It Was No More* (Princeton University Press, 2005).

14. The buoys' locations were agreed to by the border agencies in 2022. In 2023, however, Russia disputed the locations of approximately half of the 250 markers. The provocation came just weeks after the repeated jamming of airline GPS signals over Tartu, which was a European Capital of Culture in 2024.

15. See J. Andrews and L. Roberts, eds., *Liminal Landscapes* (Routledge, 2012).

16. For more on the topic, see M. D. Frederiksen and I. H. Knudsen, "What Is a Grey Zone and Why Is Eastern Europe One?," in *Ethnographies of Grey Zones in Eastern Europe*, ed. I. H. Knudsen and M. D. Frederiksen (Anthem Press, 2015), 1–25; and Č. Brković, *Managing Ambiguity* (Berghahn, 2017).

17. In Simmel's critique of modern life, he refers to this boundary as a tragedy, since it entails the objectification of our relationships. Despite this bleak picture, Simmel suggested that the alienation brought about by modernity can be resisted in the most intimate sphere. In his view, an interior withdrawal is the only—or at least, the most effective—way to preserve individuality. For Simmel, social withdrawal is equivalent to hiding, "the crudest and, externally, most radical manner of concealment," capable of paralyzing systemic relations and making them appear pointless. See Georg Simmel, *The Philosophy of Money* (Routledge and Kegan Paul, 1978), 364.

18. Georg Simmel, *The Sociology of Georg Simmel* (Free Press, 1950 [1906]), 330.

19. Michel Serres refers to a border as a fuzzy area, an open space for intervention where the residual is not hidden and the engagement with dirt is prescribed. This is therefore a zone where the irrational can overcome the normative. Michel Serres, *Detachment* (Ohio University Press, 1989). Michel de Certeau also wrote about the creative practices deployed by people to bypass the institutional organization of space. These practices might take the form of inventive ruses, rituals, and tricks, composing, when together, an antidisciplinary network. Michel de Certeau, *L'invention du quotidien* (Union générale d'éditions, 1980).

20. Borders stand simultaneously inside and outside a given system (rather than in opposition). R. Shields, *Places on the Margin: Alternative Geographies of Modernity* (Routledge, 1991); J. Dahl, E. Fihl, and B. Schepelern Johansen, eds., *A Comparative Ethnography of Alternative Spaces* (Palgrave, 2013).

21. Concerned with the role of spatialization in social transformations, historian Karl Schlögel distinguished between "hot" and "cold" locations. Hot ones appear transient, while cold locations are areas of fixed, consolidated assumptions. Constantly in the making and without an imposed hierarchy, hot locations alleviate and bridge, yet they often appear dirty and impure, a source of disorder. In contrast, history stops in cold locations; there, things have already been converted into culture, well classified and with solid narratives written by this time. Karl Schlögel, *Im Raume lesen wir die Zeit* (Hanser, 2003).

22. Michel Foucault, "Of Other Spaces," *Diacritics* 16 (1986): 22–27.

23. For more on borderland practices of belonging, see A. Jašina-Schäfer, *Everyday Belonging in the Post-Soviet Borderlands: Russian Speakers in Estonia and Kazakhstan* (Lexington, 2021).

24. This subjunctive and communal dimension of the limen was noted by Victor Turner in his study of initiation rites. He described how a sense of passage from one social status to another is often accompanied by a passage in space—a dislocation from one place to another. Additionally, Turner referred to a limen not as a borderline but as "a very long threshold; a corridor almost, or a tunnel which may become a pilgrim's road." He articulated a model that combines transformation with integration at the interstices of

central institutions, concluding that liminal gaps are necessary for changes in structure. Victor Turner, *Blazing the Trail* (University of Arizona Press, 1992), 49.

25. They rid themselves of prevailing classifications and status incumbencies, seeking other kinds of interactions. Victor Turner, *The Ritual Process* (Cornell University Press, 1969).

26. Victor Turner, "Liminal to Liminoid, in Play, Flow, and Ritual: An Essay in Comparative Symbology," *Rice University Studies* 60 (1974) 53–92, quotation at 59.

27. Fredrik Barth, ed., *Ethnic Groups and Boundaries* (Universitetsforlaget, 1969).

28. See Sarah Green, "Borders and the Relocation of Europe," *Annual Review of Anthropology* 42 (2013): 345–61; and "Lines, Traces, and Tidemarks: Further Reflections on Forms of Border," in *The Political Materialities of Borders*, vol. 2, ed. O. Demetriou and R. Dimova (Manchester University Press, 2018), 67–83.

29. That was indeed the conclusion of John W. Cole and Eric R. Wolf after investigating two peasant communities with different ethnic backgrounds and customs in a single Alpine valley. As they explained, conceptualizations about the border (as an epistemic construction) influence the kind of relations taking place therein—between people themselves, with the surroundings, and also with state institutions. John W. Cole and Eric R. Wolf, *The Hidden Frontier: Ecology and Ethnicity in an Alpine Valley* (Academic Press, 1974).

30. While Thomas M. Wilson and Hastings Donnan foreground how state power is intensely contested and administered in these locations, anthropologist Robert Álvarez places the emphasis on crossings in his study of the Mexican–US frontier, describing the types of connectivity that a border zone particularly creates. Thomas M. Wilson and Hastings Donnan, *Border Identities: Nation and State at International Frontiers* (Cambridge University Press, 1998); Robert Álvarez, "Borders and Bridges: Exploring a New Conceptual Architecture for (U.S.–Mexico) Border Studies," *Journal of Latin American and Caribbean Anthropology* 17 (2012): 24–40.

31. Karolina S. Follis, *Building Fortress Europe* (University of Pennsylvania Press, 2012).

32. Eléonore de Montesquiou, *Narva/Ivangorod* (Argo, 2010), 53.

33. Martínez, "Narva as Method."

34. *Rohkem Põlevkivi!*, May 5, 1946.

35. Tarmo Pikner, M. Metsar, and H. Palang, "Hajutatud linnamaastik: Aiamaaga seonduvad praktikad Narvas" [Dispersed Urban Landscape: Practices in the Allotment Gardens in Narva], in *Piir ja jõgi*, ed. M. Ivask (Narva Muuseum, 2014), 219–54; Francisco Martínez and Tarmo Pikner, "Infrastructural Side Effects of Geopolitics," *Roadsides* 1 (2019): 1–11; T. Pikner, K. Willman, and A. Jokinen, "Urban Commoning as a Vehicle Between Government Institutions and Informality," *International Journal of Urban and Regional Research* 44 (2020): 711–28; T. Pikner, and H. Palang, "Movements, Care, and Dispersed Periurban Landscapes Evoked by Dacha Allotment Gardens of Narva," in *Landscapes of Affect and Emotion*, ed. M. Häyrynen, J. Häkli, and J. Saarinen (Brill, 2021), 49–72.

36. Turner, *Ritual Process*.

37. Pikner, Willman, and Jokinen, "Urban Commoning."

38. Jaanika Kingumets, "From Paradise to the Town of No Hope: Home-Making Among the Soviet-Era Russian-Speakers in Narva, Estonia" (PhD diss., Tampere University, 2022), 183.

39. Caitlin DeSilvey, "Cultivated Histories in a Scottish Allotment Garden," *Cultural Geographies* 10, no. 4 (2003): 442–68.

40. Ronan Hervouet, *Datcha Blues. Existences ordinaires et dictature en Biélorussie* (Belin, 2009).

41. Melissa Caldwell, *Dacha Idylls* (University of California Press, 2011), 42.

42. Melissa Caldwell, "Dacha Labors: Preserving Everyday Soviet Life," in *Seasoned Socialism: Gender and Food in Late Soviet Everyday Life*, ed. A. Lakhitikova, A. Brintlinger, and I. Glushchenko (Indiana University Press, 2019), 165–92, quotation at 166.

43. Caldwell, *Dacha Idylls*, 4.

44. Pikner argues that dacha practices contribute to investing meaning in the landscape and are also an effective way of giving space to citizens. He notes, too, the capacity to accumulate informality within different political and economic regimes, as well as the multiplicity of involvements taking place there. See Pikner, Willman, and Jokinen, "Urban Commoning."

45. Kingumets, "From Paradise to the Town of No Hope," 170. Also, she notes that the gardening skills among residents demonstrate years of dedication to this practice which, paradoxically, cannot be performed outside the respective place and time.

46. Lovell, *Summerfolk*.

47. They have the legal status of a garden partnership; in Russian, *sadovyh tovarišestvo*.

48. Haruki Murakami, *Sputnik Sweetheart* (Penguin, 2023).

49. This sense of continuity and bonding is also noted in the research of Pikner, Caldwell, and Kingumets.

50. A. Corsín Jiménez, "Auto-construction Redux: The City as Method," *Cultural Anthropology* 32, no. 3 (2017): 450–78; T. Caldeira, "Peripheral Urbanization: Autoconstruction, Transversal Logics, and Politics in Cities of the Global South," *Environment and Planning D* 35 (2017): 3–20; G. Pozzi, "If Buildings Could Speak: Makeshift Urbanity on the Outskirts of Lisbon," in *Politics of Recuperation in Post-crisis Portugal*, ed. Francisco Martínez (Bloomsbury, 2020), 75–99.

51. On August 23, 2023, I attended the Sputnik Garden Day organized by Annela Samuel, Saara Mildeberg, and Lilian Pungas. During the festival, we enjoyed dancing and eating with the residents of Sputnik.

52. The installation was displayed at the EKA Gallery in Tallinn in 2023.

53. A. Bonnett, *Off the Map* (Aurum, 2014).

54. C. Tilley, "From the English Cottage Garden to the Swedish Allotment: Banal Nationalism and the Concept of the Garden," *Home Cultures* 5 (2008): 219–50.

8. CRYPTO-COLONIALISM

1. An example of this is T. Tuvikiene, W. Sgibnev, and C. Neugebauer, eds., *Post-Socialist Urban Infrastructures* (Routledge, 2019), which presented these legacies as obdurate, heavy, time-consuming, and expensive to upgrade.

2. All forms of infrastructure are built on an installed base and inherit its already existing strengths and limitations, insists sociologist Susan L. Star in "The Ethnography of Infrastructure," *American Behavioral Scientist* 43 (1999): 377–91; see also K. Ruhleder and Susan L. Star, "Steps Toward an Ecology of Infrastructure: Design and Access for Large Information Spaces," *Information Systems Research* 7 (1996): 111–34.

3. See, by Asta Vonderau, "Scaling the Cloud: Making State and Infrastructure in Sweden," *Ethnos* 84, no. 4 (2019): 698–718; and "Storing Data, Infrastructuring the Air: Thermocultures of the Cloud," *Culture Machine* 18 (2019): 1–12.

4. Email conversation with the author.

5. See K. Härma, "Kaevanduslinna võtavad üle krüptokaevandajad" [Crypto Miners Take Over a Mining Town], *Äripäev*, February 21, 2018, accessed May 2024, https://www.aripaev.ee/uudised/2018/02/21/kaevanduslinna-votavad-ule-kruptokaevandajad.

6. CoinsPaid, the world's biggest cryptocurrency payment company, is run from Tallinn. The owner, Max Krupyshev, was born in Ukraine but lives in Berlin. He explained

his reasons for keeping his company in Estonia this way: "Because the nation is small, regulators still have the time to speak with businesses—to understand the business, ask questions, receive and analyze the answers. Based on this understanding, they may change their minds about some things. It's a constant dialogue with the regulator." See S. Tambur, *Estonian World*, January 13, 2023, https://estonianworld.com/technology/worlds-biggest-cryptocurrency-payment-company-is-run-from-tallinn/.

7. See the coverage in the newspaper *Põhjarannik*, "Ida-Virumaalt pärit miljonärid rajavad Narva 10 miljonit eurot maksva andmetöötluskeskuse," July 8, 2019, accessed May 2024, https://pohjarannik.postimees.ee/6724713/ida-virumaalt-parit-miljonarid-rajavad-narva-10-miljonit-eurot-maksva-andmetootluskeskuse.

8. The Central Criminal Police and the FBI had been investigating their activity and accused them of creating a company acting as a Ponzi scheme.

9. The project, which was expected to cost 2 billion euros, aimed to build small modular reactors with a capacity of three hundred megawatts. The Canadian company GEH was announced as the winning bidder and signed a project development and preliminary works contract. See the coverage by the Estonian News Agency, for instance, "Nuclear Power Plant Development Plan to Go Ahead Despite Missing Laws," February 25, 2025; and the Postimees, "Our First Steps Towards Building a Nuclear Power Plant," January 21, 2025, <https://news.postimees.ee/8176805/kalev-kallemets-our-first-steps-towards-building-a-nuclear-power-plant>.

10. C. Lemanski, "Infrastructural Citizenship: The Everyday Citizenships of Adapting and/or Destroying Public Infrastructure in Cape Town, South Africa," *Transactions of the Institute of British Geographers* 45 (2020): 589–605; D. Boyer, "Infrastructural Citizenship and Geosolidarity: Making Green Infrastructure in Petroliberal Houston," *American Ethnologist* 51 (2024): 338–49.

11. T. Loloum, S. Abram, and N. Ortar, eds., *Ethnographies of Power* (Berghahn, 2021).

12. K. Polanyi, *The Great Transformation* (Beacon, 1944); M. Flinders and J. Buller, "Depoliticisation: Principles, Tactics and Tools," *British Politics* 1 (2006): 293–318.

13. Political scientist Caroline Kuzemko has studied different forms of depoliticization in the UK and highlighted a number of strategies that remove the most problematic aspects of national energy systems from public debate. For instance, she has observed how institutional forms of concealment occur through the transfer of issues from government to technocratic circles, and from the public to the private sphere and market forces. See Caroline Kuzemko, "Energy Depoliticization in the United Kingdom: Destroying Political Capacity," *British Journal of Politics and International Relations* 18 (2016): 107–24.

14. O. Kuchinskaya, *The Politics of Invisibility: Public Knowledge About Radiation Health Effects After Chernobyl* (MIT Press, 2014); V. Ferrario and B. Castiglioni, "Visibility/Invisibility in the 'Making' of Energy Landscape: Strategies and Policies in the Hydropower Development of the Piave River (Italian Eastern Alps)," *Energy Policy* 108 (2017): 829–35.

15. F. Libertson, J. Velkova, and J. Palm, "Data-Centre Infrastructure and Energy Gentrification: Perspectives from Sweden," *Sustainability: Science, Practice and Policy* 17 (2021): 153–62.

16. Herzfeld used the term "crypto" to address a practice of colonialism that is concealed and hidden. As he describes it, this colonial form of relating is enacted through a hierarchy of cultural value and as an imposition of a foreign time—rendering, in turn, local timelines meaningless or irrelevant. See Michael Herzfeld, "The Absent Presence: Discourses of Crypto-Colonialism," *South Atlantic Quarterly* 101, no. 4 (2002): 899–926.

17. As scholars Sheila Jasanoff and Sang-Hyun Kim explain, visions from science and technology are embedded in materiality, meaning, and morality, then publicly performed and institutionally stabilized. Sheila Jasanoff and Sang-Hyun Kim, "Containing the Atom:

Sociotechnical Imaginaries and Nuclear Power in the United States and South Korea," *Minerva* 47 (2009): 119–46, esp. 120.

18. S. Budnitsky, "A Relational Approach to Digital Sovereignty: E-Estonia Between Russia and the West," *International Journal of Communication* 16 (2022): 1918–39.

19. Taavi Kotka (Estonia's chief information officer between 2013 and 2017) and Kaspar Korjus (e-Residency Program director between 2014 and 2019) published a paper correlating the development of digital technologies with Estonia's national sovereignty. In their view, attention to territoriality is outmoded, and "soft ties to people abroad may help to deter future conflicts or generate increased international support should Estonia find itself in a conflict." See Taavi Kotka, C. Vargas Alvarez, and Kaspar Korjus, "Estonian E-residency: Benefits, Risk and Lessons Learned," in *Electronic Government and the Information Systems Perspective*, ed. A. Kő and E. Francesconi (Springer, 2016), 3–15, quotation at 11.

20. Francisco Martínez, "The Baltic as a Hybrid Border Zone," *Journal of Cultural Economy*, under review.

21. See R. Mäe, "The Story of E-Estonia," *Baltic Worlds* 1–2 (2017): 32–44; L. A. Kaljund, "Restoration Doctrine Rebooted: Codifying Continuity in the Estonian Data Embassy Initiative," *PoLAR* 41 (2018): 5–20; and Epp Annus, "A Post-Soviet Eco-Digital Nation? Metonymic Processes of Nation-Building and Estonia's High-Tech Dreams in the 2010s," *East European Politics and Societies and Cultures* 36 (2022): 399– 422.

22. L. Winner, "Do Artefacts Have Politics?," *Daedalus* 109 (1980): 121–36.

23. Estonia's total peak consumption in a colder winter month is close to 1,500 megawatts, with cryptocurrency mining accounting for 1 percent of that consumption during peak periods. See the national news agency ERR, "Peak Period Crypto Mining Makes Up 1 Percent of All Electricity Consumption," January 2022, https://news.err.ee/1608463286/peak-period-crypto-mining-makes-up-1-percent-of-all-electricity-consumption.

24. L. Swartz, "What Was Bitcoin, What Will It Be? The Techno-Economic Imaginaries of a New Money Technology," *Cultural Studies* 32 (2018): 623–50.

25. "The steady addition of a constant amount of new coins is analogous to gold miners expending resources to add gold to circulation. In our case, it is CPU [central processing unit] time and electricity that is expended." See Satoshi Nakamoto, "Bitcoin: A Peer-to-Peer Electronic Cash System," 2008, accessed July 2024, https://bitcoin.org/bitcoin.pdf.

26. See Z. Zimmer, "Bitcoin and Potosí Silver: Historical Perspectives on Cryptocurrency," *Technology and Culture* 58 (2017): 307–34.

27. F. Calvão, "Crypto-Miners: Digital Labor and the Power of Blockchain Technology," *Economic Anthropology* 6 (2019): 123–34.

28. Primavera De Filippi and Benjamin Loveluck, "The Invisible Politics of Bitcoin: Governance Crisis of a Decentralised Infrastructure," *Internet Policy Review* 5, no. 30 (2016): 1–28.

29. M. Graham, ed., *Digital Economies at Global Margins* (MIT Press, 2019); P. Mitchell et al., "Geolocation: Locating Trust in Digital Platforms and Economies," panel presented at AoIR, 20th Annual Conference of the Association of Internet Researchers, Brisbane, Australia, 2019.

30. "Cryptobro" refers to someone who is asocial and celibate, hiding in a basement with his computer, living through video games and his investments.

31. This recalls Simmel's designation of not-knowing as a specific kind of knowledge (not its absence) that is productive of meanings and entails an awareness of what is not known. Very few coins are still mined (generally the oldest remaining blockchains), and those that are (like Bitcoin) do not rely on a DAO (decentralized autonomous organization). A DAO sets the rules following a peer-to-peer monitoring of interactions; it appeared alongside narratives of "horizontality" and "transparency." Interestingly, the

philosophy behind digital currencies resonates with some of Simmel's ideas on money and non-knowledge, which were developed more than a century ago. For more on the topic, see Georg Simmel, *The Philosophy of Money* (Routledge and Kegan Paul, 1978); and J. Hou, "Making Ends Meet by Mining on Blockchain: Subalternity, Materiality, and Yearnings of Chinese Amateur Crypto Miners," *Journal of Digital Social Research* 5 (2023): 80–117.

CONCLUSION

1. R. Macfarlane, *Underland: A Deep Time Journey* (Hamish Hamilton, 2019).

2. Søren Kierkegaard, *Stages on Life's Way* (1845; Princeton University Press, 1988); Henry David Thoreau, *Walden* (1854; Princeton University Press, 2016).

3. Pockets vary in size but not in purpose. They began to appear in attire by the late seventeenth century, nesting and concealing things while keeping them accessible. B. Burman and A. Fennetaux, *The Pocket: A Hidden History of Women's Lives, 1660–1900* (Yale University Press, 2019).

4. Georg Simmel, "The Sociology of Secrecy and of Secret Societies," *American Journal of Sociology* 11 (1906): 441–98, quotation at 462.

5. This has also been noted by Gilbert Herdt in his ethnography of male initiation practices and the formation of sexual cultures in New Guinea, as well as by Gerald Creed, who, after studying different forms of masquerade in rural Bulgaria, concluded that mumming is a sort of premodern drag allowing an ambivalent inclusion in the present. They both referred to secrecy as an ordinary cultural practice, questioning the belief that it would lose relevance in the contemporary order of things. Originally, Simmel posited two types of secret formations: a primitive one, in which a subversive group is itself hidden from the rest of the community, and a more complex one in which the existence of the secret arrangement is known by the society but not the identity of its members. Herdt adds a third form of secrecy: one in which individual members are known and recognized as such by the public, to the point where state institutions themselves might be those promoting relationships of concealment (especially at historical junctures and in situations of unstable relationships). Herdt regarded secrecy as both a social product and a performative structure, having a strong impact in the creation of selfhood. Gilbert Herdt, *Secrecy and Cultural Reality* (University of Michigan Press, 2003). In the case of Creed, he uses *kukeri* (traditional mumming performances) to illustrate the limited alternatives available to cope with cultural dispossession. Gerald W. Creed, *Masquerade and Postsocialism: Ritual and Cultural Dispossession in Bulgaria* (Indiana University Press, 2011).

6. In the German language, the folding screen is called a *Spanische Wand* because the distribution of this device all over Europe was initiated by the Spanish kingdom in the sixteenth century, following the visit of a delegation of Japanese Christians to King Philip II. E. Vila-Matas, "Paradoja del biombo," *El País*, October 14, 2014.

7. Raymond Williams, *Marxism and Literature* (Oxford University Press, 1977).

8. For more on how Russian speakers are perceived, see Alina Jašina-Schäfer's ethnography of everyday belonging within the post-Soviet borderlands.

9. Along with Anton Serdjukov and Eduard Zentsik, Semjon organized the Territory festival on August 5, 2023. The lineup featured bands of different genres, from funk to bossa nova, ambient, Krautrock, hip hop, and electronic music. Through these cultural practices, they are updating traditional ideas of identity and attachment to places. "We are organizing the festival to make people happy, both ourselves and visitors to Sillamäe," said Semjon. "It is gratifying to see that there has been a response, that we are not just on our own, because all those who have worked to organize the festival are art people," added Anton.

10. Marika Kirch and Aksel Kirch, "Search for Security in Estonia: New Identity Architecture," *Security Dialogue* 26 (1995): 439–48.

11. Andrey Makarychev, "Reactive Re-Bordering, Geopolitics and Biopolitics: Estonia at Europe's Eastern Flank," *Alternatives: Global, Local, Political* 49 (2024): 127–37.

12. James Scott, *Seeing Like a State* (New Haven: Yale University Press, 1998).

13. Elliott Prasse-Freeman, "Resistance/Refusal: Politics of Manoeuvre Under Diffuse Regimes of Governmentality," *Anthropological Theory* 22 (2022): 102–27.

14. Residents of the eastern region decline to restrict themselves to the prevailing representations, or game, as Goffman would put it. He described social order as a set of ordinary gatherings and narrative-like enactments. This kind of dramaturgical understanding of public interactions relies on people's performance of anticipated social roles, "shared cognitive presuppositions," and "self-sustained restraints." Erving Goffman, "The Interaction Order: American Sociological Association, 1982 Presidential Address," *American Sociological Review* 48 (1982): 1–17, quotations at 4.

15. James Scott highlights the importance of mundane forms of resistance when direct confrontation with authority is impossible or ineffective. These hidden scripts comprise actions such as sabotage, false compliance, dissimulation, gossip, and social withdrawal. James C. Scott, *Weapons of the Weak* (Yale University Press, 1985). Indeed, attempts to rationalize and simplify societies caused some of the disasters of the twentieth century, like collectivization and totalitarianism.

16. Homi K. Bhabha, *The Location of Culture* (Routledge, 1994), 4.

17. It is done by placing power relations in historical context while revaluating local forms of knowledge, ideally with emancipatory ends. See Tim Beasley-Murray, Wendy Bracewell and Michał Murawski, eds., *Anti-Atlas: Critical Area Studies from the East of the West* (UCL Press, 2025).

18. In her study of dirt and purity taboos, Douglas argued that cultures create order by putting chaotic experiences into categories. Social ordering thus follows two phases: first, the categorization of what does not fit and its physical rejection; and second, a process of dissolving any characterization, which leads to its utter invisibilization and loss of identity. She did not pay enough attention, however, to the intransitive character of such a gesture, in the sense that the designation of the alien and irrational in modern contexts entails a boomerang ordering effect toward the core, which might become oppressively tight and ordered. Furthermore, and as noted by Michael Thompson years later, things may move into and out of the category of waste. Mary Douglas, *Purity and Danger* (Routledge, 1966). See also Michael Thompson, *Rubbish Theory* (Oxford University Press, 1979); and Zsuzsa Gille, *From the Cult of Waste to the Trash Heap of History* (Indiana University Press, 2007).

19. The modern failure at naming and categorizing everything produces a problem of classification and the multiplication of ambivalent social beings. Zygmunt Bauman, *Modernity and Ambivalence* (Polity, 1991). The adjective "ambivalent" refers to a multivocal and poly-directional position, to taking more than one side at once. Nonetheless, the condition of ambivalence, exemplified in mixed feelings or contradictory ideas about something, can also become pathological—producing mental disorders—on the failure to generate an emotional synthesis or because of the intensity of one of those feelings. For more on the topic, see E. Bleuler, *Dementia Praecox oder Gruppe der Schizophrenien* [Dementia Praecox or Group of Schizophrenias], (Deuticke, 1911); and Sigmund Freud, *The Standard Edition of the Complete Psychological Works of Sigmund Freud*, vol. 12 (1912; Hogarth Press, 1958).

20. Erving Goffman, *Behavior in Public Places* (Free Press, 1966).

21. In this vein, sociologist Andrea Mubi Brighenti argues that visibility is a field of contention, and attentive management of how we are seen allows us to reconceive traditional relations of authority and equally challenge them. Andrea Mubi Brighenti, ed., *The*

New Politics of Visibility (Intellect, 2022). For more on the topic, see B. L. Bellman, "The Paradox of Secrecy," *Human Studies* 4 (1981): 1–24; C. D. Piot, "Secrecy, Ambiguity, and the Everyday in Kabre Culture," *American Anthropologist* 95 (1993): 353–70; C. Smart, "Families, Secrets and Memories," *Sociology* 45, no. 4 (2011): 539–53; G. Jones, "Secrecy," *Annual Review of Anthropology* 43 (2014): 53–69; and S. Woodward and C. Mayr, "Secret Objects in the Home: Potency, (In)visibility and Everyday Relationships," *Cultural Sociology* (2023): 1–16.

22. Shoshana Zuboff, *The Age of Surveillance Capitalism* (Public Affairs, 2019).

23. For more on "inoperosity," see Giorgio Agamben, *Means Without End* (University of Minnesota Press, 2000).

24. Francisco Martínez, "Doing Nothing: Anthropology Sits at the Same Table with Contemporary Art in Lisbon and Tbilisi," *Ethnography* 20, no. 4 (2018): 541–59.

25. A hydraulic drainage system is used to transport ash to the dumping field, where the ash is washed with water and pumped through pipes. The remaining water spills into sediment ponds and is pumped back into the power plant. As noted by both Eesti Energia and the Ministry of Environment, the water from the sedimentation lagoons circulates in a closed system. Nevertheless, water must be discharged from time to time into the Narva River, yet only after a cleaning treatment.

26. Alexandre Monnin, "The Negative Commons: Between Waste and Ruins," *Études* 9 (2021): 59–68; and D. Boyer, "Revolutionary Infrastructure," in *Infrastructures and Social Complexity: A Companion*, ed. P. Harvey, J. C. Bruun, and A. Morita (Routledge, 2017), 174–86.

27. For how infrastructural harm extends to other arrangements, see Y. Kallianos, A. Dunlap, and D. Dalakoglou, "Introducing Infrastructural Harm: Rethinking Moral Entanglements, Spatio-temporal Dynamics, and Resistance(s)," *Globalizations* 20, no. 6 (2022): 829–48.

28. In his ethnography of the Western Apache in Arizona, anthropologist Keith Basso described the performative character of our sense of place. Keith Basso, *Wisdom Sits in Places* (University of New Mexico Press, 1996).

29. M. Tironi, "Soil Refusal: Thinking Earthly Matters as Radical Alterity," in *Thinking with Soils*, ed. J. F. Salazar et al. (Bloomsbury, 2020), 175–90.

30. S. Ureta, "Chemical Rubble: Historicizing Toxic Waste in a Former Mining Town in Northern Chile," *Arcadia* 20 (2016), Rachel Carson Center for Environment and Society, https://doi.org/10.5282/rcc/7704.

31. Francisco Martínez and Marika Agu, "Postcards from the Edge: Territorial Sacrifice and Care in Eastern Estonia," *Roadsides* 5 (2018): 68–76.

32. F. Anderl, ed., *Epistemologies of Land* (Rowman & Littlefield, 2024).

33. Exhibited at the Container Gallery of the Telliskivi Creative City in Tallinn in 2024.

34. H. Spriggs, "From Basement to De-basement? A Probing Response to Opacity," *Etnográfica* 28 (2024), https://etnografica.cria.org.pt/en/article/22/18.

35. The concept of ecological memory first appeared in these two articles: Darryl Bruce, "The How and Why of Ecological Memory," *Journal of Experimental Psychology* 114 (1985): 78–90; and Judit Padisák, "Seasonal Succession of Phytoplankton in a Large Shallow Lake (Balaton, Hungary): A Dynamic Approach to Ecological Memory, Its Possible Role and Mechanisms," *Journal of Ecology* 80 (1992): 217–30.

36. Thus, he invited us "to let our understanding prefer the gesture of giving-on-and-with." Édouard Glissant, *Poetics of Relation* (University of Michigan Press, 1997), 190.

37. Anthropologist Christina Schwenkel has proposed this concept in relation to visual tools mobilized to enact political goals. Christina Schwenkel, "Spectacular Infrastructure and Its Breakdown in Socialist Vietnam," *American Ethnologist* 42 (2015): 520–34.

Index

Note: Page numbers in *italics* refer to illustrations.

www.ingramcontent.com/pod-product-compliance
Lightning Source LLC
Chambersburg PA
CBHW020532270326
41927CB00006B/537